Site Formation Processes of Submerged Shipwrecks

A co-publication with the Society for Historical Archaeology

UNIVERSITY PRESS OF FLORIDA

Florida A&M University, Tallahassee
Florida Atlantic University, Boca Raton
Florida Gulf Coast University, Ft. Myers
Florida International University, Miami
Florida State University, Tallahassee
New College of Florida, Sarasota
University of Central Florida, Orlando
University of Florida, Gainesville
University of North Florida, Jacksonville
University of South Florida, Tampa
University of West Florida, Pensacola

Site Formation Processes of
Submerged Shipwrecks

Edited by Matthew E. Keith

University Press of Florida
Gainesville · Tallahassee · Tampa · Boca Raton
Pensacola · Orlando · Miami · Jacksonville · Ft. Myers · Sarasota

This book may be available in an electronic edition.

21 20 19 18 17 16   6 5 4 3 2 1

Library of Congress Cataloging-in-Publication Data
Site formation processes of submerged shipwrecks / edited by
Matthew E. Keith.
pages cm
Includes bibliographical references and index.
ISBN 978-0-8130-6162-7
1. Shipwrecks. 2. Underwater archaeology. 3. Excavations (Archaeology)
I. Keith, Matthew E., author.
G525.S557 2016
930.1'0285—dc23
2015030172

The University Press of Florida is the scholarly publishing agency for the State
University System of Florida, comprising Florida A&M University, Florida
Atlantic University, Florida Gulf Coast University, Florida International
University, Florida State University, New College of Florida, University of
Central Florida, University of Florida, University of North Florida, University
of South Florida, and University of West Florida.

University Press of Florida
15 Northwest 15th Street
Gainesville, FL 32611-2079
http://www.upf.com

Contents

Illustrations

.

Tables

1

Introduction

Site Formation Processes of Submerged Shipwrecks

IAN OXLEY AND MATTHEW E. KEITH

Shipwrecks have captured people's imaginations for millennia, and with the development of the field of maritime archaeology over roughly the last half century, we have learned a great deal about the past through the systematic study of submerged shipwreck sites. As with any field of study, our collective knowledge base is continually expanding as techniques, tools, and methods become increasingly sophisticated. Although the importance of understanding wreck site formation has been recognized in the field of maritime archaeology since the beginning (Dumas 1962; Frost 1962; Throckmorton 1965; Nesteroff 1972), the expansion of lines of inquiry into the study of wreck site formation have been relatively slow to develop (as noted by Bass 1980; Gibbins 1990; Murphy 1997; Stewart 1999).

Site formation processes consist of a wide range of both punctuated and ongoing events and processes that contribute to the condition of a shipwreck site at a given point in time. Formation on submerged sites begins with the initial deposition event and evolves depending on the subsequent effects of the natural environment and human activity. These processes are affected by deposition (e.g., sinking, scuttling) and depositional environment (e.g., water depth, seafloor composition) followed by the subsequent effects of processes such as wave action, storms, bioturbation, pressure, salinity, temperature, chemical reactions, and human activity. Maximizing the effectiveness of archaeological interpretation is predicated upon attaining a sound appreciation of site formation processes. In depth study of site formation processes can lead archaeologists to a better understanding of a site's matrix, inform heritage managers so that they may better preserve and protect archaeological sites, and inform conservators so they can properly stabilize artifacts and site components (both in the field and in the laboratory).

THE DEVELOPMENT OF SITE FORMATION THEORY IN MARITIME ARCHAEOLOGY

The relationship between field practice and theoretical research in shipwreck archaeology can be characterized by the delay between its development and acceptance and the integration of theoretical concepts into mainstream shipwreck archaeological practice. For many years, few publications of wreck site investigations paid any attention to site formation. Those that discussed the subject often did not include reference to theoretical concerns, and specific site formation considerations were even scarcer. Undoubtedly one factor is that most maritime archaeological sites are still reported only at interim level, and few sites worldwide are comprehensively published (cf. Red Bay, *Mary Rose*). In recent years calls have been made for a unifying methodology and theory for maritime archaeology based, among other things, on a comprehensive treatment of site formation theory (Gibbins 1990; Stewart 1999; Martin 2011), but this was not always the case.

THE EARLY YEARS

Shipwreck archaeology has slowly emerged from a past tainted by indiscriminate artifact collection, treasure salvage, and the unrecorded destruction of sites. From the earliest archaeological investigations of shipwreck sites, it was evident that the destructive effects of marine life were more pronounced on rocky substrates as opposed to the more sterile sandy environments (Nesteroff 1972). Frost (1962) and Dumas (1962) pioneered studies of wreck formation, putting forward generalized models for the sinking and wrecking of Classical ships, the so-called tumulus sites (referring to the mounds of ballast stone that overlay the site), while Throckmorton (1965) developed empirical models using a series of dated and documented sites at Methone in southwest Greece.

THE 1970s

In the seventies the requirement to identify suitable materials to contain nuclear waste buried under the sea provided an unusual impetus for considering formation processes in the deep ocean environment (Tylecote 1977). In terrestrial archaeology this period saw the introduction of the concept of transforms. Schiffer and Rathje (1973) put forward the proposition that linking the past to the present depends upon studying the archaeological record in the context of developing and applying the principles from two areas of archaeological theory: n-transforms (interactions through time between culturally deposited assemblages and the specific environmental conditions in which they were placed) and c-transforms (the spatial, quantitative, and association attributes of archaeological materials as functions of the cultural system that produced them). The late seventies included the further application of such concepts to shipwreck archaeology. Clausen and Arnold (1976) discovered remains of colonies of benthic organisms adhering to the upper two thirds of large concretions, providing evidence that the depth of the sediment in the area had fluctuated over the period of deposition: at least once in the past the conglomerates were largely, or perhaps entirely, exposed long enough to permit these organisms to flourish. Bascom (1976) concentrated on the marine environment of the Mediterranean and Black Sea as preservation media for the purposes of optimizing any search strategy.

Keith Muckelroy attempted to combine these concepts into a comprehensive and systematic approach to underwater site depositional processes. Muckelroy (1977) developed models for addressing what he felt were the basic conceptual concerns in the archaeology of the wrecking event that took place between the ship's existence as a functioning entity and the discovery of shipwreck remains by the archaeologist. In a further refinement (1978) he represented the evolution of a shipwreck as a flow diagram comprising five subsystems: the process of wrecking; salvage operations; the disintegration of perishables; seabed movement; and the characteristics of excavation methodologies. The inputs to the system are the ship itself and any material subsequently deposited on the site, whereas outputs are the material that has floated away, been salvaged, or disintegrated. Within the system the subsystems of sea bed movement, disintegration of perishables, and salvage are linked by positive feedback loops; that is, salvage operations will disturb the sea bed, and material will deteriorate due to the loss of the state of relative equilibrium. Muckelroy divided these mechanisms into two categories: scrambling processes and extracting filters. Scrambling processes are those that disturb the site matrix, making it difficult to interpret archaeological context, while extracting filters are mechanisms that remove artifacts or objects away from the wreck. Scrambling processes begin during the process of wrecking, and include such post-depositional processes as waves and currents, sea bed movement, and bioturbation (Muckelroy 1978; Stewart 1999:567).

Muckelroy put forward a site classification system based on an environmental model that ranked physical attributes (e.g., topography, particle size of deposit, slope, sea horizon, and fetch) and interpreted the results on the basis of the completeness of the archaeological record. He acknowledged the role of natural formation processes (i.e., chemical and biological), stating that explanation must lie in variations in the composition of the objects concerned, in the chemistry of the sea bed deposits, in the quality of the seawater in the area, and other such chemical and biological factors.

THE 1980s

The eighties saw a resurgent interest in archaeological "knowability" (i.e., how do we know what we know?) and a parallel urgency in most Western countries for archaeologists to participate in government planning and cultural resource management. There was also an increased emphasis on the study of impacts to archaeological sites (Wildesen 1982), site formation as an aid to predictive modeling and survey, and general concepts of management archaeology.

Parker (1981) advocated a flexible approach, concluding that even "tumulus" sites may be the subject of contamination. Jumbled so-called ships' graveyard sites can also be of value, as can individual wrecking events identified with detailed recording and careful analysis, even when the remains are scattered, mingled, and denuded by illicit excavation. Also there was an increasing awareness of processes and inter-relationships between site formation, materials preservation, and site assessment (MacLeod and Killingley 1982).

Around the same time Murphy (1983) stated that the application of a multidisciplinary approach to shipwreck studies was long overdue and that little was known about the environmental impact on wrecks and, conversely, the impact of wrecks on the environment.

In his seminal book *Formation Processes of the Archaeological Record*, Schiffer (1987) pointed out that because degradation can be caused by specific processes, and not necessarily simply by the passage of time, deposits formed at the same time but subject to different formation processes vary in their degree of preservation. Therefore useful information can be derived from badly degraded deposits, and some information of archaeological interest (e.g., ecofacts) can be added through environmental mechanisms.

Work conducted at the Terence Bay site in Canada during the early part of the decade included observations of the biophysical environment surrounding the wreck site as part of the collection of non-artifactual data.

This assessment had three elements: sediments within the wreck, the surrounding bathymetry, and the biological species present. The information gathered helped reconstruct the wrecking event and the subsequent development of the site (Kenchington et al. 1989) and also provided cross-disciplinary insight into the impacts of fishing on historic cod populations (Kenchington and Kenchington 1993).

The 1990s and Beyond: The Rise of Heritage Management

The importance of shipwreck site formation research began to be stressed repeatedly by organizations in countries with relatively mature heritage management structures, usually associated with central government. This increased emphasis on management of both individual sites and submerged bottom lands is at least partially responsible for an expanded emphasis on site formation studies commencing in the 1990s. Examples include the U.S. National Park Service Submerged Cultural Resources Unit (Lenihan and Murphy 1981), the U.K. Archaeological Diving Unit (Oxley 1992), the beginnings of the involvement of U.K. heritage agencies, and Australia's state maritime archaeologists. These specialist functions, by necessity, had sensitivity to the archaeological resource base, which faced threats from increased development and fishing activities. Moreover, as effective management is dependent upon high quality information, managers sought opportunities to understand and manage the resource better, which included expanded study of site formation.

Frost (1962) stated that during site investigation, it was evident that knowledge of general principles of site formation can help identify at an early stage the likely levels of preservation, thus helping the likely return of archaeological data compared with the resources required for the investigation. This cost-benefit analysis was becoming increasingly important in shipwreck heritage management archaeology, although even today comparatively little attention is paid to site formation theory in many cases. This is particularly perplexing as the trends are toward management in situ, predictive survey, and the consideration of archaeological areas rather than individual sites, all areas of research that can benefit substantially from site formation study.

Approaches to Shipwreck Site Environment Investigation

Rather than concentrating on characteristics on the scale of the site as a whole, as proposed by Muckelroy, the prediction of the preservation and/

or degradation of shipwrecks could be approached by trying to understand particular processes operating in the present day (Gregory 1996). The objective of determining which of these processes were important in terms of the formation of the submerged archaeological record and which affect future management in situ can be achieved by measuring the deterioration of materials and monitoring various chemical and biological parameters operating in the natural marine environment.

This work reinforced a trend that could be seen in some shipwreck investigations and post-excavation analysis whereby attention was being paid to smaller and smaller types of evidence. Led by the conservation sciences, there is an increasing focus on detail, ranging from specific biozones and interfaces between artifacts and burial environments (Florian 1987) to a concentration on microorganisms that clearly play an important role in the development of submerged archaeological sediments (Guthrie et al. 1995). This trend has clearly been influenced by the emergence of archaeologists with specific scientific expertise who promote the use of analytical methodologies that are recognized by and acceptable to the established marine sciences (Ferrari 1994; Gregory 1996).

IMPACTS

There was also much to learn about natural and cultural impacts, including the type of impact resulting from a *process*; the characteristic features of each impact type—degree, duration, extent, and distribution in time and space; and the degree of distortion caused by impacts on the archaeological record. Ferrari (1994) drew attention to the varied impacts that can affect submerged sites and the idea that an initial assumption of a continual reduction in both the quantity and quality of data over time has been replaced by the assertion that these patterns can be detected and archaeological interpretation can be refined accordingly.

SITE DETERIORATION MODELS

Understanding of the real effects of natural degradation and related impacts has been gained from modeling site deterioration. Research on quantifying site deterioration models has explored innovative ways of depicting such processes on the scale of the site as a whole.

Mathewson (1989) proposed a concept of archaeological site decay adapted from models of forest succession, while accepting that a forest is renewable while archaeological sites are not. The archaeological model shows a uniform decay rate for a specific component of a site, and external impacts can either increase or retard this rate. Factors that complicate the decay model are given as site component, physical, chemical, and biological variability. While admitting that the work required to build a generic, quantitative site decay model was felt to be excessively complex and economically unrealistic, the author claimed that it was reasonable to propose the development of a logic-based, qualitative decay model that related to the impact of an induced change in the site environment for each site component and spatial relationship.

In an alternative approach Ward and colleagues (1998) pointed out that most existing models for wreck disintegration were based on the form of the wreck at various phases of breakdown and the identification of generalities about factors affecting wreck formation. In addition, the environmental processes that influenced wreck disintegration at the various stages had not, up until that point, been used as the basis for formation models. A process-based model for wreck evolution proposed utilizing the influence of wreck depositional history on such processes as biological decay and chemical corrosion of wreck materials and on wreck evolution itself.

As part of a long-term management strategy employed by the National Park Service, extensive research has been conducted to analyze and model the USS *Arizona* site. These data were utilized by the National Institute of Standards and Technology to perform a finite element analysis with the goal of determining the structural integrity of the ship's hull and of modeling the expected time until collapse (Foecke et al. 2009).

By developing and expanding deterioration models, archaeologists and conservators can better understand how a site developed, and heritage managers can obtain the data necessary to manage wreck sites properly.

In Situ Management

Management in situ (or, as it is less accurately termed, preservation in situ) came to be recognized as an important component of submerged heritage management in that it enabled some archaeological sites, or parts of them, to be protected from deterioration processes (Oxley 2001). It also represented, and represents, a viable alternative to emergency excavation and recovery of materials. Techniques used can range from the relatively unsophisticated application of sand-bags to the application of geotextiles and elegantly designed structures to deflect fishing trawls.

Early on these projects suffered from a lack of available data for proper guidance. Strategies were often driven by contingency, implemented as short-term, stop-gap measures that frequently were not followed up by further studies and longer-term solutions. An environment for protecting one archaeological material or context will not necessarily be conducive to preserving another. Furthermore, it was apparent that the real effects of even simple stabilization strategies such as sand-bagging were not fully understood.

Exceptions to these less successful early attempts at management in situ range from the well-researched approach taken by Parks Canada to the intentional reburial of the Red Bay wreck timbers, following total excavation and comprehensive recording (Waddell 1994), to work conducted under the Reburial and Analysis of Archaeological Remains (RAAR) Project in Marstrand, Sweden (Gregory 2007; Richards et al. 2012). In the former case, the construction of the reburial pit (which contains over 3,000 timbers) incorporates facilities for the periodic collection of interstitial seawater and representative wood samples for analysis. Over the coming years this work will continue to provide important data on the utility of reburial strategies and the behavior of archaeological materials in seawater. As reburial strategies are normally based upon mimicking the original burial environment, this work will inform all the required stages of assessing, replicating, and monitoring that environment. Today ongoing projects and research (Björdal and Gregory 2012; Richards and McKinnon 2009; Oxley, chapter 10, this volume) are following these strategies of collecting data and expanding knowledge of site formation to enhance the capability to preserve submerged wreck sites.

Researchers in the field of maritime archaeology have long acknowledged the importance of site formation but have neither accepted a systematic theory to integrate it nor adopted widespread practices to do so. This is in part due to researchers focusing on specific research interests but more often derives from lack of funding, limited time, and lack of access to the specialists necessary to perform such work.

Moving Forward: Current Research in Site Formation

The increased focus on management of submerged resources in the last quarter decade, coupled with the increased emphasis on in situ preservation, has made the need to understand site formation a central focus of modern archaeology.

This volume brings together researchers from various backgrounds all with the commonality of working to enhance our understanding of the formation processes that impact submerged shipwrecks. Throughout the volume the authors discuss the fundamentals of their topic as well as their own research, highlighting new approaches that may prove useful in understanding how sites are formed and preserved. The volume is divided into three primary sections pertaining to specific aspects of site formation processes: natural processes, cultural processes, and the application of site formation data in heritage management.

Chapters in section 1 focus on natural processes that impact submerged shipwreck sites. Ben Ford (Indiana University of Pennsylvania, Department of Anthropology); Carrie Sowden (Great Lakes Historical Society); Katie Farnsworth (Indiana University of Pennsylvania, Department of Geology); and M. Scott Harris (College of Charleston, Department of Geology), discuss the geologic and geomorphologic impacts to shipwreck sites in coastal and inland environments and how these processes affect shipwreck sites. They highlight the case of the Red River wreck along the Texas-Oklahoma border and their current research in the Black River region of Lake Ontario to underscore their points. Matthew E. Keith and Amanda M. Evans (Tesla Offshore, LLC) take the discussion further offshore with an emphasis on the important role that seafloor properties play on the wrecking event and subsequent deterioration of a wreck site. In chapter 4 Rory Quinn (Centre for Maritime Archaeology, University of Ulster); Robin Saunders (Innervision Design); Ruth Plets (Centre for Maritime Archaeology University of Ulster); Kieran Westley (Centre for Maritime Archaeology, University of Ulster); and Justin Dix (School of Ocean and Earth Science, University of Southampton), discuss their leading research into the role of scour on shipwreck sites in predominantly sandy environments. In chapter 5 Ian D. MacLeod (Western Australian Maritime Museum) discusses the impact of corrosion on shipwreck sites, the utility of corrosion analysis, and the insight that this work can provide to archaeological analysis. In chapter 6 David Gregory (National Museum of Demark) discusses the degradation of wood and what this information can tell us about a shipwreck site, providing examples of how this information can aid in archaeological interpretation.

Section 2 of the volume consists of chapters pertaining to the impact of human activities on shipwreck sites. These impacts can range from actions performed leading up to the sinking event through modern impacts to wreck sites, whether intentional or accidental. In chapter 7 Amanda M. Evans and Antony Firth (Fjordr Limited) discuss impacts from offshore development projects (such as oil and gas operations, offshore wind farms, and harbor improvements) and management responses to these activities.

In chapter 8 Michael Brennan (Ocean Exploration Trust) discusses the impacts of bottom trawling on shipwreck sites and his research into quantifying the impacts of trawling on shipwreck sites in the Mediterranean and the Black Sea. In chapter 9 Martin Gibbs and Brad Duncan (University of New England, Australia) discuss the economics of ship loss and the broad spectrum of cultural activities leading up to and following a ship's sinking in an attempt to recover value from the wreck site.

The final section of the volume includes chapters that highlight the applications of site formation processes and the role this research plays by looking at research performed in the interests of heritage management, by both public and private entities. In order to manage shipwrecks within their jurisdiction properly, many heritage management agencies have developed unique strategies to bring about a more thorough understanding of a wide range of processes that take place across a diversity of environments. In Chapter 10, Ian Oxley (Historic England) discusses the role of site formation in underpinning the management and research performed by his agency. After detailing the development of English Heritage policies and their impact on management strategies, he discusses specific examples of projects and programs that integrate or specifically hinge upon site formation. Chapters 9 and 10 discuss research performed through partnerships between government agencies and private entities in studying deep-water wreck sites in the U.S. Gulf of Mexico. In Chapter 9 Daniel Warren (C & C Technologies, Inc.) discusses the use and efficacy of positioning technology in mapping deep-water wrecks and how it has influenced research into a series of deep-water wreck sites. In Chapter 10 Robert Church (C & C Technologies, Inc.) discusses his "equation of site formation" developed for modeling site distribution on metal-hulled deep-water wrecks. This unique research was developed from years of study for the goals of predicting the debris distribution pattern of metal-hulled wreck sites, aiding archaeologists in better understanding the site itself, assisting heritage managers in developing science-based avoidance criteria, and even assisting in reconstructing the events of the sinking.

While we acknowledge that a volume of this size can only scratch the surface of the wide range of topics and variables that impact submerged shipwreck sites throughout the world, we hope this work will fill a vacuum in the field of maritime archaeology by serving as an important reference tool that brings together many of the key concepts influencing site formation on submerged shipwreck sites. The research discussed throughout represents significant contributions to the field that we must continue to develop and expand upon in order to maximize our understanding of our past while ensuring the protection of these resources for future generations.

References Cited

Bascom, Willard
1976   *Deep Water, Ancient Ships: The Treasure Vault of the Mediterranean.* David and Charles, Newton Abbot.

Bass, George F.
1980   Marine Archaeology: A Misunderstood Science. *Ocean Yearbook* 2:137–152.

Björdal, Charlotte, and David Gregory
2012   *Wreck Protect: Decay and Protection of Archaeological Wooden Shipwrecks.* Archaeopress, Oxford.

Clausen, Carl J., and J. Barto Arnold III
1976   The Magnetometer and Underwater Archaeology: Magnetic Delineation of Individual Shipwreck Sites, a New Control Technique. *International Journal of Nautical Archaeology* 5(2):159–169.

Dumas, Frederic
1962   *Deep-Water Archaeology.* Translated by Honor Frost. Routledge and Kegan Paul, London.

1972   Ancient Wrecks. In *Underwater Archaeology: A Nascent Discipline*, pp. 27–34. UNESCO, Paris.

Ferrari, Ben J.
1994   *Physical, Biological and Cultural Factors Influencing the Formation, Stabilisation and Protection of Archaeological Deposits in UK Coastal Waters.* Ph.D. dissertation, University of St. Andrews.

Florian, Mary-Lou E.
1987   The Underwater Environment. In *Conservation of Marine Archaeological Objects*, edited by C. Pearson, pp. 1–20. Butterworths, London.

Foecke, Tim, Li Ma, Matthew A. Russell, David L. Conlin, and Larry E. Murphy
2009   Investigating Archaeological Site Formation Processes on the Battleship USS *Arizona* Using Finite Element Analysis. *Journal of Archaeological Science* 37(5):1090–1101.

Frost, Honor
1962   Submarine Archaeology and Mediterranean Wreck Formations. *Mariner's Mirror* 48:82–89.

Gibbins, David
1990   Analytical Approaches in Maritime Archaeology: A Mediterranean Perspective. *Antiquity* 64:376–89.

Gregory, David J.
1996   *Formation Processes in Underwater Archaeology: A Study of Chemical and Biological Deterioration.* Ph.D. dissertation, University of Leicester.

2007   Environmental Monitoring. Reburial and Analyses of Archaeological Remains: Studies on the Effects of Reburial on Archaeological Materials Performed in Marstrand, Sweden 2002–2005. In *The RAAR Project*, edited by T. Bergstrand and I. N. Godfrey, pp. 59–90. Bohusläns Museum, Uddevalla.

Guthrie, Jodi N., Linda L. Blackall, David J. W. Moriarty, and Peter Gesner
1994   Wrecks and Marine Microbiology Case Study from the *Pandora*. *Bulletin of the Australian Institute of Maritime Archaeology* 18(2):19–24.

Kenchington, T. J., J. A. Carter, and E. L. Rice
1989   The Indispensability of Non-Artifactual Data in Underwater Archaeology. In *Underwater Archaeology Proceedings from the Society for Historical Archaeology Conference, Baltimore, Maryland*, edited by J. Barton Arnold III, pp. 111–120. Society for Historical Archaeology, Pleasant Hill, California.

Kenchington, T. J., and E.L.R. Kenchington
1993   An Eighteenth Century Commercial Length-Frequency Sample of Atlantic Cod, *Gadus morphua*, Based on Archaeological Data. *Fisheries Research* 18:335–347.

Lenihan, Daniel J., Toni L. Carrell, Stephen Fosberg, Larry E. Murphy, Sandra L. Rayl, and John A. Ware (editors)
1981   *The Final Report of the National Reservoir Inundation Study*. Volumes I–II. National Park Service, Southwest Cultural Resources Center, Santa Fe.

Lenihan, Daniel J., and Larry Murphy
1981   Considerations for Research Designs in Shipwreck Archaeology. In *Underwater Archaeology: The Challenge Before Us. The Proceedings of the Twelfth Conference on Underwater Archaeology, New Orleans, Louisiana*, edited by Gordon P. Watts, pp. 69–75. Fathom Eight Special Publication No. 2, San Marino, California.

MacLeod, Ian D., and J. S. Killingley
1982   The Use of Barnacles to Establish Past Temperatures on Historic Shipwrecks. *International Journal of Nautical Archaeology* 11(3):249–252.

Martin, Colin
2011   Wreck-Site Formation Processes. In *Oxford Handbook of Maritime Archaeology*, edited by Alexis Catsambis, Ben Ford, and Donny Hamilton, pp. 47–67. Oxford University Press, New York.

Mathewson, C. C. (editor)
1989   *Interdisciplinary Workshop on the Physical-Chemical-Biological Processes Affecting Archaeological Sites*. Environmental Impact Research Program Contract Report EL-89-1. U.S. Army Corps of Engineers, Waterways Experimental Station, Vicksburg, Mississippi.

Muckelroy, Keith
1977   Historic Wreck Sites in Britain and Their Environments. *International Journal of Nautical Archaeology* 6(1):47–57.
1978   *Maritime Archaeology*. Cambridge University Press, Cambridge.

Murphy, Larry
1983   Shipwrecks as Database for Human Behavioural Studies. In *Shipwreck Anthropology*, edited by R. A. Gould, pp. 65–89. School of American Research Advanced Series, Santa Fe, New Mexico.

1997   Site Formation Processes. In *Encyclopedia of Underwater and Maritime Archaeology*, edited by James P. Delgado, pp. 386–388. Yale University Press, New Haven.

Nesteroff, W. D.

1972   Geological Aspects of Marine Sites. In *Underwater Archaeology: A Nascent Discipline*, pp. 175–184. UNESCO, Paris.

Oxley, Ian

1992   The Investigation of the Factors Which Affect the Preservation of Underwater Archaeological Sites. In *Underwater Archaeology Proceedings from the Society for Historical Archaeology Conference, Kingston, Jamaica*, edited by D. H. Keith and T. L. Carrell, pp. 105–110. Society for Historical Archaeology, Tucson, Arizona.

2001   Towards the Integrated Management of Scotland's Cultural Heritage, Examining Historic Shipwrecks as Marine Environmental Resources. *World Archaeology* 32(3):413–426.

Parker, A. J.

1981   Stratification and Contamination in Ancient Mediterranean Shipwrecks. *International Journal of Nautical Archaeology* 10(4):309–335.

Richards, Vicki, David Gregory, Ian MacLeod, and Henning Matthiesen

2012   Reburial and Analyses of Archaeological Remains in the Marine Environment: Investigations into the Effects on Metals. In *Conservation and Management of Archaeological Sites. Special Issue: Preserving Archaeological Remains in Situ*, edited by David Gregory and Henning Matthiesen, pp. 35–47. Maney Publishing.

Richards, Vicki, and Jennifer McKinnon (editors)

2009   *In Situ Conservation of Cultural Heritage: Public, Professionals and Preservation.* Flinders University Program in Maritime Archaeology, Past Foundation, Columbus, Ohio.

Schiffer, Michael B.

1987   *Formation Processes of the Archaeological Record.* University of New Mexico Press, Albuquerque.

Schiffer, Michael B., and W. L. Rathje

1973   Efficient Exploitation of the Archaeological Record: Penetrating Problems. In *Research and Theory in Current Archaeology*, edited by C. L. Redman, pp. 169–179. John Wiley and Sons, London.

Stewart, David

1999   Formation Processes Affecting Submerged Archaeological Sites: An Overview. *Geoarchaeology: An International Journal* 14(6):565–587.

Throckmorton, Peter

1965   Wrecks at Methone. *Mariners Mirror* 51(4):305–319.

Tylecote, R. F.

1977   Durable Materials for Seawater: The Archaeological Evidence. *International Journal of Nautical Archaeology* 6(4):269–283.

Waddell, Peter

1994   Long Range Shipwreck Timber Storage. *Bulletin Australian Institute for Maritime Archaeology* 18(1):1–4.

Ward, I.A.K., P. Larcombe, and P. Veth
1998   Towards a New Process-Orientated Model for Describing Wreck Disintegration: An Example Using the *Pandora* Wreck. *Bulletin of the Australian Institute for Maritime Archaeology* 22:109–114.
Wildesen, L. E.
1982   The Study of Impacts on Archaeological Sites. In *Advances in Archaeological Method and Theory*, Vol. 5, edited by Michael B. Schiffer, pp. 51–96. Academic Press, New York.

I

Natural Processes

2

Coastal and Inland Geologic
and Geomorphic Processes

BEN FORD, CARRIE SOWDEN, KATHERINE FARNSWORTH,
AND M. SCOTT HARRIS

Submerged archaeological sites are environmental anomalies, and many of the coastal and inland site formation processes result from the site and the environment reaching equilibrium with each other. As the site affects the environment and is in turn integrated into the environment, the two become inextricably linked. The site excavated by archaeologists is as much a result of the environment as it is the original human deposition. The formation of each site is, consequently, different, because of variations in the type of site (e.g., wooden hull or steel hull), the way the site was deposited (e.g., shipwreck or abandonment), and the environment (i.e., the factors acting on the wreck; Martin 2011). However, environmental site formation processes are uniformitarian and with proper study they can be stripped away. Once the results of site formation processes have been removed, the remaining patterns have an increased likelihood of being the result of past human activity (Murphy 1998; Will and Clark 1996). In addition to isolating human activity from patterns formed by natural processes, it is useful to understand how sites form, and why preservation varies, as means to understanding better the linkages between the data recovered by archaeologists and the past human activities that formed those data. These aims all fall within what is often called middle-range theory (Binford 1978).

The uniformitarian nature of site formation processes, and in particular geomorphic site formation processes, led to their early consideration by underwater archaeologists. Frederic Dumas discussed the effects of geomorphic variations in site burial rates in his 1962 *Deep-Water Archaeology*, and Keith Muckelroy devoted a substantial portion of his foundational *Maritime Archaeology* (1978) to geomorphic site formation processes (as did his terrestrial counterpart Michael Schiffer). Of Muckelroy's eleven factors affecting site formation, four were geomorphic, including the three that he found to be the most important in determining the survival of archaeological remains: underwater topography, the nature of the coarsest deposits, and the nature of the finest deposits (Muckelroy 1978:163).

This chapter builds on these early observations to discuss how geologic and geomorphic processes affect coastal and inland archaeological site formation. Following a synthesis of previous studies, we present two case studies that illustrate how these processes affect shipwreck sites and the search for shipwrecks.

Coastal and Inland Geologic and Geomorphic Site Formation Processes

Any submerged inland or coastal region is apt to contain multiple sites and multiple types of sites, all of which are affected by geomorphic processes. Consequently this section focuses on site formation factors instead of specific site types. For example, erosion is a formation process along coasts and rivers and affects both prehistoric and historic habitations as well as shipwrecks. However, erosion does not work alone to form a site; it is just one part of a complex suite of variables "ranging from the width and depth of the Continental Shelf to seasonal changes in regional high pressure systems" (Conlin 2005:169). The processes discussed here include the interaction between the availability, sources, and characteristics of bottom material and the movement of water through the region; topography; changes in water level and erosion; and human alterations to the region.

Many of the formation processes discussed in this chapter are physical and apply to both coastal and inland environments. Chemical and biological formation processes, however, tend to vary between salt and fresh water and bear some mention before proceeding. These considerations are also discussed in more detail in chapters 5 and 6. The most notable difference between fresh and salt environments is the presence of shipworms (*Teredo navalis*) and boring crustaceans of the genus *Limnoria*, which live only in seawater. Wood borer infestation is dependent on temperature, salinity, depth, and dissolved oxygen content, with oxygen content playing the dominant role, so their presence will also vary within the coastal zone and into deeper waters (Gregory 2004; Leino et al. 2011; Paola 2005). Bacteria and fungi of different types appear in both fresh and seawater. These infestations, which emit an enzyme that breaks down the cellulose in wood, tend to be less destructive to wood than are marine borers, but they can have an effect on the long-term preservation of a shipwreck. They can also create microenvironments that influence site preservation; for example, when decay creates a hydrogen sulfide–rich layer (Gregory 2004; Leino et al. 2011; Singley 1988). The availability of oxygen is the principal determinant of fungi and bacteria infestation, so that neither thrives more than a few centimeters below the surface. As discussed later in this chapter, how quickly a shipwreck is buried and whether it remains buried is a major determinant of how well it is preserved. Finally, the effects of water chemistry vary between inland and coastal environments. Seawater contains a relatively constant amount of salts, while bodies of freshwater can vary widely due to local conditions such as use of de-icing salts and fertilizers. The greater amounts of salts in seawater tend to cause more iron corrosion through an electrochemical galvanic cell reaction (Cronyn 1996; Matthiesen et al. 2004; Rayl et al. 1981; Singley 1988; Ware and Rayl 1981). In some tests higher concentrations of salts have led to greater wood weight loss than fresh water (Ware and Rayl 1981). It is possible, in some environments, for there to be enough salts present in fresh water to cause similar effects (Singley 1988).

Sediment Characteristics and Movement

The type of sediment and its rate of accumulation are fundamental to the preservation of submerged archaeological sites. Generally, rapidly accumulating fine sediments lead to the best preservation (Muckelroy 1978; Quinn et al. 2007:1458; Ward et al. 1999:43). A site that is evenly and gently enveloped in sediment is removed from oxygenated and abrasive environments so that physical, biological, and chemical deterioration slow dramatically. Anecdotally, this pattern is apparent in the comparison of the Yorktown wrecks and the *Adelaar*. Some of the British vessels sunk at Yorktown were in areas of strong currents and erosion. These vessels were much less preserved than those vessels, including *Betsy*, that were protected by deep layers of silt (Broadwater 1980:231–232, 1998:471). As a counterpoint to *Betsy*, *Adelaar* sank in an exposed and abrasive environment off Scotland, where even the historically recorded cargo of bricks was ground to nothing (Martin 2011:57). Building on similar observations at the *Pandora* site, Ward and colleagues (1999) developed a quantitative model of sediment accumulation and its implications for site preservation. Their model moved beyond anecdotal observations by collecting on-site current, wave, and sediment data to compare with the archaeological record and create a more complete understanding of how the environment and the hull interacted as the site formed. While burial is generally beneficial, the pattern of burial is important, and there are exceptions where filling and burial have damaged a shipwreck site. For example, *Swan* and *Invincible* both accumulated sediments unevenly, leading to significant hull deformation (Martin 2011:65; Quinn et al. 1998:133). Of course the archaeologists were able to record this deformation only because sediment continued to accumulate over the site, preserving the timbers in their twisted and broken state.

Sediment sources include rivers and in situ eroding parent material, but the sediment does not always remain in one place; waves, tides, and currents regularly redistribute sediment so that the direction of this water movement and the position of a site relative to sediment traps also influence if and how a site is buried. The velocity of this water movement and the type of sediment (particle size, density, and cohesion) govern the frequency and distance of sediment suspension, movement, and deposition. These complex relationships are illustrated by Hjulström (fig. 2.1) and Shields diagrams.

Waves dominate the movement of sediments in the nearshore because they provide the energy to mobilize sediments and combine with currents to govern sediment movement (Conlin 2005:141; Hayes et al. 1984:3; Ward et al. 1999:50). This process can bury or expose an archaeological site through the movement of sediments, but it can also lead to the burial or movement of a site through direct action on artifacts. Artifacts in the nearshore are a part of the sediment budget of that shore system and susceptible to erosion, movement, and redeposition just like any other shore sediment (Will and Clark 1996:504). Less dense materials move in the direction of littoral drift, but denser artifacts often settle in place. The wave energy tends to place near-surface sediments into suspension, which allows denser materials to drop vertically to the base of the suspended sediments. The depth that the artifact settles below the sediment surface is dependent on the size and velocity of the waves (Murphy 1990:15; Waters 1992:270). This process results in a secondary deposition of artifacts that is analogous to a terrestrial site deflated by wind processes. Older and younger materials are deposited at the same level, dictated by the wave base, regardless of the time between their depositions (Muckelroy 1978:177; Murphy 1990:52). Since the process is governed by wave energy, the highest energy event since a dense item was deposited will dictate the depth of its burial. High energy events will also tend to encapsulate dense artifacts below the depth affected by normal waves. The longer a site has been submerged, the greater its opportunity to

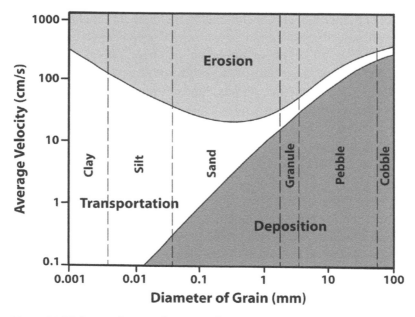

Figure 2.1. Hjulström diagram illustrating the erosion, transportation, and deposition velocities of various grain sizes.

have been affected by a high energy event, so the law of superposition may still hold. Over time, however, the dense components of a wave-affected site will tend to be winnowed to a consistent depth.

In addition to waves, tides and currents affect site formation processes. While, unlike waves, these forces have been found to have mixed or limited impact on the fragmentation of shipwrecks (Martin 2011; Quinn et al. 1998:113; Ward et al. 1999:50), they do play a significant role in the movement of sediments. Longshore currents, which result from the prevailing wave pattern and tidal flow, are responsible for eroding sediments around some sites and depositing sediments on other sites (Conlin 2005:137; Millet and Goiran 2007). Strong currents, such as spring tides, eddies, and storm-driven currents, are also among the primary drivers of sand wave migration. The movement of sand waves across the seafloor can result in the cyclical burial and exposure of an archaeological site, with preservation, deterioration, and abrasion depending on how often and how long the site is exposed or buried (Caston 1979:200; Ward et al. 1999:51).

Rivers also play a role in the movement of sediments. Rivers have their own currents and sediment budgets, which affect the burial and exposure of riverine archaeological sites. The water and sediment flowing out of rivers also affect coastal sites by contributing to the regional sediment regime. The current velocity and amount of sediment flowing through and out of a river are linked to larger environmental patterns, such as temperature and precipitation, as these ultimately govern the river flow and erosion in the region (Conlin 2005:142). As was true for artifacts in the coastal zone, artifacts within a river are part of that river's sediment budget and are as susceptible to transport and redeposition as any other similar-density particle (Quinn et al. 2007:1457).

The forces that move sediments are often governed by factors beyond the immediate region, such as the width of the continental shelf, proximity to major currents (e.g., Gulf Stream), and weather patterns (Conlin 2005:137, 140). These forces, and the sediment and current characteristics, are all inter-related in terms of regional geomorphic site formation processes. For example, sediment type, sediment migration, waves, and currents all bear on the burial and exposure of shipwreck sites through scour. Scour is more fully discussed later in this book (see Quinn et al., chapter 4, this volume), but a brief description will serve to illustrate the interplay between regional site formation processes. Scour can be explained by Bernoulli's principle: when a current encounters an obstruction (such as a shipwreck), pressure increases on that side of the obstruction, causing a decrease in velocity and a decrease in the ability of the current to transport sediment; but as the current moves past the obstruction, pressure decreases and velocity increases, allowing the current to mobilize and transport sediment. The result is the possible removal of sediment down-current of the obstruction, if the force of the pressure difference exceeds that of gravity, and the formation of a scour trench. The obstruction can then settle into the scour trench. This process is governed by the speed and direction of the current relative to the obstruction, which are influenced by conditions such as water depth, location, weather, and tides as well as the composition of the bottom material. Sandy sediments are the most susceptible to scour because they require less velocity to erode than do cohesive clays and silts. The process of scouring and settling can continue until the obstruction is buried or it comes to rest on a more cohesive stratum. Thus the geology as well as the geomorphology of the region is important. If the shipwreck comes to rest on a sediment layer that cannot be scoured, a portion of the vessel may remain above the sediment surface and is unlikely to be preserved. Once the obstruction has been removed, either through settling or deterioration, the scouring process ends (Caston 1979; Conlin 2005; McNinch et al. 2006). Burial through scour and settling can also be accelerated or undone by other geomorphic processes. Migrating sand waves can overtake and bury an exposed shipwreck (Caston 1979:200). As the sand wave migrates away, the scour process may resume. Changes in currents can also uncover a site previously buried by scouring. For example, a shift in a tidal inlet may cause erosion across a site, reexposing the site. Once a site is reexposed, the process of scouring and settling will resume until the obstruction settles beneath the new sediment surface (McNinch et al. 2006:304). Clearly there are causal links between the physical processes of sediment movement, and those processes are further interconnected as they operate in concert and opposition to form an archaeological site.

TOPOGRAPHY

Bottom topography figures into sediment movement by controlling depth, interrupting or channeling currents, and mobilizing sediments, but the morphology of the submerged surface also influences site formation in other ways. The slope of the bottom, combined with gravity, influences the break-up and deposition of a shipwreck site. The hull tends to collapse down-slope, and timbers and other materials become concentrated in that portion of the site (Bernier 2007, 4:281; Quinn et al. 2007:1458). At the microtopography level, the presence of geomorphic features such as gullies, cracks, or karst solution cavities may trap artifacts and prevent them from being further eroded (Horrell et al. 2009; Martin 2011). Denser artifacts are the most likely to become lodged in these locations, and in some cases they may be trapped not far from where they were deposited, helping to preserve the context of the site.

EROSION

The process of erosion relates to both topography and sediment movement. The shape of the region and the nature of its geology influence how riverbanks and coasts erode, and the sediment mobilized by this erosion becomes part of the sediment budget for the region. Scour, sand waves, and other processes already described are aspects of erosion, but this section deals specifically with sites located in active, or once active, erosive environments, such as coasts or riverbanks.

The location of the coast is not fixed, but moves with changes in sea level, and has been generally moving landward in fits and starts since the last glacial maximum, circa 18,000 years ago. In the case of submerged sites, rising sea levels can help preserve them by reducing the effects of wave action on the site and generally lowering the energy of the site environment (Conlin

2005:137; Ford et al. 2009; Murphy 1990:52). However, for sites that were originally subaerial, inundation is often a destructive process (Kelley et al. 2010; National Trust 2005; Sear et al. 2011; Stright et al. 1999). The same is true in rivers, lakes, and reservoirs, where rising water erodes archaeological sites as well as changing their physical, biological, and chemical environments (Lenihan et al. 1981; Mcphail et al. 2009).

The direct action of waves on archaeological deposits and the matrix supporting archaeological sites causes much of the destruction along coasts. Waves and currents disturb the site context, move artifacts horizontally, erode features, abrade artifacts, place sediments in suspension so that artifacts and ecofacts move vertically, and generally leave little if any useful archaeological information (Erlandson 2008; Head 2000; Mcphail et al. 2009:49; Westley et al. 2011a). In high latitudes, ice can also play a role in coastal and littoral erosion. The weight and movement of ice can damage sites and move artifacts considerable distances in addition to contributing to shoreline erosion (Bernier 2007, 4:285; Will and Clark 1996).

These processes are acting constantly, eroding sites as the sea inches landward, and can be significantly exacerbated by major storms. It is estimated that millions of archaeological sites are damaged or lost annually to erosion, and hurricane Katrina in 2005 destroyed an estimated 1,000 historical and archaeological sites in a single storm (Erlandson 2008:168). These processes are likely to accelerate during the next century if storm activity increases as predicted by climatologists (Westley et al. 2011a:352).

The destruction of coastal sites, however, is not absolute, as certain geologic and geomorphic attributes tend to lead to site preservation. The rate of local sea level rise—which is determined not only by the global rate of water rise (eustatic change) but also by the slope of the shore and whether the region is experiencing isostatic rebound or subsidence—plays a major role in whether a site is preserved. Generally, the less time that the site is directly acted on by waves and the less time that it has the possibility of experiencing a major storm event, the more likely it is to be preserved. The presence of protective features, such as islands or barrier beaches, also tends to mitigate the destructive forces of marine transgression (the movement of the waterline across the site). Thus bedrock topography and the geomorphology of the coast play a role in whether a site is preserved. Finally, the depth of the site below the ground surface influences its preservation. The deeper a site is buried, the farther it is removed from the erosive power of waves, wind, and ice (Kelley et al. 2010:695; Murphy 1990:52; Waters 1992:278). For example, preservation of the Douglass Beach submerged terrestrial site was the result of barrier island formation and migration. The site was inhabited when it was in an upland or back-barrier lagoonal margin environment, and as sea level rose a barrier island first protected the site from high energy waves and, later, migrated across the site, burying it and protecting it until the coastline had moved far enough inland that the site was not directly exposed to wave action (Murphy 1990:52).

Barrier beach migration also plays a role in shipwreck site formation. Barrier beaches tend to be mutable; their formation and movement governed by tides, currents, waves, and wind as well as sediments originating from farther offshore and nearby rivers. These forces can lead to the reshaping of islands through littoral drift and aeolian processes, the landward movement of the island (transgression) through wave and tidal action, and the seaward expansion of the island (progradation) through sediment accumulation (Damour 2002; Waters 1992). Because they are always changing, barrier beaches may accumulate more shipwrecks than stable shorelines where charts remain reliable. They also lead to dynamic site formation processes, in which a shipwreck's environmental energy and exposure changes throughout the life of the wreck.

The shipwrecks around Dog Island and St. George Island, barrier islands on Florida's Gulf Coast, offer a good example of the processes at work in these environments (Damour 2002; Horrell 2005; Meide et al. 2001). These shipwrecks have been variously exposed or buried as the beach moves landward. Melanie Damour (2002) has also argued that the movement of St. George Island has confounded past attempts to locate the HMS *Fox* (lost in 1799) and that it is possible the hull is buried within the island. A similar fate appears to be befalling the *Vale*, which was lost on the landward side of Dog Island in 1899. While the wreck was partially exposed or shallowly buried in 1999, it has since been completely buried as the island transgresses (Meide et al. 2001; Chuck Meide, pers. comm., 2013). Meanwhile, a hull associated with the fishing vessel *Priscilla*, lost in 1914 only a few hundred meters from the *Vale* but on the seaward side of the island, has become increasingly exposed as the island moves away from the wreck (Meide et al. 2001).

Shipwrecks such as the *Priscilla*, subjected to coastal erosion on exposed sections of beach, are among the least likely to be preserved. In these high energy environments, often only the heavy iron portions of the wreck remain on the beach, the sea having broken up and carried away the wooden components (Russell 2005). Where articulated hull fragments remain, it is largely a result of the amount of energy present in the beach system. The energy of the beach environment is a significant determinant of the sediment grain size of that beach, and portions of hulls are better preserved on sandy beaches, where they can become buried, but are nearly absent on rocky beaches (Russell 2004, 2005). Because of these site formation processes, beached shipwrecks are one of the many instances where natural site formation processes may mask our understanding of the material record. Matthew Russell (2004:382) has hypothesized that site formation processes are the primary reason that most beached shipwreck sites date to the nineteenth and twentieth centuries; the majority of earlier beached wrecks have been obliterated by the destructive and nearly constant geomorphic processes of the coast.

Erosion is not limited to the coasts; it is also an active process at riverine sites. As a river meanders it erodes sediments in one place and deposits them in another; all things being equal, the erosion and deposition are balanced. However, once an archaeological site has been eroded, much of its information potential is lost, so that each shift in river erosion has the potential to erase a portion of the region's archaeological record. This process can damage terrestrial sites as well as ship hulls embedded in riverbanks (Horrell et al. 2009:31–32; Milne et al. 1997; Simms and Albertson 2000). The presence of archaeological sites along rivers also complicates the site formation process of sites within rivers. As a river erodes its banks, or as storms wash artifacts from nearby sites into the river, the river acts as a trap, and the archaeological materials become part of the sediment budget of the river. The eroded archaeological materials might be deposited on a second archaeological site within the river, since sites often trap materials coming downstream, or the eroded materials may be deposited in a lower-energy portion of the river. Because artifact density and river velocity control where the materials are deposited, many artifacts are likely to accumulate in one portion of the river, creating what appears to be a site. The Flintlock Site, Florida, demonstrates this phenomenon: it consists of archaeological materials eroded from upland sites that became concentrated in a stretch of the Apalachicola River where the discharge from a power plant deflects the river current, reducing its velocity and allowing the artifacts to accumulate (Horrell et al. 2009).

Anthropogenic Factors

The role of humans in creating the Flintlock Site, both by inhabiting sites near rivers and changing the regional fluvial system, brings us to their effects in coastal and inland geomorphic site formation processes. The regional geology and geomorphology influenced where people settled by controlling slope, aspect, access to potable water, harbor formation, and other considerations (Quinn et al. 2007; Westley et al. 2011b). The locations of harbors as well as ship-traps, shoals, and other geologic features similarly influenced trade route and wreck locations. Thus geologic and anthropogenic forces interact in site formation, both at the establishment of the site and throughout its history.

Humans affect geomorphic processes by changing sediment transport regimes in rivers and along coasts, by changing water quality, by altering channels through dredging and armoring, by raising or lowering water levels, by trapping sediments behind dams, by influencing the global climate, and through many other intended and unintended consequences of our actions (Broadwater 1980:231; Erlandson 2008; Halpern et al. 2008; Horrell et al. 2009:12; Lenihan et al. 1981; Walter and Merritts 2008; Wilkinson and Murphy 1986). The archaeological record is full of evidence of anthropogenic change to the environment, past and present (Ford 2011), but two examples will suffice. Millet and Goiran (2007) have argued that by separating their eastern and western harbors with the Heptastadion, the ancient Alexandrians prevented the eastern harbor from filling with sand. In this case a man-made feature was used to affect a local geomorphic pattern and change the sediment regime in a harbor. It is also a good example of how studying an archaeological feature in a regional context can provide a new interpretation of its use. Studying modern anthropogenic forces, Adams and Black (2004) have identified how regional cultural forces such as dredging and shipping routes have changed the geomorphology of shipwreck sites at St. Peter Port, Guernsey. Through channel dredging and propeller-wash erosion, formerly compact and stable sediments have begun to erode. In addition to exposing hull timbers, this process has exposed items such as galley fuel, rope, and shoe fragments—items that until recently were protected within the hull of the shipwrecks and that are unlikely to survive in situ once exposed.

Change and Continuity

The current environment does not always resemble the past environment. Meandering rivers, rising sea levels, and changes in sediment regimes are all geomorphic processes that change the regional environment and, in the process, affect how submerged archaeological sites form. These changes mean that we cannot always apply our current perception of the environment to the past, but through an understanding of the underlying processes we can strip them away to re-create what the environment was like when the site was deposited and how the environment influenced the formation of the site. The regional geologic and geomorphic processes are perhaps the most uniformitarian of all the site formation processes and are consequently the most knowable through careful study of stratified sediment and bottom characteristics, current and past flora and fauna, the site itself, and geomorphic models.

It is also important to note that all these changes become more pronounced with time and proximity to the coast. The amount of time that has passed since a site was deposited increases the likelihood that the site has been notably affected by ongoing processes (e.g., sea-level rise) and specific events (e.g., hurricanes). Similarly, the number of factors and the force of individual factors both increase near the shore. Coasts are higher in energy than deep-water environments, and the intensity of that activity translates directly to site formation processes.

Finally, the geomorphic component of a site's formation process is made up of several separate but interrelated processes, which in turn interact with other biological, chemical, physical, and anthropogenic forces, the timing of which is important. Site formation is not simply a sum of the forces acting on a site but a process where future events act on the environment and site created by past events. David Conlin's (2005:164) analysis of the interplay between hurricane Hugo (1989) and the wrecks of *Housatonic* and *Hunley* illustrates this point. The wrecks had scoured to the Pleistocene clay layer by 1989 and were buried, so that when Hugo passed over them they were unaffected. However, the hurricane caused a large amount of sediment to wash out of Charleston Harbor. The offshore transport of these sediments was probably augmented by the man-made jetties that help clean the harbor. As a result, the wrecks were buried under additional sediment. Because the new sediments were deposited under hurricane conditions, they were not readily removed by normal nearshore processes, resulting in a net increase in the burial of the wrecks. If these events had happened in a different order, such as a hurricane immediately following the wrecking event, a different outcome would have resulted.

Case Studies

Red River, Oklahoma

In 1990, with the shifting of the Red River in Choctaw County, Oklahoma, the steamboat *Heroine* was exposed after being encased under 40 feet of sediment and a farmer's field for 147 years (fig. 2.2). The river systems of the western United States lend themselves to such surprise discoveries due to the gradual movement of rivers as well as quick changes in path caused by avulsion events during floods (Corbin 1998). The *Heroine* sank during the first season of navigation on the upper section of the Red River, on May 7, 1838, on her way to deliver supplies to the military outpost at Fort Towson, Indian Territory (Brown and Crisman 2005; Crisman 2005; Crisman and Lees 2003; Crisman et al. 2013; Lees and Arnold 2000).

Figure 2.2. Case study locations.

Prior to 1838 much of the Red River was non-navigable due to the Great Log Raft. With Henry Shreve's invention of the "snagboat," the upper Red River was cleared for navigation by 1838, and ships were able to deliver supplies and settlers to the area with more regularity. However, the river remained hazardous because of its changing nature and the threat of hidden dangers just below the surface. The *Heroine* was caught on one of those dangers in the spring of 1838 when her hull was punctured by a log snag that was just below the waterline. Some of her cargo and her engine were salvaged, but the ship and any remaining goods were left to the river (Crisman 2014; Crisman et al. 2013).

Site Formation Processes

The river quickly enveloped the shipwreck and deposited sediment into the hold, while portions of the superstructure likely protruded temporarily from the water. Like many shipwreck events in high velocity areas, the upper works of the ship were quickly washed away with the rush of the river current; however, the hull of the ship was left mostly intact due to the quick sedimentation.

Beginning in 1843, when a massive flood caused the river channel to migrate south, erosion abandoned the shipwreck in floodplain deposits and eventually buried it under 12 meters (40 feet) of sediment, which became part of an Oklahoma hay field. The site was rediscovered when the river channel migrated northward again and eroded portions of the farmer's field due to another massive storm and flood in 1990. The *Heroine* was first noticed sticking out of the bank of the river on the Oklahoma side. Over the course of subsequent years, the river continued to meander until the shipwreck was in the thalweg, or deepest part, of the river.

Colin Martin (2011:48) has conceived of wreck formation in three phases: the wrecking event, an unstable or dynamic phase, and a stable phase. These phases are generally sequential as the wreck is incorporated into the physical environment, but Martin notes that the stable phase can revert to a dynamic phase. In the case of the *Heroine*, the hull went through the dynamic phase twice; once when initially sunk in 1838, and then again when it was reexposed in the early 1990s. During these dynamic phases it was subjected to currents, scour, differential sediment deposition, abrasion, and anthropogenic factors, but it was also buried in sediment for long periods of time, leading to a generally good state of preservation.

When the *Heroine* struck the snag in the river, the captain was unable to release the ship. The snag occurred aft of the forward bulkhead (a snag locker designed to help the vessel survive striking a snag), and held the ship in place as it filled with water. Because it was held in place at the bow, and due to the direction of the current, sand was scoured from around the bow. The end product of this is a shipwreck lowest at the bow: there was difference in elevation of approximately 3 m between the bow and the stern over the ship's length of 51.7 m (136 feet 8 inches).

Fieldwork directed by Kevin Crisman of the Institute of Nautical Archaeology and supported by the Oklahoma Historical Society took place over five seasons. Observations made during this time demonstrated that the river system fluctuated substantially day to day and year to year. Some years the water was high, obscuring all of the wreck, and the current ran very fast, making work difficult. In other years the water was very low with a slow current, making work much easier. However, the movement of river sediment created the biggest hurdle—but allowed for observation of the dynamics of the Red River and how the river interacted with the wreck to form the site.

During the excavation of the *Heroine*, specific sediment layers were observed that could be easily correlated with the historical record. Of most interest was a layer of rocks and pebbles inside the hull. The movement of items of such size, to create such a layer within the hull of the ship, must have been related to a large event, likely the 1843 flood. This flood eroded the river banks and caused the river to shift south and bury the shipwreck entirely. At this time the *Heroine* entered Martin's stable phase, until exposed again in 1990 by another great flood (Martin 2011).

In years when the river was running fast and high, excavation on the shipwreck was slow and frustrating. The excavators would clear portions of the wreck for 5–6 hours, finally clearing a section enough to document. By the next morning, the entire space would be completely filled again with sediment as well as logs, branches, twigs, and other light material that was being carried down the river. The space inside the hull created a lull in the flow of the river, allowing for these items to drop out of the water column and rest in the space that had been freshly cleared. This process likely happened at a similar rate immediately after the vessel wrecked and explains the good state of preservation inside the hull, where intact withy bound barrels of pork were discovered.

It was also helpful to watch the dynamic phase of Martin's process over the course of five years while working on this project. The movement of sediment-laden water clearly had a detrimental effect on anything that was not buried. The structure that could be viewed above the water eroded away year by year. Precluding human control of the river system, the exposed portion of the wreck will continue to erode until the next major flood shifts the river again and reburies the *Heroine*.

While the changing Red River is not unusual, it is a different river than it was in 1838. The Red River and its tributaries have been dammed for water control and to create hydroelectric power. This anthropogenic regional pressure creates a different environment, with the flow of the river now fluctuating on a sometimes daily rather than seasonal basis. In today's river, even with the shallow draft of a western river steamboat, it would be impossible to navigate the *Heroine* in this area. This portion of the river is now considered non-navigable by the Army Corps of Engineers, suggesting that the modern river has a lower energy than the historic river.

Black River Bay, New York

In 2011 a consortium of Indiana University of Pennsylvania, College of Charleston, and Great Lakes Historical Society worked to locate and identify shipwrecks sunk after the War of 1812 in the Black River Bay, New York (see fig. 2.2). The purpose of the project was twofold: (1) to locate and identify two War of 1812 ships, and (2) to gather data to understand the geology of the area better. With that in mind, a two-part project was designed utilizing both archaeologists and geologists, looking to gain double the information out of a single set of data.

The area of Black River Bay was selected for its important role in the War of 1812 naval efforts. Sackets Harbor was the United States naval station on Lake Ontario, and at the end of the war many of the newly built naval ships were laid up in there as well as farther up the bay in Storrs Harbor. While still a freshwater fluvial system, the Black River Bay is significantly different from the previous example in Oklahoma. The area under study ranges from a deep navigable bay that ends in Lake Ontario to shallows with moving and drifting sand bars. The goals of the study were to survey the entire bay floor up to the shallows with a side-scan sonar, magnetometer, and sub-bottom profiler. The geologists would use the data to develop a better understanding of how the bay formed and what processes were ongoing; the data would also be used by the archaeologists aiming to identify a War of 1812 shipwreck, the *Mohawk*, that may have been towed out of Sackets Harbor and sunk in the deeper waters of the river. Additionally there was a recursive relationship between the geological and archaeological studies, with the potential that a shipwreck of known age could act as a marker horizon to understand sedimentation better and with the likelihood that geologic information about lake floor morphology and shoreline formation would inform the archaeological work.

Mohawk was suspected to be within the survey area due to several lines of circumstantial evidence. Following the War of 1812 *Mohawk* was not removed from the harbor with the majority of the fleet. Instead it was resting on the bottom in 1829 when William Vaughan was contracted to remove it. Vaughan's contract does not specify how he was to dispose of the vessel, and one hypothesis was that he refloated the demasted hull and resank it immediately outside the harbor, where the bay is approximately 18 m deep. This would have been the most expedient option to remove the ship as a hazard to navigation. This hypothesis was supported by an early marine remote sensing survey that identified a rise in the bay floor accompanied by a magnetic anomaly (Murphy 1976) as well as by anecdotal reports from fishermen of recovering large hull fragments from the bay.

After completing the survey, however, neither the side-scan sonar nor magnetometer data suggested that the remains of a large vessel were present within the bay. Modern small craft, dock fragments, and tree trunks were identified in the remote sensing records, but diver inspections of the possible and ambiguous targets were negative. Furthermore, the sub-bottom profiler data indicated that there was less than 1 m of soft sediment overlying a much harder substrate, most likely bedrock. Subsequent geologic sampling confirmed that the soft surficial sediment was silt and fine sands but was unable to penetrate the substrate. This environment makes it unlikely that the hull of *Mohawk* is buried within the thin layer of silt and suggests that the bottom of the bay did not provide a protective environment. If *Mohawk* was scuttled in the bay, and it may not have been, it has either completely deteriorated or was flushed into the lake.

Despite more than two hundred years of European occupation and evidence of Native American habitation near Black River Bay extending back millennia, only mid to late twentieth-century materials were identified in the main channel of the bay. This observation suggests that the channel is not conducive to the preservation of archaeological sites, likely because of the current through the channel and the relatively thin layer of soft sediment overlaying a hard substrate. The research described here was designed as an integrated geologic and archaeological survey, with the same data used to address both lines of inquiry. However, if the surveys had been conducted sequentially, the geologic data and an appreciation of fluvial site formation processes could have rendered an archaeological survey unnecessary. In areas where preexisting geologic and geomorphic data is

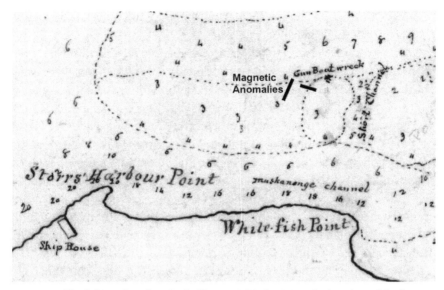

Figure 2.3. Black River Bay chart by R. Vinton, 1829, depicting the location of the "gunboat wreck" and magnetic anomalies.

available, assessing site formation processes makes it possible to model the likelihood of site preservation.

The second part of the archaeological project was to search for a 75-foot armed barge that had been laid up in Storrs Harbor but had broken its mooring and caught on a sandbar near where the Black River and Muskellunge Creek join at the head of the bay. Unlike the main channel of the bay, the shape of which has remained largely unchanged over the past two centuries, a comparison of modern and historic maps of the region indicates that the shallows of the bay have shifted significantly in the last two centuries, in particular since increasing regional agriculture led to more upland erosion (Ford 2009). Within the shallows, islands and shoals present in the early nineteenth century have disappeared, while others have formed or moved. A map from 1829 (fig. 2.3) clearly labels the armed barge wreck location ("Gun Boat wreck"), but the shoreline in this region has shifted slightly, an adjacent island has expanded substantially, and the shoals in the region have changed considerably, making it difficult to pinpoint the wreck location. The discordance between the historic and modern maps illustrates the necessity to understand sediment movement when attempting to locate a buried shipwreck. Furthermore, the possibility that the wreck was in good condition, having been encapsulated in a shoal, was based on an understanding of the site formation processes of shipwrecks in fluvial systems.

In order to explore this site, a magnetometer survey was conducted that indicated two lines of anomalies in the vicinity of the armed barge wreck. A more detailed geophysical survey was undertaken by towing a ground penetrating radar (GPR) instrument across the frozen surface of the bay. This survey took advantage of the shifting sediments, in that the shallow water in the survey area allowed the GPR to penetrate approximately 4 meters (13 feet) of bottom sediment. The GPR survey produced a high amplitude anomaly approximately 23 meters (75 feet) long (fig. 2.4), which was investigated with a test excavation. The excavation did not locate the armed barge wreck; instead it encountered a series of apparently natural stones at the depth indicated in the GPR records.

While this wreck has yet to be found, the search for it has been heavily influenced by an understanding of site formation processes within the Black River. It is hypothesized that the armed barge became lodged on a dynamic sand bar formed by rapidly shifting sediment in the shallow headwaters of Black River Bay near where Muskellunge Creek joins the bay. Once embedded in the sand bar, the armed barge was subjected to repeated scour and settling cycles as the river current moved around the hull. These cycles may well have been punctuated by major floods that occasionally affected the river during the historic period as well as by ice erosion during the winter. The hull was likely buried by new sediments entering the river system through agricultural erosion. It is possible that the armed barge is actually encapsulated in the adjacent island, not unlike Damour's (2002) argument that HMS *Fox* is within St. George Island. In both cases, changes in islands and bars make locating the shipwreck difficult, even with solid historical cartographic evidence (Damour 2002:117). In the case of the Lake Ontario armed barge, this situation has been exacerbated by the St. Lawrence Seaway, which maintains Lake Ontario at a level slightly higher than its historical average. This anthropogenic change makes the historic charts harder to interpret, but it also has broader site formation process implications by changing the environment of the shoreline and more deeply submerging sites.

Differences in site formation potential between the navigable portion of Black River Bay and the sandy shallows, within 2 km of each other, are striking. The active channel appears to be a destructive environment, while the also active but sediment-rich shallows may contain sites buried by 3 m or more of sediment. This juxtaposition suggests how dynamic river

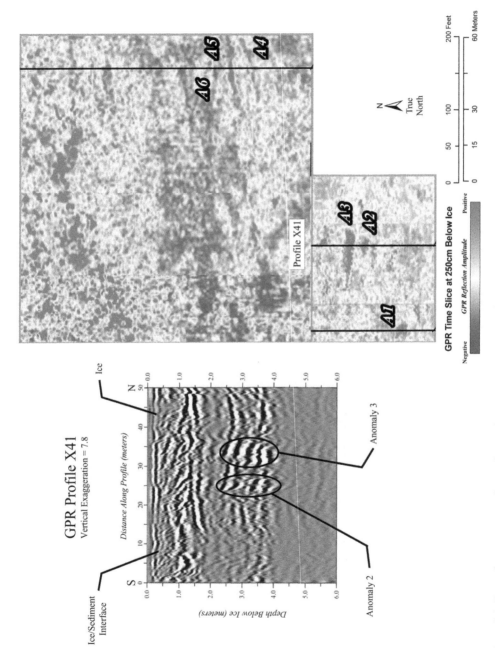

Figure 2.4. Ground penetrating radar results, gunboat survey area. Anomaly A3 was tested and appears to be associated with naturally occurring stones. Figure by Peter Leach.

systems are and the need to approach archaeology in these systems from a regional or local perspective.

SUMMARY AND CONCLUSION

While the two case studies focus on environments dominated by fluvial processes, the regional site formation factors of currents, sediments, and humans are evident. The potentially destructive force of current is apparent in the removal of *Heroine*'s superstructure, and when combined with suspended sediment the Red River current has quickly abraded the exposed portion of the hull. The combination of sediment and current, however, has also aided in site preservation. The quick burial of *Heroine* preserved nearly the entirety of its hull, much of the drive mechanism, and many fragile items such as footwear and softwood crates (Crisman 2014). This preservation resulted from the hull and its contents being encased within the soft bottom and riverbank within five years of sinking—effectively removing it from physical, chemical, and biological deterioration. It is worth noting that these same shifting sands were also the cause of many western river shipwrecks, thus initiating the formation of many sites. The Red River scenario is in direct opposition to the main channel of Black River Bay, where the remote sensing survey identified primarily late twentieth-century materials, likely because the river bottom does not readily protect archaeological materials.

The type of sediment in both rivers also plays a role in site formation. The hypothesized preservation of the Black River armed barge is largely a result of scour and settling, which occur most readily in sandy environments because sands are rapidly mobilized and deposited. Similarly, the sandy sediments of the Red River in part determined how the *Heroine* filled as the sands were quickly deposited in the reduced-velocity environment within the hull. *Heroine* also appears to have scoured and settled into the sandy bottom. Finally, both rivers were subjected to anthropogenic changes that affected site formation processes. The damming of the Red River has disrupted the natural cycles of the river, but how this change will affect the shipwreck is unknown. It is unclear if the fluctuating water levels will cause the hull to deteriorate faster, or if the reduced volume of water through the river will slow or alter the migration of the channel, leaving the wreck exposed for a longer period. Along the Black River, historic farming has added to the river's sediment budget and possibly buried the armed barge under a thick layer of sand.

Interpretation of the physical processes relevant to site formation within the Black River Bay benefited from the geological inputs of our geoscience colleagues in terms of both data and regional perspectives. This observation has lead us to embrace what Michael Schiffer termed the "Geoarchaeological Mandate"—the need to include a geoarchaeologist or geologists in the early stages of a field project in order to understand the processes of deposition and erosion that occurred due to regional site formation processes (Schiffer 1987:256–257; see also Milne et al. 1997:135). The deeper understanding of site formation processes that comes with including geoscientists is a tremendous benefit to archaeologists attempting to determine where sites are likely to be preserved and what techniques are most likely to yield positive results. These collaborations also benefit our geological colleagues because a shipwreck of a known date can serve as a marker horizon that is helpful in measuring change and development within the sediment system. Finally, as research monies become scarcer, the combination of geoscience and archaeology surveys not only provides twice as much return for each research dollar but also often generate an understanding of the region's human and geologic history that exceeds what either survey would have produced alone.

ACKNOWLEDGMENTS

The Black River geology and archaeology survey was funded by a generous grant from the National Geographic Society/Waitt Grants Program, as well as support from Indiana University of Pennsylvania, Great Lakes Historical Society, the College of Charleston, the Institute of Nautical Archaeology, and the Sackets Harbor Battlefield State Historic Site. We also sincerely appreciate Kevin Crisman, the Oklahoma Historical Society, and the Institute of Nautical Archaeology for providing us access to the *Heroine* data. Peter Leach was instrumental in collecting the ground penetrating radar data.

REFERENCES CITED

Adams, Jonathan, and Jennifer Black
2004   From Rescue to Research: Medieval Ship Finds in St Peter Port, Guernsey. *International Journal of Nautical Archaeology* 33(2):230–252.
Bernier, Marc-André
2007   Site Formation Process and Break-Up of the 24M Vessel. In *The Underwater Archaeology of Red Bay: Basque Shipbuilding and Whaling in the 16th Century*, Vol. 4, edited by Robert Grenier, Marc-André Bernier, and Willis Stevens, pp. 215–290. Parks Canada, Ottawa.

Binford, Lewis
1978   *Nunamiut Ethnoarchaeology.* Academic Press, New York.
Broadwater, John
1980   The Yorktown Shipwreck Archaeological Project: Results from the 1978 Survey. *International Journal of Nautical Archaeology and Underwater Exploration* 9(3):227–235.
1998   Yorktown Shipwrecks. In *Encyclopedia of Underwater and Maritime Archaeology*, edited by James Delgado, pp. 471–472. Yale University Press, New Haven.
Brown, Heather, and Kevin Crisman
2005   News from the Red River: A Mid-Season Update on the Steamboat *Heroine*. *INA Quarterly* 32(4):3–6.
Caston, G. F.
1979   Wreck Marks: Indicators of Net Sand Transport. *Marine Geology* 33:193–204.
Conlin, David L.
2005   Environmental Context: A Multidisciplinary Approach. In *USS* Housatonic: *Site Assessment*, edited by David L. Conlin, pp. 129–170. National Park Service, Submerged Resources Center, Naval Historical Center, and South Carolina Institute of Archaeology and Anthropology.
Corbin, Annalies
1998   Shifting Sand and Muddy Water: Historic Cartography and River Migration as Factors in Locating Steamboat Wrecks on the Far Upper Missouri River. *Historical Archaeology* 32(4):86–94.
Crisman, Kevin
2005   The *Heroine* of the Red River. *INA Quarterly* 32(2):3–10.
2014   The Western River Steamboat *Heroine*, 1832–1838, Oklahoma, USA: Construction. *International Journal of Nautical Archaeology* 43(1):128–150.
Crisman, Kevin, and William Lees
2003   Beneath the Red River's Waters: The Oklahoma Steamboat Project, Part 1. *INA Quarterly* 30(2):3–8.
Crisman, Kevin, William B. Lees, and John Davis
2013   The Western River Steamboat *Heroine*, 1832–1838, Oklahoma, USA: Excavations, Summary of Finds, and History. *International Journal of Nautical Archaeology* 42(2):365–381.
Cronyn, J. M.
1996   *The Elements of Archaeological Conservation.* Routledge, New York.
Damour, Melanie
2002   *Looking for HMS* Fox *(1799): A Model for Applying Barrier Island Geomorphology to Shipwreck Survey.* Master's thesis, Florida State University, Tallahassee.
Dumas, Frederic
1962   *Deep-Water Archaeology.* Translated by Honor Frost. Routledge and Kegan Paul, London.
Erlandson, Jon M.
2008   Racing a Rising Tide: Global Warming, Rising Seas, and the Erosion of Human History. *Journal of Island and Coastal Archaeology* 3(2):167–169.

Ford, Ben

2009   *Lake Ontario Maritime Cultural Landscape.* Ph.D. dissertation, Texas A&M University, College Station.

2011   Coastal Archaeology. In *Oxford Handbook of Maritime Archaeology*, edited by Alexis Catsambis, Ben Ford, and Donny Hamilton, pp. 763–785. Oxford University Press, New York.

Ford, Ben, Amy Borgens, and Peter Hitchcock

2009   The "Mardi Gras" Shipwreck: Results of a Deep-Water Excavation, Gulf of Mexico, USA. *International Journal of Nautical Archaeology* 39(1):76–98.

Gregory, David

2004   Degradation of Wooden Shipwrecks: Threats. *MoSS Newsletter*, March 2004. Electronic document, http://moss.nba.fi/download/moss_newsletter7.pdf, accessed September 22, 2014.

Halpern, Benjamin, Shaun Walbridge, Kimberly Selkoe, Carrie Kappel, Fiorenze Micheli, Caterina D'Agrosa, John Bruno, Kenneth Casey, Colin Ebert, Helen Fox, Rod Fujita, Dennis Heinemann, Hunter Lenihan, Elizabeth Madin, Matthew Perry, Elizabeth Selig, Mark Spalding, Robert Steneck, and Reg Watson

2008   A Global Map of Human Impact on Marine Ecosystems. *Science* 319:948–952.

Hayes, Miles, Thomas Moslow, and Dennis Hubbard

1984   *Beach Erosion in South Carolina.* U.S. Department of Commerce, Washington, D.C.

Head, Lesley

2000   *Cultural Landscapes and Environmental Change.* Arnold, London.

Horrell, Christopher

2005   *Plying the Waters of Time: Maritime Archaeology and History on the Florida Gulf Coast.* Ph.D. dissertation, Florida State University, Tallahassee.

Horrell, Christopher, Della Scott-Ireton, Roger Smith, James Levy, and Joe Knetsch

2009   The Flintlock Site (8JA1763): An Unusual Underwater Deposit in the Apalachicola River, Florida. *Journal of Maritime Archaeology* 4:5–19.

Kelley, Joseph T., Daniel F. Belknap, and Stefan Claesson

2010   Drowned Coastal Deposits with Associated Archaeological Remains from a Sea-level "Slowstand": Northwestern Gulf of Maine, USA. *Geology* 38(8):695–698.

Lees, William, and J. Barto Arnold III

2000   Preliminary Assessment of a Wreck in the Red River, Choctaw County, Oklahoma, USA. *International Journal of Nautical Archaeology* 29(1):120–125.

Leino, Minna, Ari Ruuskanen, Juha Flinkman, Jussi Kaasinen, Ulla Klemelä, Riikka Hietala, and Niko Nappu

2011   The Natural Environment of the Shipwreck *Vrouw Maria* (1771) in the Northern Baltic Sea: An Assessment of Her State of Preservation. *International Journal of Nautical Archaeology* 40(1):133–150.

Lenihan, Daniel J, Toni L. Carrell, Stephen Fosberg, Larry Murphy, Sandra L. Rayl, and John A. Ware (editors)

1981   *Final Report of the National Reservoir Inundation Study.* 2 vols. National Park Service, Southwest Cultural Resources Center, Santa Fe.

Martin, Colin

2011   Wreck-Site Formation Processes. In *Oxford Handbook of Maritime Archaeology*, edited by Alexis Catsambis, Ben Ford, and Donny Hamilton, pp. 47–67. Oxford University Press, New York.

Matthiesen, Henning, Eva Salomonsen, and Birgit Sørensen

2004   The Use of Radiography and GIS to Assess the Deterioration of Archeological Iron Objects from Water Logged Environments. *Journal of Archaeological Science* 31:1451–1461.

McNinch, Jesse E., John T. Wells, and Arthur C. Trembanis

2006   Predicting the Fate of Artefacts in Energetic Shallow Marine Environments: An Approach to Site Management. *International Journal of Nautical Archaeology* 35(2):290–309.

Mcphail, Richard I., Michael J. Allen, John Crowther, G. M. Cruise, and John E. Whittaker

2009   Marine Inundation: Effects on Archaeological Features, Materials, Sediments and Soils. *Quaternary International* 214:44–55.

Meide, Chuck, James McClean, and Edward Wiser

2001   *Dog Island Shipwreck Survey 1999: Report of Historical and Archaeological Investigations*. Research Reports no. 4. Program in Underwater Archaeology, Florida State University, Tallahassee.

Millet, Bertrand, and Jean-Philippe Goiran

2007   Impacts of Alexandria's Heptastadion on Coastal Hydro-sedimentary Dynamics during the Hellenistic Period: A Numerical Modeling Approach. *International Journal of Nautical Archaeology* 36(1):167–176.

Milne, Gustav, Martine Bates, and Mike Webber

1997   Problems, Potential and Partial Solutions: An Archaeological Study of the Tidal Thames, England. *World Archaeology* 29(1):130–146.

Muckelroy, Keith

1978   *Maritime Archaeology*. Cambridge University Press, Cambridge.

Murphy, Larry E.

1990   *8SL17: Natural Site-Formation Process of a Multiple-Component Underwater Site in Florida*. Southwest Cultural Resources Center Professional Papers no. 39. National Park Service, Submerged Cultural Resources Unit, Santa Fe.

1998   Site Formation Processes. In *Encyclopedia of Underwater and Maritime Archaeology*, edited by James Delgado, pp. 386–388. Yale University Press, New Haven.

Murphy, R. Joseph

1976   *Excavation of Revolutionary War Vessel and Ethnohistorical Study of the Area*. Report submitted to the National Science Foundation and New York State Parks and Recreation Commission, Division of Historic Preservation.

National Trust

2005   *Shifting Shores: Living with a Changing Coastline*. National Trust for Places of Historic Interest and Natural Beauty, London.

Palma, Paola

2005   Monitoring Shipwreck Sites. *International Journal of Nautical Archaeology* 34(2):323–331.

Quinn, Rory, Jonathan Adams, Justin Dix, and Jonathan Bull
1998   The *Invincible* (1758) Site—an Integrated Geophysical Assessment. *International Journal of Nautical Archaeology* 27(2):126–138.

Quinn, Rory, Wes Forsythe, Colin Breen, Donal Boland, Paul Lane, and Athman Lali Omar
2007   Process-based Models for Port Evolution and Wreck Site Formation at Mombasa, Kenya. *Journal of Archaeological Science* 34:1149–1460.

Rayl, Sandra, George Simmons Jr., and Robert Benoit
1981   Field Studies of Differential Preservation in Freshwater Environments: Brady Creek Reservoir, Texas; Claytor Lake Reservoir, Virginia, and Virginia Polytechnic Institute and State University. In *The Final Report of the National Reservoir Inundation Study,* vol. 2, edited by Daniel Lenihan, pp. 6-i–6-88. National Park Service, Southwest Cultural Resources Center, Santa Fe.

Russell, Matthew
2004   Beached Shipwrecks from Channel Islands National Park, California. *Journal of Field Archaeology* 29(3–4):369–384.
2005   *Beached Shipwreck Archaeology: Case Studies from Channel Islands National Park.* Submerged Resources Center Professional Reports No. 18. National Park Service, Submerged Resources Center, Intermountain Region, Santa Fe.

Schiffer, Michael
1987   *Formation Processes of the Archaeological Record.* University of New Mexico Press, Albuquerque.

Sear, D. A., S. R. Bacon, A. Murdock, G. Doneghan, P. Baggaley, C. Serra, and T. P. LeBas
2011   Cartographic, Geophysical and Diver Surveys of the Medieval Town Site at Dunwich, Suffolk, England. *International Journal of Nautical Archaeology* 40(1):113–132.

Simms, Janet, and Paul Albertson
2000   Multidisciplined Investigation to Locate the *Kentucky* Shipwreck. *Geoarchaeology* 15(5):441–468.

Singley, Katherine
1988   *The Conservation of Archaeological Artifacts from Freshwater Environments.* Lake Michigan Maritime Museum, South Haven, Michigan.

Stright, Melanie J., Eileen M. Lear, and James F. Bennett
1999   *Spatial Data Analysis of Artifacts Redeposited by Coastal Erosion: A Case Study of McFaddin Beach, TX.* Minerals Management Service, Herndon, Virginia.

Vinton, R.
1829   *Sketch (a vue) of the Mouth of Black River and Waters Adjacent, Jefferson County, New York.* RG 77 Civil Works Map File D77. National Archives, Washington, D.C.

Walter, Robert, and Dorothy Merritts
2008   Natural Streams and the Legacy of Water-Powered Mills. *Science* 319:299–304.

Ward, Ingrid, Piers Larcombe, Richard Brinkman, and Robert Carter
1999   Sedimentary Processes and the *Pandora* Wreck, Great Barrier Reef, Australia. *Journal of Field Archaeology* 26(1):41–53.

Ware, John, and Sandy Rayl
1981   Laboratory Studies of Differential Preservation in Freshwater Environments. In

The Final Report of the National Reservoir Inundation Study, vol. 2, edited by Daniel Lenihan, pp. 3-i–3-108. National Park Service, Southwest Cultural Resources Center, Santa Fe.

Waters, Michael, R.
1992   *Principles of Geoarchaeology: A North American Perspective.* University of Arizona Press, Tucson.

Westley, Kieran, Trevor Bell, M.A.P. Renouf, and Lev Tarasov
2011a   Impact Assessment of Current and Future Sea-Level Change on Coastal Archaeological Resources—Illustrated Examples from Northern Newfoundland. *Journal of Island and Coastal Archaeology* 6(3):351–374.

Westley Kieran, Rory Quinn, Wes Forsythe, Ruth Plets, Trevor Bell, Sara Benetti, Fergal McGrath, and Rhonda Robinson
2011b   Mapping Submerged Landscapes Using Multibeam Bathymetric Data: A Case Study from the North Coast of Ireland. *International Journal of Nautical Archaeology* 40(1):99–112.

Wilkinson, T. J., and P. Murphy
1986   Archaeological Survey of an Intertidal Zone: The Submerged Landscape of the Essex Coast, England. *Journal of Field Archaeology* 13(2):177–194.

Will, Richard, and James Clark
1996   Stone Artifact Movement on Impoundment Shorelines: A Case Study from Maine. *American Antiquity* 61(3):499–519.

3

Sediment and Site Formation in the Marine Environment

MATTHEW E. KEITH AND AMANDA M. EVANS

Natural or environmental site formation processes contribute to the decay and disarticulation of a submerged shipwreck over time. Archaeologists, even those not explicitly focused on site formation processes, are in some way concerned with interpreting the formation processes that have transformed the vessel from its original, intact form into the wreck site investigated on or beneath the seafloor. By understanding how site formation occurs, archaeologists can more accurately understand artifact distribution and wreck decay, resulting in a more complete and accurate reconstruction of life aboard the vessel (Muckelroy 1978:176–181). Site formation studies are extremely important for informing long-term management strategies and can also be used to inform strategies designed to search for shipwreck sites.

Natural site formation processes include a number of variables that influence the degree of preservation that a shipwreck will experience in a given environment. As Ford and colleagues note (chapter 2, this volume), wrecks in high energy shallow water environments can be destroyed or very well preserved depending on the conditions present. Deeper-water wrecks are often well preserved at and below the mud-line, but the upper portions of the hull exhibit levels of collapse similar to that of their shallow water counterparts (as exhibited by wrecks discussed in Jones 2004; Ford et al. 2008; Søreide 2011), due to a variety of factors (e.g., through the wrecking event, gravity, and impacts of biologic and chemical processes).

In most environments the seafloor itself is the most important factor in influencing the potential decay or preservation of a submerged shipwreck. The thickness and composition of seabed sediments, coupled with external factors that shape and move sediments, determine whether a shipwreck becomes entirely or partially buried or remains exposed on the seabed. Currents, tides, and waves are the dominant external impacts on seabed sediments and influence sediment deposition, erosion, and scour. Currents and tides play a more important role in shallow water, while mid- and deep-water environments are more likely to be shaped by currents and punctuated events, such as those generated by extreme storm events or tsunamis. This chapter addresses sediment types encountered in the open ocean, factors controlling sediment movement, and the impact of sediment on shipwrecks, followed by a case study examining the role of sediment movement at a number of offshore wreck sites located in the northern Gulf of Mexico.

Chapter 2 of this volume addresses nearshore processes that result in major changes to the landscape, such as shifting rivers, changing coastlines, eroding barrier islands, and the challenges these introduce to the study of shipwrecks located in nearshore and inland environments. As in nearshore environments, the properties of and subsequent movement of seabed sediments in an offshore environment are perhaps the most significant factors in protecting or endangering many wreck sites throughout the world. Marine sediment—through deposition, accretion, scour, mass transport, and stability—impacts both shipwreck site preservation potential and as the archaeologist's ability to identify a previously unknown wreck site. As the availability of increasingly advanced technologies allows archaeologists to investigate growing numbers of shipwreck sites in deeper environments, it becomes imperative that an understanding of these environments is reached to inform research and help put shipwreck sites into their proper context.

The Role of Burial in Shipwreck Preservation

Perhaps the most significant factor contributing to the preservation of shipwrecks and their associated artifacts is burial beneath seabed sediments. Chemical and biologic processes are responsible for breaking down organics (such as wood, rope, and floral and faunal remains) and some types of inorganic materials (such as metal), especially in areas where the wreck remains exposed above the seafloor in the water column. Many wrecks have been documented that consist solely of inert materials exposed at the seafloor, such as ceramics or ballast stone, and with organic remains later identified buried below the seafloor or ballast (e.g., Keith and Simmons 1988). Certain environmental conditions, including low temperature, low salinity, and/or low dissolved oxygen, can significantly slow the decay of both organic and inorganic materials but will not prevent deterioration. Burial beneath the seabed often has the largest direct impact on site preservation by preventing exposure to biologic organisms, such as marine borers and shipworms (Gregory, chapter 6, this volume) and environmental conditions that influences corrosion and deterioration (MacLeod, chapter 5, this volume). While the properties of the sediments themselves (such as pH and microbiology) can limit the preservation of materials, and exceptions exist (MacLeod, chapter 5, this volume), the preservation potential of buried materials is more often than not significantly greater than equivalent materials exposed above the seafloor.

Working with a sample of wrecks in U.K. waters, Keith Muckelroy (1978) examined the primary factor in shipwreck preservation, determining that properties directly associated with the composition of the seabed are the dominant contributor to preservation. His work was an important step in identifying variables that impact wreck burial.

As Muckelroy (1978:160) observed: "From the earliest days of archaeological investigation under water it was apparent that, as on land, ancient remains were more likely to have been preserved within soft substrates than within rocky ones." Despite the importance of factors such as temperature, salinity, and dissolved oxygen content, the composition of seabed sediments is often the one broad category that is most likely to impact wreck preservation. The wreck of *Stirling Castle*, lost in 1703 off the east coast of Kent, England, illustrates the importance of wreck burial. First observed in 1979 due to shifting of the local Goodwin Sands sand bank, the hull was originally noted to be exceptionally well preserved after 276 years below the seafloor. Continual monitoring has noted that the wreck has rapidly decayed in the intervening years since exposure was first noted (English Heritage 2007; Wessex Archaeology 2003). It is therefore imperative to understand the nature and movement of sediments surrounding a given shipwreck site to understand fully the issues related to preservation.

The Marine Environment

The marine environment can be divided into three principal zones. These are continental margins, deep-ocean basins, and the mid-ocean ridges (Trujillo and Thurman 2008:80). Passive continental margins are defined by a relatively flat continental shelf, gradual continental slope, and a continental rise that extends to the deep-ocean basin. Active margins exhibit a narrow shelf, followed by a steep slope and offshore trench where the continental plates converge with the oceanic plates. A hallmark of the deep-ocean basins are the essentially flat abyssal plains punctuated by volcanic peaks, arcs, and deep-ocean trenches. Finally, the mid-ocean ridge is dominated by a series of underwater mountains of volcanic origin that were created by spreading along divergent plate boundaries. The mid-ocean ridge is estimated to cover 23% of the Earth's surface (Trujillo and Thurman 2008:91).

To date virtually all offshore archaeological investigations have been concerned with wrecks located along continental margins, specifically continental shelves and slopes. The deep-ocean basins and mid-ocean ridges, therefore, represent virtually unexplored portions of the seabed (National Ocean Service 2013). A study performed by Bascom (1976) based on mid-nineteenth-century insurance records indicated that while 80% of documented wrecks occurred close to shore, as many as 20% may have occurred in deep water. Extrapolating from this to the long history of seafaring, one could surmise that countless wrecks are located in areas farther from coastlines and in deep-water areas yet to be investigated.

OFFSHORE SEDIMENT DEPOSITION, SEDIMENT PROPERTIES, AND SEDIMENT MOVEMENT

The primary factors that impact the initial impact and subsidence of a shipwreck on the seafloor are sediment composition and cohesion. Sediments have differing properties that react variably to external forces, therefore subsequent and continued burial of the wreck depend upon sediment deposition rates, scour processes and erosion, possible sediment liquefaction, and long-term bedform migration (Keith and Evans 2009).

ROLE OF THE SEABED IN THE WRECKING EVENT

Muckelroy (1978), Stewart (1999), and others have noted that site formation processes begin with the wrecking event and continue throughout the life of the wreck site. The initial wrecking event has an important role in the condition and potential burial of a wreck site. A vessel striking a hard bottom may be immediately broken and scattered (as in the case of the *Kennemerland* wreck (Muckelroy 1978:172–174)), while a hull settling onto a soft seabed may experience subsidence or self-burial and therefore immediate preservation of at least a portion of the wreck.

Attempting to quantify sediment types, Keith and Evans (2009) discussed the utility of employing engineering measurements, such as shear strength, as a method for estimating the rate of initial subsidence. Based on a limited data sample some correlation was observed between areas of low shear strengths and seafloors that appeared to accommodate a degree of wreck burial. Ward and colleagues (1999a) summarized research by Riley, who observed that the lower half of a ship typically settles into the seabed up to the waterline when wrecked upright on a sandy seabed, and by Mc-Carthy, who identified varying rates of settlement in soft seabed sediments versus harder sediments. Wachsmann (2011:206) discussed how a wooden wreck occurring in deep water typically rights itself, sinking keel first, generating a pressure wave that can displace unconsolidated sediments, and in some cases burying a portion of the wreck upon impact.

While the initial impact plays a significant role in the burial and condition of a sunken ship, the properties of the seafloor sediments, coupled with external forces that act upon them (e.g., waves and currents) will have an ongoing impact in the preservation of a shipwreck site.

SEDIMENTATION

Marine sediments are derived from multiple sources, including land (terrigenous), marine organisms (biogenous), seawater (hydrogenous), and space (cosmogenous). Terrigenous deposits, primarily derived from rivers, coastal erosion, and landslides, dominate the continental margins and are the most abundant marine sediment type by volume. Wind-derived (aeolian) and volcanic terrigenous deposits are more widespread and can be found throughout the world's oceans, although generally they are preferentially deposited along coastal margins. Deposits formed through biogenesis are the next most common, but are even more widespread than terrigenous deposits. Deposits formed through hydrogenesis and cosmogenesis are much less common but are widely distributed.

Another common type of nearshore sediment encountered frequently by archaeologists consists of carbonate shelves and reefs formed through biogenesis in warm shallow waters with low rates of terrigenous sedimentation. Major carbonate shelves include the Florida and Yucatan coasts, the Persian Gulf, northern Australia, and parts of the South Pacific between Indonesia and the Philippines. Reefs, typical of carbonate shelves, are common throughout warm coastal waters between approximately 30 degrees north and 30 degrees south latitude.

Pelagic deposits in deep-ocean basins are dominated by calcareous oozes (~48%), terrigenous abyssal clays (~38%), and biogenic siliceous oozes (~14%; Trujillo and Thurman 2008:121). Worldwide, nearshore terrigenous sediments are deposited at an average rate of 1 meter per 1,000 years; deposition rates in pelagic zones are significantly lower, less than 1 centimeter per 1,000 years (Trujillo and Thurman 2008:122). Along certain continental shelf margins, sediment deposition rates are much higher, usually the result of alluvial deposition. Areas of higher deposition typically correlate with the presence of higher magnitude rivers, such as those found along the eastern coast of North and South America, the Gulf of Mexico, the northwest coast of Africa, and the Indian Ocean, which introduce significant quantities of sediment into the marine environment.

In areas with high rates of sedimentation, a wreck may eventually become buried. It has to be understood though that sedimentation rates are not constant; for example, alluvial sedimentation rates may decrease as a river meanders or changes gradient. Therefore it is possible that a wreck may have been in an area of low deposition soon after the wrecking event, only to be buried following years of exposure, or conversely, may have been buried relatively rapidly after it first wrecked even though modern sedimentation rates are extremely low. Since sedimentation rates are generally measured in millimeters per year, normal sediment deposition or accretion is not usually the primary cause of ship burial.

There are two classes of marine sediments: cohesive sediments and cohesionless sediments. Cohesion typically increases as grain size decreases, therefore cohesive sediments include clays and some silts and are composed of extremely small, plate-shaped mineral grains (Grabowski et al. 2011:103). The chemical content of the cohesive sediment attracts water to the plates through electrostatic forces (Grabowski et al. 2011:104). Clay exhibits a wide range of properties based on water content and chemical composition. When dry, clay is hard and rigid due to a close attraction between the grains; when wet, clay exhibits a soupy consistency (Grabowski et al. 2011:103–105). In an offshore environment, clay particles remain suspended in the water column longer than other sediment types, until they settle out of suspension and are deposited on the seafloor (TxDOT 2008). Clays that have been subaerially exposed above sea level are typically very firm since the water is removed from the clay through evaporation. In the case of clays that have been deposited in a stable marine environment, water is slowly squeezed from the deposited clay by the weight of subsequently deposited overlying layers of sediment. The result is typically very soft surface clay that gradually increases in strength with depth. Water-saturated clays and silts are generally referred to as muds (Grabowski et al. 2011:102).

Cohesionless grains are larger and more rounded particles than clay

Table 3.1. Grain size scales

Grain Size Scales and Conversion Table

Millimeters	Phi (Φ)	Wentworth Size Class
4096 to 256	-12 to -8	Boulder
256 to 64	-8 to -6	Cobble
64 to 4	-6 to -2	Pebble
4 to 2	-2 to -1	Granule
1.00	-1 to 0.0	Very coarse/Coarse sand
0.84–0.59	0.25–0.75	Coarse sand
0.50	1.0	Coarse/Medium sand
0.42–0.30	1.25–1.75	Medium sand
0.25	2.0	Medium/Fine sand
0.210–0.149	2.25–2.75	Fine sand
0.125	3.0	Fine/Very Fine sand
0.105–0.074	3.25–3.75	Very fine sand
0.0625	4.0	Very fine sand/coarse silt
0.053–0.037	4.25–4.75	Coarse silt
0.031	5.0	Coarse/Medium silt
0.0156	5.5–6.5	Medium silt
0.0078	7.0–7.5	Fine silt
0.0039	8.0–8.5	Very Fine silt
0.0020–0.00024	9.0–12.0	Clay

Note: Based on data compiled from Folk 1980 and Shackley 1975.

(table 3.1). Cohesionless grains are classified by size and include sands, gravels, cobbles, and boulders. Due to the larger grain sizes in cohesionless sediments, they interact by mechanical as opposed to chemical means (Tx-DOT 2008; Jain and Kothyari 2010:35). Pure cohesionless sediment is free flowing when dry and has little to no cohesion when submerged (United States Army Corps of Engineers 2002). Although shear strengths (a measure of the amount of stress necessary for sediments to shear laterally and therefore accommodate self-burial) of sands are low, strength can occur in cohesionless soils due to "apparent cohesion" created by the capillary tension in the pore water pressure (TxDOT 2008). Cementation caused by the presence of calcium carbonate and silica can also enhance peak strength within cohesionless sediments (Chaney and Demars 1985:540). Apparent cohesion and cementation can create extremely hard seafloors that inhibit initial subsidence or burial. Measures of sediment properties such as bulk density and plasticity are also important to understand the likelihood of sediment mobilization (Rego et al. 2012; Lick and McNeil 2000).

With regard to sediment deposition, it is important to note that coarser-grained sediments fall out of suspension first; therefore fine silts and clays travel farther than coarser-grained sands or gravels (Masselink and Hughes 2003). This is why many of the world's coasts are characterized by sands and gravels. Continental shelf and slope margins are dominated by coarser-grained silts and clays, which travel farther into the marine system from their fluvial source, while pelagic sediments, which travel the farthest, are predominantly very fine-grained clays or oozes.

In most deep-water environments, from continental slopes basinward, depositional rates are so slow that any sedimentation experienced by even the oldest wrecks will be negligible. However, deep-water environments can also be subject to mass wasting events, called turbidity currents, that occur along steep slope breaks and submarine canyons. These deposits can carry massive quantities of sediment from the outer shelf out to the deep ocean, which has the potential to impact severely, move, or bury a shipwreck site (Church et al. 2007:28).

The physical properties of seafloor sediments are one factor in determining the amount of force necessary to mobilize sediments; the other factor is the shear stress caused by currents and waves (Whitehouse 1998:64; Jain and Kothyari 2010:33).

WAVES AND CURRENTS

Shipwrecks in shallow water depths experience significant wave impacts and can be subjected to strong along-shore currents or strong tidal migrations (as discussed by Ford et al. chapter 2, this volume, and evidenced by McNinch et al. 2006). Shallow water environments are higher energy than deeper water due primarily to the effects of waves and currents. Although the impacts of waves, and to some degree currents, decrease as water depth increases, given certain conditions they can still have substantial impact on the seafloor and, by extension, seafloor sediments.

External water movement (through waves or currents) may mobilize unconsolidated sandy sediments, but consolidated silts and clays require a greater amount of force to mobilize and provide more resistance to instigating sediment movement (Curray 1960). Areas of coarse-grained unconsolidated deposits are much more likely to encounter regular sediment movement through scour (as discussed by Quinn et al., chapter 4, this volume; Whitehouse 1998:62; Ward et al. 1999b) or through bedform migration, as in the example of the shifting sand banks over the *Stirling Castle* wreck.

Waves are formed in a number of ways. Ocean waves are primarily wind driven, although internal waves formed due to density differences, known as pycnoclines, can also occur. Tides are technically another form of wave, resulting from the gravitational pull of the sun and moon, while man-made waves such as those generated from a ship's wake may also impact seabed sediments. Finally, waves caused by singular geologic events such as earthquakes or mudslides can also have a significant impact on the seafloor.

Surface waves influence the seabed only in relatively shallow waters. The depth to which a wave causes significant impacts below the water surface is known as the wave base. The wave base is typically equal to half the wavelength (which can be measured as either crest to crest or trough to trough; Trujillo and Thurman 2008:250; Waters 1992:249–251). Wavelengths vary in different bodies of water. In the Gulf of Mexico and Caribbean the average wavelength has recently been measured at 70 m (230 feet), and in the open waters of the western Atlantic Ocean the average wavelength was 120 m (394 feet; Peters and Loss 2012). Given that the wave base is half the wavelength, the average wave will not impact the seabed in the Gulf of Mexico at depths greater than 35 m (115 feet) or depths greater than 60 m (197 feet) in the open Atlantic. However, the strength of a wave's impact dissipates with depth, so even though some impact to the bottom may occur in these water depths, the strength of these impacts may not be sufficient to mobilize sediments until much shallower water is encountered. For this reason, it is generally believed that in deeper water depths along continental shelves, seafloor sediments are generally only impacted by surface waves in the case of extreme storm events (Curray 1960; Davies 1983; Rego et al. 2012).

In shallow water, wind-derived surface waves are relatively predictable and mobilize sediment in a specific direction. Surface waves derived from local storm events may have a more dramatic effect on bottom sediments but are far less predictable (Davies 1983:1). Which impact is more important on a given shipwreck site depends on the area in question and the likelihood of exposure to storms. Waves traveling along the continental shelf have little to no influence on the seabed until water depth decreases to the point that the surface wavelength becomes greater than the local water depth. Only when wave base is greater than water depth does the wave energy begin to impact the seabed. Wave energy becomes increasingly intense as the water becomes shallower and can result in sediment transport (where the seabed is erodible), bottom percolation (where the seabed is permeable), or bottom motion (where the seabed consists of soft muds; Davies 1983:1). The preceding discussion of waves is intentionally simplified and does not explore the complexity of all wave patterns, such as deep-water internal waves. Pertinent to the shipwreck archaeologist is that wave-induced sediment transport can result from a variety of wave patterns and combinations.

Like waves, currents can have an impact on seabed morphology by inducing scour or depositing sediments on site (Quinn 2006; Quinn et al., chapter 4, this volume). There are two types of ocean currents: surface and deep-water currents. Surface currents are wind-driven currents that exist above the pycnocline, a layer of density/salinity change at 300–1,000 m (984–3,280 feet) that exists in the mid-latitudes. Deep-water currents are density-driven currents that occur below the pycnocline, are the result of temperature and salinity changes that occur at the surface, and are greatly influenced by sinking water in the extreme northern and southern latitudes (Trujillo and Thurman 2008:241). Deep-water currents affect larger amounts of water but move more slowly than surface currents. According to Søreide, current speeds of 1 to 2 cm/second (0.19 to 0.39 knots) are typical in deep water (2011:161). Still, in certain parts of the ocean, deep-sea currents in 4,000 m (13,123 feet) of water have been measured at 0.83 knots and observed to erode the seafloor, creating scour and ripple marks (Capurro 1970:149). To put this into perspective, according to Curray (1960:233), "a velocity of 35 cm/second (~0.68 knots) is . . . the approximate mean velocity at 1 meter above the bottom which is required to pick up and move fine quartz sand."

Shipwreck preservation rates have been demonstrably linked to burial by seafloor sediments (Muckelroy 1978; Wessex Archaeology 2003; English Heritage 2007). Sediment deposition, properties, and movement influence how a given shipwreck site looks upon its initial discovery and continue to influence the site long after the archaeological investigation has concluded. It is imperative, therefore, that as part of long-term management strategies, archaeologists and especially heritage managers understand the dynamic conditions impacting sediment.

An understanding of sediment properties is also an important consideration in the search for shipwreck sites. Wrecks that are partially or entirely buried dictate a search strategy emphasizing a very tight survey grid that is reliant on technologies such as magnetometers designed to identify buried ferromagnetic materials. Conversely, a search in a deep-water environment with low depositional rates and limited impacts from waves might rely on acoustic imaging of the seafloor using wider survey grid coverage to search for targets sitting at or above the seafloor.

Case Study: Gulf of Mexico Shipwreck Study

Heritage management agencies, as demonstrated by other chapters within this volume, have a vested interest in studying site formation processes relevant to historic wrecks in marine environments. The U.S. Department of the Interior through the Bureau of Ocean Energy Management (BOEM) manages all federal bottom lands leased for energy extraction in United States federal waters. Since 1974 BOEM and its predecessor agencies have been responsible for managing cultural resources and ensuring that they are not impacted by offshore energy development activities. In order to manage existing and potential wrecks better in the face of offshore development, BOEM has had to address the question of site formation processes, to understand if shipwrecks are likely to be preserved, and how best to identify them based on the surrounding environment. BOEM has commissioned multiple studies in recent years that emphasize site formation as part of their research design. These include segments of the ongoing Lophelia project (Church et al. 2007), and a study designed to model the impacts of hurricanes on shipwrecks on the outer continental shelf (OCS; Gearhart et al. 2011).

Another recent BOEM-funded study was designed to investigate a series of possible shipwreck sites for evaluation of historic significance (Evans et al. 2013). A secondary goal of the study was to assess the impact of site formation processes on each wreck site. The contracted scope of work required that coring be performed to assess site formation processes but left development of the remaining portion of the research design up to the contractor. Tesla Offshore, LLC, was contracted to perform the study, in partnership with personnel from the University of West Florida, Louisiana State University, and University of Texas at Austin. This study illustrates the challenges and opportunities of assessing sediment-related site formation processes.

Methodology

Existing literature in the fields of oceanography, geomorphology, engineering, and other disciplines provides a wealth of information about potential impacts to shipwrecks. At the commencement of the Tesla-BOEM study, a number of methods from archaeological studies and other disciplines were evaluated for their ability to identify ongoing impacts to the wrecks included as part of the study, considering both practicality and cost-efficiency.

Methods for studying the oceanographic, geologic, and geomorphologic processes that impact the marine environment are diverse and numerous. Some of the most common techniques for assessing seabed characteristics are geophysical data acquisition, oceanographic modeling, and physical measurements of the seabed and water column. These tools can be used for long-term monitoring of a region or specific site as well as to collect data during a single site visit that can be added to models or analyzed to provide information about conditions at a specific point in time.

Fieldwork for the study was conducted from 2009 to 2011. A total of eleven potential wreck sites were investigated; verified shipwrecks were identified at nine of the sites. The study wrecks are located at water depths of 11–36.5 m (36–120 feet) across the north-central and northwestern Gulf of Mexico, along the Louisiana and northeast Texas coasts (fig. 3.1). Of the nine wrecks investigated, eight were steel-hulled vessels ranging in age from the early twentieth century up to relatively modern wrecks. The other wreck was a casualty of the U.S. Civil War, constructed primarily of iron and dated to the mid-nineteenth century. Four of the wrecks were inverted on the seabed with the keel facing up.

Shipwreck burial and the role of sediment in site formation are not often at the forefront of archaeological investigations, and the Tesla-BOEM work provides a recent case study in methodology. The study used three primary methods of analysis related to seafloor sediment: geophysical remote sensing, sediment coring, and oceanographic modeling. Although the results of the study are specific to the actual environments encountered, the methods used and detailed here are applicable to a wide range of sites across various environments.

Geophysical Remote Sensing

Geophysics, and most commonly acoustics, can be used to identify the seafloor and near seafloor stratigraphy and give a qualitative assessment of these conditions (Quinn et al. 1997). Advances in quantifying acoustic signatures for seabed classification based on sonar backscatter continue to improve and may someday be a cost-efficient and more rapid method of seafloor classification than direct measurements (Ishtiak and Demsar 2013). Geophysics can also be used for long-term monitoring at sites. High resolution bathymetry can be used to assess a site's condition, as in the yearly evaluations of the SS *Richard Montgomery* performed on behalf of the U.K. Maritime and Coastguard Agency and Ministry of Defense (MCA 2012), and has also been established as a method for identifying net sediment erosion or scour (Quinn 2006; Gregory 2009). Side-scan sonar may

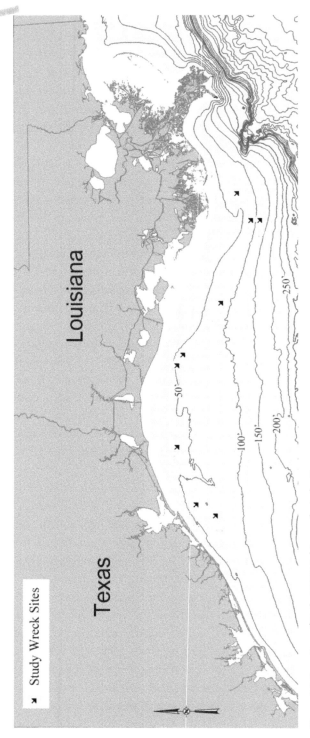

Figure 3.1. Location of Tesla-BOEM shipwreck study sites.

Subbottom Profiler Image A.

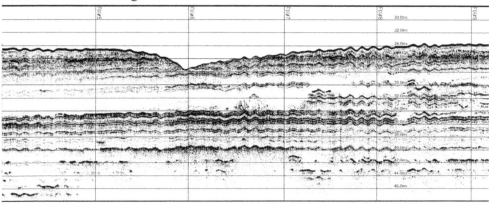

Subbottom Profiler Image B.

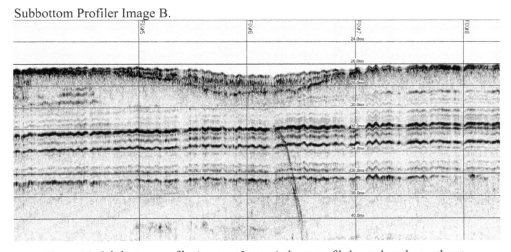

Figure 3.2. Sub-bottom profiler imagery. Image A shows profile located on the southeast side of probable *R. W. Gallagher*, approximately 15 m (49 feet) from the wreck. Image B shows profile on west side of probable *Cities Service Toledo*, approximately 20 m (66 feet) from the wreck. Horizontal scale in increments of 150 m (492 feet); vertical scale in increments of ~1.5 m (~5 feet; Evans et al. 2013).

also be used as a qualitative measurement of scour or sediment change (Quinn 2006; Evans et al. 2013).

Stationary Acoustic Doppler Current profilers can provide measurements of current speed, while tidal buoys can measure tides and waves, which are particularly useful during extreme storm events. Satellite altimeters can also be used for measuring water column properties that can provide information about ocean currents or tides.

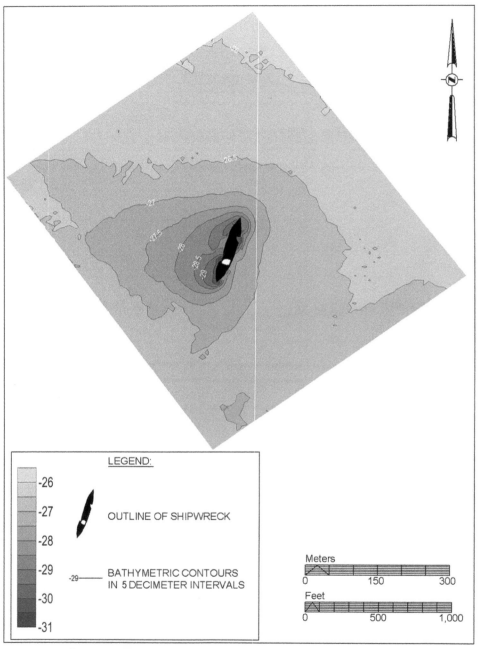

Figure 3.3. Bathymetry contours surrounding the wreck of probable *R. W. Gallagher* in 5 decimeter intervals (~4 inches; Evans et al. 2013).

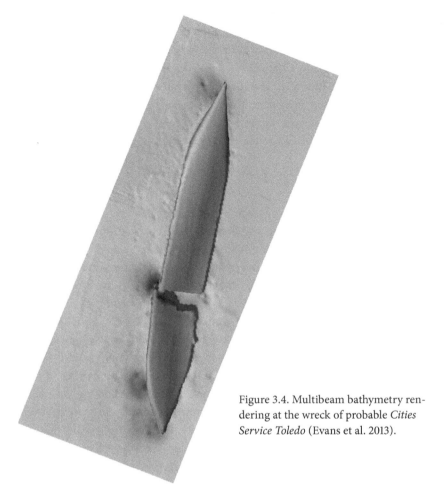

Figure 3.4. Multibeam bathymetry rendering at the wreck of probable *Cities Service Toledo* (Evans et al. 2013).

For the BOEM study, geophysical data acquired over each wreck site during the initial survey cruise included side-scan sonar, multibeam and singlebeam bathymetry, magnetometer, and sub-bottom profiles. A 3D scanning sonar was utilized at three of the wreck sites, and a sector scanning sonar was used at a number of the wreck sites during diving operations. The results of the geophysical data provided imagery of the wreck sites, allowed overall site plans to be developed, identified site extents and distribution, provided water depth and seafloor gradient information, identified scour patterns surrounding sites, and provided imagery of sub-seafloor stratigraphy.

The geophysical data were most useful in identifying the extent and depth of scour patterns around each wreck site (figs. 3.2, 3.3, 3.4). Geophysical data recorded clear scour patterns at every wreck site, and in some cases more recent in-fill was evident on sub-bottom profiles. Figure 3.2 highlights sub-bottom profiles adjacent to the wreck sites of the probable *R. W. Gallagher* and probable *Cities Service Toledo*, illustrating evidence of in-filled scour at the latter site. The majority of sites exhibited broad shallow scour zones extending away from the wreck site (fig. 3.3). Scour zones were typically larger and deeper surrounding the bow and stern of each wreck and at breaks in the hull, likely due to localized acceleration of flow regimes (fig. 3.4).

Sediment Coring

Direct sediment properties of seafloor sediments can be tested using a variety of techniques, including soil borings, box cores, grab samples, or in situ measurements such as cone penetrometer tests. Analysis of sediment core data can provide information about the geochemical and biological properties of sediments (Camidge et al. 2009) as well as the grain size and geotechnical properties of sediments along the core's profile.

Diver-deployed sediment cores were acquired at each site included in the Tesla-BOEM study. Sediment properties were analyzed by logging each core, measuring grain size with a mass spectrometer, and conducting radio isotope analysis. Grain size has been described as "a property of first-order importance" (Masselink and Hughes 2003:102) and, along with shear strength measurements, provided information concerning the physical properties of the sediments at each study site. Information concerning the physical properties of the individual grains was necessary in order to build locally specific models of sediment transport potential during extreme storm events (Keith and Evans 2009; Rego et al. 2012). Measured grain sizes were commonly silts and clays in the eastern portion of the survey area, closer to the mouth of the Mississippi River, while sand, silt, and clay dominated the samples from the western sites (Evans et al. 2013:401–410). Distance offshore was also found to impact grain size distributions. The grain size curves indicated patterns of sedimentation and in some cases revealed evidence of repeated episodes of scour and in-fill. Figure 3.5 highlights variations in sedimentation patterns by comparing sediment core logs at two sites in similar water depths that are both approximately 21 nautical miles offshore. The primary differences between these sites are sediment type, current flow regimes, and proximity to historic storms.

Cores were sampled for radio isotope analysis, with the goal of using this data as a proxy indicator for local sedimentation rates and scour (Allison

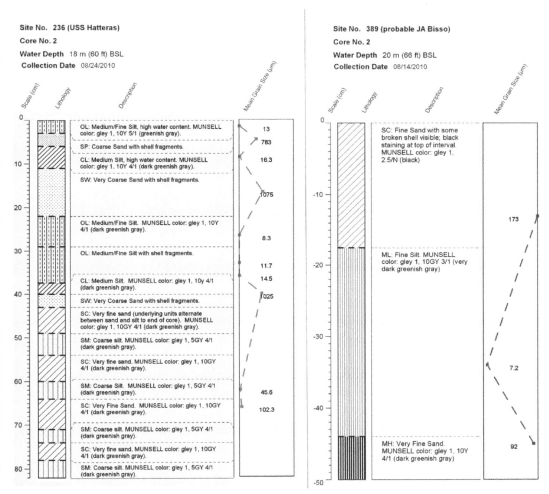

Figure 3.5. Core logs illustrating lithology and mean grain size at sites of USS *Hatteras* and probable *J. A. Bisso* (based on data compiled for Evans et al. 2013).

and Lee 2004; Allison et al. 2005; Neil and Allison 2005). Due to their short half-life duration, radio isotope tracers, particularly Lead-210 (^{210}Pb) and Cesium-137 (^{137}Cs), can provide an indication of recent processes and were chosen for analysis as part of the study. Lead-210 is naturally occurring, with a half-life of 22.3 years, while ^{137}Cs was introduced into the atmosphere through thermonuclear testing (1954–72) and has a half-life of 30 years. Measurements of ^{210}Pb and ^{137}Cs were used to develop decay curves, in which it was possible to identify interruptions and possible erosion/scour events within the overall profiles.

Radio isotope analysis was designed to determine post-disturbance sediment accumulation rates or erosion signatures that would contribute to an understanding of the likelihood and rates of shipwreck burial or scour—similar to analyses conducted at the sites of *Housatonic* (Conlin 2005) and *Hunley* (Lenihan and Murphy 1998:16)—both of which are related to site preservation.

Radio isotope analysis did not identify signatures of more recent (within the last 30 years) storm events in the core profiles. The lack of recent storm evidence may have been due to poor retention of the uppermost sediments within the core sleeve during acquisition. However, discrete disruptions in the radio isotope decay curve were identified for all but one of the sites examined. In some cases the observed disruptions appear to correspond with known historic storms; in other cases it was postulated that the disturbance may have been caused by the wrecking event itself, although the sample interval and available data were insufficient in the study to determine this with certainty.

Radio isotope decay curves indicated that rates of sediment deposition are relatively low at all of the sampled study sites. The highest recorded accumulation rates ranged from 0.14 to 0.17 centimeters/year; the lowest rates ranged from 0.06 to 0.08 cm/year. Based on the identified linear accumulation rates it would take 100 years to accumulate between 6 and 17 cm (2.4 to 6.7 inches) of sediment at the study sites, not accounting for the effects of compaction and dewatering. The results of the radio isotope analysis indicated that ongoing sediment accretion alone was unlikely to play a significant role in burying site components at any of the study sites.

Modeling

Oceanographic modeling was utilized to determine long-term sediment accretion and removal rates and to identify areas where storm events had resulted in significant bottom impacts (Evans et al. 2013; Rego et al. 2012). Oceanographic research for this study focused on the potential for sediment transport and mobility at the study sites, including accretion and scour, as they relate to site exposure. Seafloor sediments surrounding the study wrecks are predominantly clays and silts, primarily terrigenic deposits derived from the Mississippi and other rivers along the Gulf coast. Due to the cohesive properties of these sediments, typical current and wave forces in these water depths were believed to be insufficient to mobilize these deposits naturally (Curray 1960). Therefore oceanographic modeling focused on extreme storm events that had occurred in recent years in order to model net sediment accretion and erosion at each site.

Modeling was performed by Deltares (Evans et al. 2013; Rego et al. 2012) and incorporated sediment property data delivered from analysis of the aforementioned sediment cores and bathymetry data, as well as H*WIND data from recent hurricanes. The modeling used this data to simulate hydrodynamics and wave action using proprietary Delft3D-FlOW and Delft3D-WAVE models. For a more detailed discussion of the methodology see Evans and colleagues (2013:21–22).

Oceanographic modeling at the study sites showed considerable variation, with depths of disturbance between 0.3 and 150 cm (0.1 and 59 inches), depending on degree of sediment consolidation and proximity to modeled storm paths. The modeling indicated that significant scour from storms could be expected at a number of the sites, followed by significant redeposition of disturbed sediment after the storms had passed (possibly illustrated by figure 3.2b), resulting in moderate net scour (and in one case net sediment accretion).

CASE STUDY SUMMARY

The results of the Tesla-BOEM study provided useful information regarding sediment deposition and scour rates occurring on a number of shipwreck sites on the northwestern Gulf of Mexico outer continental shelf. The results of the study also provide insight into the utility and applicability of different techniques for modeling and measuring site formation processes on submerged shipwreck sites (Evans et al. 2013). The geophysical data, while useful in addressing a number of research objectives, were essential in illustrating specific sediment movement patterns at the site level. Oceanographic modeling was used to demonstrate potential impacts from the punctuation of extreme storm events and, for management purposes, to provide estimates of net sediment movement.

The radio isotope analysis was implemented in an attempt to determine the age of sediments at the sites and, therefore, to serve as a proxy for sediment accretion and erosion rates.

The results of the study raised questions about the strength of annual flow velocities surrounding wreck sites and about whether induced flow is sufficient to mobilize the predominantly cohesive sediments throughout the region, or if storm-induced conditions are necessary. Current measurements around selected wreck sites coupled with additional sediment core data that account for plasticity and water content would help answer these questions as part of a future research program.

The most challenging aspect of site formation studies is developing a cost-effective and efficient research design. The methods employed in the Tesla-BOEM study were not the only possible options but, given the parameters of the contract, were believed to be the best options to extract maximum long-term data during a relatively short duration project. The methodology therefore focused on techniques that could provide the maximum amount of information based on a single visit to the study sites. Alternatively, examples of methodologies used for long-term monitoring of sites are discussed by Oxley (chapter 10, this volume) and evidenced by Camidge et al. (2009), Wessex (2003), Ward et al. (1999b), Dix et al. 2007; and MCA (2012).

Conclusions

Understanding the characteristics and interactions of bottom sediments can provide a wealth of information. An understanding of regional sediments can inform strategies and interpretation when searching for shipwreck sites; site specific studies can provide information regarding the burial history of the wreck site (Lenihan and Murphy 1998; Evans et al. 2013); and this line of inquiry can inform the management strategies of heritage managers and conservators.

As archaeologists and other partners in heritage management are increasingly responsible for the protection and/or management of shipwreck sites, it becomes increasingly apparent that understanding seabed properties is an important first step. While it is not feasible to change the ocean's salinity or remove wood boring organisms from the equation, reburial of material is a practical and commonly employed method for protecting wreck sites (Gregory 2009; and Gregory and Manders 2011). A proper understanding of sediment properties and the macro and micro environments surrounding a wreck site is important to ensure the efficacy and improvement of in situ preservation practices.

Acknowledgments

We would like to thank the U.S. Department of the Interior, Bureau of Ocean Energy Management, for funding the research discussed in the case study. Radio isotope analysis for this study was performed by Dr. Mead Allison of the University of Texas at Austin; oceanographic modeling was performed by Deltares under the direction of Dr. João Lima Rego. Dr. Patrick Hesp assisted with analysis of geophysical data and analysis of results.

References Cited

Allison, Mead A., and M. T. Lee
2004   Sediment Exchange between Amazon Mudbanks and Shore-Fringing Mangroves in French Guiana. *Marine Geology* 208:169–190.
Allison, Mead A., A. Sheremet, M. A. Goñi, and Greg W. Stone
2005   Storm Layer Deposition on the Mississippi-Atchafalaya Subaqueous Delta Generated by Hurricane Lili in 2002. *Continental Shelf Research* 25:2213–2232.
Bascom, Willard
1976   Deep Water, Ancient Ships: The Treasure Vault of the Mediterranean. Doubleday, Garden City, New York.
Camidge, K., C. Johns, P. Rees, M. Canti, M. Hoskin, I. Panter, and J. Rees
2009   *Royal Anne Galley Marine Environmental Assessment Phase 2 Field Assessment Report.* Report for English Heritage. Historic Environment Projects, Cornwall County Council, Truro. Available from http://www.cornwall.gov.uk/idoc. ashx?docid=c59b2bef-7eec-461e-8a23-ced7c5383490&version=-1.
Capurro, Luis R. A.
1970   *Oceanography for Practicing Engineers.* Barnes and Noble, New York.
Chaney, Ronald C., and K. R. Demars
1985   *Strength Testing of Marine Sediments: Laboratory and In-Situ Measurements.* American Society of Testing and Materials, Baltimore, Maryland.
Church, Robert, Daniel J. Warren, Roy Cullimore, Lori Johnston, Morgan Kilgour, James Moore, Nicole Morris, William Patterson, William Schroeder, and Tom Shirley
2007   *Archaeological and Biological Analysis of World War II Shipwrecks in the Gulf of Mexico: Artificial Reef Effect in Deepwater.* OCS Study MMS 2007–015. U.S. Department of the Interior, Minerals Management Service, New Orleans.
Conlin, David L. (editor)
2005   *USS* Housatonic: *Site Assessment.* Submerged Resources Center Professional Report no. 19. National Park Service, US DOI, Santa Fe, New Mexico.
Conlin, David L., and Matthew A. Russell
2009   Site Formation Processes Once-Removed: Pushing the Boundaries of Interdisciplinary Maritime Archaeology. In *ACUA Underwater Archaeology Proceedings 2009, Toronto, Canada,* edited by Erika Laanela and Jonathan Moore, pp. 83–90. Advisory Council on Underwater Archaeology.
Curray, J.
1960   Sediments and History of Holocene Transgression, Continental Shelf, Northwest Gulf of Mexico. In *Recent Sediments, Northwest Gulf of Mexico,* edited by F. Shepard and T. J. Van Andel, pp. 221–266. American Petroleum Institute Symposium, American Association of Petroleum Geologists.

Davies, A. G.

1983   Wave Interactions with Rippled Sand Beds. In *Physical Oceanography of Coastal and Shelf Seas*, edited by B. Johns, pp. 1–66. Elsevier Science Publishers, New York.

Dix, J. K., D. O. Lambkin, M. D. Thomas, and P. M. Cazenave

2007   *Modeling Exclusion Zones for Marine Aggregate Dredging*. English Heritage Aggregate Levy Sustainability Fund Project 3365 Final Report.

English Heritage

2007   *Stirling Castle: Conservation and Management Plan*. Electronic document, http://www.english-heritage.org.uk/content/imported-docs/p-t/mgmtplan-stirlingcastlevfinal.pdf, accessed April, 2014.

Evans, Amanda M., Matthew E. Keith, Erin E. Voisin, Patrick Hesp, Greg Cook, Mead A. Allison, Graziela da Silva, and Eric Swanson

2013   *Archaeological Analysis of Submerged Sites on the Gulf of Mexico Outer Continental Shelf*. OCS Study BOEM 2013-01110. U.S. Department of the Interior, Bureau of Ocean Energy Management, Gulf of Mexico OCS Region, New Orleans.

Folk, Robert L.

1980   *Petrology of Sedimentary Rocks*. Hemphill Publishing, Austin.

Ford, Ben, Amy Borgens, William Bryant, Dawn Marshall, Peter Hitchcock, Cesar Arias, and Donny Hamilton

2008   *Archaeological Excavation of the Mardi Gras Shipwreck (16GM01), Gulf of Mexico Continental Slope*. Prepared by Texas A&M University for the Minerals Management Service, Gulf of Mexico OCS Region, U.S. Department of the Interior, New Orleans.

Garrison, E. G., C. F. Giammona, F. J. Kelly, A. R. Tripp, and G. A. Wolff

1989   *Historic Shipwrecks and Magnetic Anomalies of the Northern Gulf of Mexico: Reevaluation of Archaeological Resource Management Zone 7—Volume I executive summary*. OCS Study MMS 89-0023. U.S. Department of the Interior, Minerals Management Service, New Orleans.

Gearhart, Robert II, Doug Jones, Amy Borgens, Sara Laurence, Todd DeMunda, and Julie Shipp

2011   *Impacts of Recent Hurricane Activity on Historic Shipwrecks in the Gulf of Mexico Outer Continental Shelf*. OCS Study BOEMRE 2011-003. U.S. Department of the Interior, Minerals Management Service, New Orleans.

Grabowski, Robert C., Ian G. Droppo, and Geraldene Wharton

2011   Erodibility of Cohesive Sediment: The Importance of Sediment Properties. *Earth Science Reviews* 105:101–120.

Gregory, David

2009   In Situ Preservation of Marine Archaeological Sites: Out of Sight but Not Out of Mind. In *In Situ Conservation of Cultural Heritage: Public, Professionals and Preservation*, edited by Vicki Richards and Jennifer McKinnon, pp. 1–16. Flinders University Program in Maritime Archaeology, Past Foundation, Columbus, Ohio.

Gregory, David, and Martijn Manders

2011   *In-situ Preservation of a Wreck Site*. In *Wreck Project: Decay and Protection of Ar-*

chaeological Wooden Shipwrecks, edited by Charlotte Gjelstrup Björdal and David Gregory, pp. 107–127. Information Press, Oxford.

Ishtiak, Kazi, and Urska Demsar

2013   Improving Seabed Classification from Multi-Beam Echo Sounder (MBES) Backscatter Data with Visual Data Mining. *Journal of Coastal Conservation* 17:559–577.

Jain, Rajesh K., and Umesh C. Kothyari

2010   Influence of Cohesion on Suspended Load Transport of Non-Uniform Sediments. *Journal of Hydraulic Research* 48:33–43.

Jones, Toby

2004   *The Mica Shipwreck: Deepwater Nautical Archaeology in the Gulf of Mexico*. Master's thesis, Department of Anthropology, Texas A&M University, College Station.

Keith, Donald H., and Joe J. Simmons III

1988   Analysis of Hull Remains, Ballast, and Artifact Distribution of a 16th-Century Shipwreck, Molasses Reef, British West Indies. *Journal of Field Archaeology* 12:411–424.

Keith, Matthew E., and Amanda M. Evans

2009   Shipwreck Subsidence: Applying Geotechnical Concepts to Archaeology. In *ACUA Underwater Archaeology Proceedings 2009, Toronto, Canada*, edited by Erika Laanela and Jonathan Moore, pp. 59–70. Advisory Council on Underwater Archaeology.

Lenihan, Daniel J., and Larry Murphy

1990   Archaeological Record. In *Submerged Cultural Resources Study: USS Arizona Memorial and Pearl Harbor National Historic Landmark*, edited by Daniel J. Lenihan, pp. 75–115. Southwest Cultural Resources Center Professional Papers no. 23, Santa Fe.

1998   Research Design. In *H. L. Hunley Site Assessment*, edited by Larry E. Murphy, pp. 15–20. National Park Service, Submerged Resources Center, Naval Historical Center, and South Carolina Institute of Archaeology and Anthropology.

Lick, Wilbert, and Joe McNeil

2000   Effects of Sediment Bulk Properties on Erosion Rates. *The Science of the Total Environment* 266(2001):41–48.

Maritime and Coast Guard Agency (MCA)

2012   SS Richard Montgomery *Survey Report 2012*. Electronic document, http://www.dft.gov.uk/mca/mca_summary_report_2012.pdf, accessed February 15, 2014.

Masselink, G., and M. G. Hughes

2003   *Introduction to Coastal Processes and Geomorphology*. Oxford University Press, New York.

McNinch, J. E., J. T. Wells, and A. C. Trembanis

2006   Predicting the Fate of Artefacts in Energetic, Shallow Marine Environments: An Approach to Site Management. *International Journal of Nautical Archaeology* 35(2):290–309.

Merritt, Olivia

2011   *AMAP2—Characterising the Potential of Wrecks*. SeaZone Ltd., for English Heritage. Bentley: SeaZone Solutions. Available from http://archaeologydataservice. ac.uk/archives/view/amap2_eh_2011/.

Muckelroy, Keith

1978   *Maritime Archaeology*. Cambridge University Press, Cambridge.

Neil, C. F., and M. A. Allison

2005   Subaqueous Deltaic Formation on the Atchafalaya Shelf, Louisiana. *Marine Geology* 214:411–430.

National Ocean Service

2013   *Ocean Facts*. National Oceanic and Atmospheric Administration, United States Department of Commerce. Electronic document, http://oceanservice.noaa.gov/facts/exploration.html, accessed January 13, 2013.

Pearson, C. E., S. R. James Jr., M. C. Krivor, S. D. El Darragi, and L. Cunningham

2003   *Refining and Revising the Gulf of Mexico Outer Continental Shelf Region High-Probability Model for Historic Shipwrecks: Final Report. Volume II: Technical Narrative*. OCS Study MMS 2003-061. U.S. Department of the Interior, Minerals Management Service, New Orleans.

Peters, Shanan E., and Dylan P. Loss

2012   Storm and Fair-Weather Wave Base: A Relevant Distinction? *Geology* 40:511–514.

Quinn, Rory

2006   The Role of Scour in Shipwreck Site Formation Processes and the Preservation of Wreck-Associated Scour Signatures in the Sedimentary Record—Evidence from Seabed and Sub-Surface Data. *Journal of Archaeological Science* 33:1419–1432.

Quinn, Rory, J. M. Bull, and Justin K. Dix

1997   Buried Scour Marks as Indicators of Paleo-Current Direction at the *Mary Rose* Wreck Site. *International Journal of Marine Geology* 140:405–413.

Rego, João Lima, Katherine Cronin, Patrick Hesp, Deepak Vatvani, Amanda Evans, and Matthew Keith

2012   *Hurricane-Induced Bottom Stirring on the Louisiana-Texas Continental Shelf*. Paper presented at the Joint Numerical Seabed Modeling Group, Brest, France.

Shackley, Myra L.

1975   *Archaeological Sediments: A Survey of Analytical Methods*. John Wiley and Sons, New York.

Søreide, Fredrik

2011   *Ships from the Depths: Deepwater Archaeology*. Texas A&M University Press, College Station.

Stewart, David J.

1999   Formation Processes Affecting Submerged Archaeological Sites: An Overview. *Geoarchaeology* 14(6):565–587.

Texas Department of Transportation (TxDOT)

2008   Soil and Bedrock Information. Electronic document, http://www.dot.state.tx.us/business/contractors_consultants/bridge/soil_bedrock.htm, accessed October, 31, 2009.

Trujillo, Alan P., and Harold V. Thurman

2008   *Essentials of Oceanography*. Pearson Prentice Hall, New Jersey.

United States Army Corps of Engineers

2002   *Coastal Engineering Manual Part III, Coastal Sediment Processes.* Publication No. EM 1110-2-1100. Corps of Engineers Internet Publishing Group, Washington, D.C. Electronic document, http://140.194.76.129/publications/eng-manuals/EM_1110-2-1100_vol/PartIII/PartIII.htm, accessed April 2012.

United States Department of the Interior, Minerals Management Service, Gulf of Mexico OCS Region (USDI MMS)

2005   *Notice to Leasees and Operators of Federal Oil and Gas Leases on the Outer Continental Shelf, Gulf of Mexico Region. Revisions to the List of OCS Lease Blocks Requiring Archaeological Resource Surveys and Repots.* NTL No. 2005-G10. New Orleans.

Wachsmann, Shelley

2011   Deep-Submergence Archaeology. In *Oxford Handbook of Maritime Archaeology*, edited by Alexis Catsambis, Ben Ford, and Donny Hamilton, pp. 763–785. Oxford University Press, New York.

Ward, I.A.K., P. Larcombe, and P. Veth

1999a   A New Process-Based Model for Wreck Site Formation. *Journal of Archaeological Science* 26:561–570.

Ward, I.A.K., P. Larcombe, R. Brinkman, and R. M. Carter

1999b   Sedimentary Processes and the *Pandora* Wreck, Great Barrier Reef, Australia. *Journal of Field Archaeology* 26(1):41–53.

Waters, Michael R.

1992   *Geoarchaeology: A North American Perspective.* University of Arizona Press, Tucson.

Wessex Archaeology

2003   *Stirling Castle Historic Wreck Site: Archaeological Desk-based Assessment.* Report for English Heritage. Available from http://www.english-heritage.org.uk/content/imported-docs/p-t/stirlingcastlearchaeologicalreport2008.pdf.

Whitehouse, Richard

1998   *Scour at Marine Structures: A Manual for Practical Applications.* Thomas Telford Publications, London.

4

Marine Scour of Cohesionless Sediments

RORY QUINN, ROBIN SAUNDERS, RUTH PLETS, KIERAN WESTLEY,
AND JUSTIN DIX

Scour occurs at the seafloor when sediment is eroded from an area in response to forcing by oscillatory flows such as waves; by directional flows—for example, tidal, river, or density induced—or by combined flows (Whitehouse 1998). Commonly scour is initiated either by migration or change in morphology of bedforms or by the introduction of an object to the seafloor intentionally, as in coastal engineering, or accidentally, as in shipwrecks (Soulsby 1997; Whitehouse 1998; Quinn 2006). Marine structures are vulnerable to erosion due to scouring by waves and tidal currents, and scour processes can ultimately lead to their complete failure and collapse (Soulsby 1997; Whitehouse 1998). Scour signatures are widely reported from the marine environment, and their development and importance in short- and long-term site evolution are noted in archaeology (Arnold et al. 1999; Caston 1979; McNinch et al. 2001; Quinn 2006; Trembanis and McNinch 2003; Uchupi et al. 1988; Ward et al. 1999a). Scour also has bearing in a range of other endeavors: biology (Eckman and Nowell 1984), coastal engineering and seabed development (Carreiras et al. 2003; Kumar et al. 2003; Sumer at al. 1997; Sumer et al. 2001); glacial and geomorphological research (Hay et al. 2005; Richardson 1968; Russell 1993; Sharpe and Shaw 1989), and mine burial and detection (Hatton et al. 2004; Smith et al. 2004).

In archaeological investigations, scour signatures are reported widely, from nearshore submerged wreck sites in shallow water (Arnold et al. 1999; Caston 1979; McNinch et al. 2001; Quinn et al. 1997; Wheeler 2002) to deepwater sites on the continental shelf and beyond (Ballard et al. 2000, 2002; McCann and Oleson 2004; Uchupi et al. 1988). Scour is reported from intact and scattered wreck sites (Arnold et al. 1999; Caston 1979; McNinch et al. 2001; Quinn 2006; Wheeler 2002) and from individual artifacts and artifact scatters (Ballard et al. 2000, 2002; McCann and Oleson 2004). In maritime archaeology the focus on site formation theory (Muckelroy 1978; O'Shea 2002; Quinn 2006; Stewart 1999; Ward et al. 1999a) and an acceptance that physical processes dominate site formation in the early stages (Ward et al. 1999a) suggest that a greater understanding of scour processes and associated depositional and erosional processes at wreck sites is important.

FLOW REGIMES AT SUBMERGED STRUCTURES

As a complete discussion on the mechanics of scour processes (and associated hydrodynamics and sediment dynamics) is beyond the scope of this chapter, this section summarizes the general principles of scour and introduces terminology relevant to this study. For those interested in learning more about scour, excellent overviews are presented in books by Soulsby (1997) and Whitehouse (1998) and in review papers by Sumer and Fredsoe (1999) and Sumer et al. (2001). Additionally, more comprehensive discussions on scour processes and signatures around shipwreck sites can be found in Caston (1979), Saunders (2005), Quinn (2006), and Dix et al. (2007).

The introduction of an object to the seafloor leads to an increase in flow velocity (due to continuity) and turbulence (due to the generation of vortices; Whitehouse 1998). Scouring subsequently results in the lowering of the seabed from some previously obtained equilibrium (or quasi-equilibrium) level, due to the flow velocity increase near the object, a resulting increase in the *local* Shields parameter (a non-dimensional number used to calculate the initiation of motion of sediment in a fluid flow), and subsequent divergences in the sediment transport regime (Voropayev et al. 2003). Therefore the introduction of an object to the seafloor causes changes in the flow regime in its immediate environs, resulting in one of the following or a combination of them: flow contraction; the formation of a horseshoe vortex in front of the structure; the formation of lee-wake vortices behind the structure (sometimes accompanied by vortex shedding); turbulence; the occurrence of reflection and diffraction waves; wave breaking; and sediment liquefaction promoting material loss from the site (Sumer et al. 2001). These processes increase local sediment transport and subsequently lead to scour (Sumer et al. 2001). When scour occurs on fine-grained (silt or clay) seabeds, the eroded material is carried away from the wreck site in suspension, leaving a seafloor depression that may not readily be in-filled by natural processes (Whitehouse et al. 2011). Where scouring takes place

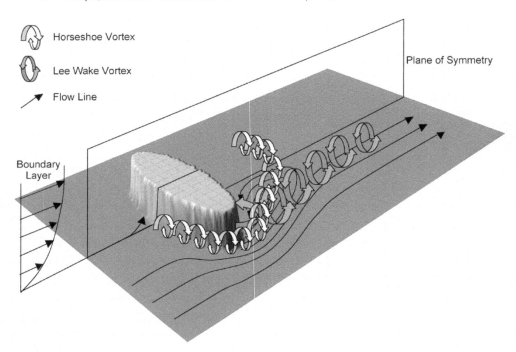

Figure 4.1. Idealized flow patterns and vortex development operating on a fully submerged wreck site (Quinn 2006). Synoptic model is based upon data and discussions presented in Eckman and Nowell (1984), Sumer et al. (1997), Sumner and Fredsoe (1999), Tetsik et al. (2005), and Voropayev et al. (2003).

in course-grained deposits (sand or gravel), it usually results in local deposition, often comprising the eroded material, in addition to scour. Since course-grained deposits fall out of solution much more rapidly, shipwrecks studied archaeologically in shallow water and coastal environments are predominantly located on sand- or gravel-dominated seabeds. The discussion and examples in this chapter are therefore specific to areas dominated by course-grained deposits. See the Keith and Evans (chapter 3, this volume) for a discussion of areas dominated by fine-grained deposits.

The flow around a fully submerged short horizontal cylinder—a good analogy for a shipwreck—is essentially three-dimensional (Testik et al. 2005) and consists of two basic flow structures: the horseshoe vortex formed at the front of the structure and the vortex flow pattern formed at the lee side of it (fig. 4.1). The horseshoe vortex is formed by the rotation of the incoming flow. Under the influence of the adverse pressure gradient produced by the structure, the boundary layer on the bed up-flow of the structure undergoes a three-dimensional separation, rolls up to form a swirling vortex around the structure, and trails off down-flow (Sumer et al. 1997; fig. 4.1). The morphology of horseshoe vortices can be strongly distorted, resulting in complicated flow patterns. One such result is vortex shedding, where self-propelling, closed ring structures are formed and transported by the flow (Testik et al. 2005).

Lee wake vortices are formed by the rotation in the boundary layer over the surface of the object (fig. 4.1). End effects (from the tips of the structure, in this case the bow and stern of a submerged vessel) play a dominant role in the flow pattern and strongly modify the structure of vortices (Testik et al. 2005). Lee wake vortices emanating from the surface of the structure are brought together in the vicinity of the structure due to flow convergence (Hatton et al. 2004; Smith et al. 2004; Testik et al. 2005). Additionally, two counter-rotating vortices form a vortical region in the near wake on the lee side of the structure (Testik et al. 2005). In practice, localized flow acceleration has been observed by Ward et al. (1999b) using two single-point current meters at the bow and stern of the HMS *Pandora* wreck site on the Great Barrier Reef.

In engineering terms, scour is often broadly classified as local scour (e.g., steep-sided scour pits at individual obstructions), global or dishpan scour (shallow broad depressions developed around installations), or general seabed movement, resulting in erosion, deposition or bedform development (Whitehouse 1998). However, the terms *local*, *global*, and *dishpan* are poorly defined and are at best qualitative descriptions. Quinn (2006) uses the terms *near-field* and *far-field* to describe scour signatures formed in the immediate area (near-field) and wake (far-field) of the wreck, while Saunders (2005) uses the terms *local* and *wake* scour to describe similar concepts. In this chapter, the terms *local* and *wake scour* are adopted.

SCOUR AND WRECK SITE FORMATION

Site formation processes at wreck sites are driven by some combination of chemical, biological, and physical processes, with physical processes dominant in initial phases (Ward et al. 1998, 1999a). Although many authors describe wrecks as being in some form of equilibrium state with the surrounding environment (Gregory 1995; Quinn et al. 1997; Ward et al. 1999a; Wheeler 2002), it is important to acknowledge that wreck sites act as open systems, with the exchange across system boundaries of both material (sediment, water, organics, and inorganics) and energy (wave, tidal, storm; Quinn 2006). Wrecks are therefore generally in a state of dynamic (not steady-state) equilibrium with respect to the natural environment, characterized by negative disequilibrium, ultimately leading to wreck disintegration (Quinn 2006).

Positive and negative feedbacks operate between physical, chemical, and biological processes in the water column, the sediment pile, and the wreck as it disintegrates and interacts with the surrounding environment (Ward et al. 1998, 1999a). Fundamental processes driving site formation are therefore dependent upon the complex erosion (net sediment/material loss) and accretion (net sediment/material deposition) history of wreck sites. Furthermore, exposed parts of wreck structures tend to be affected by aerobic bacteria, wood borers, and increased corrosion rates, while buried wreck components tend to be affected by anaerobic bacteria (Ward et al. 1998). Therefore even major chemical and biological processes contributing to site formation are constrained by the physical process of scour (Quinn 2006).

Seabed scour operates on a variety of temporal scales, with scouring at permanent (static) structures initially occurring rapidly, over a period of days to weeks, but approaching ultimate (equilibrium) values asymptotically (Whitehouse 1998). Due to the dynamic and mobile nature of submerged wreck sites and artifact scatters in the nearshore zone, the process of scouring can therefore occur at a wide range of temporal scales (hours to decades) as sites and objects are invariably covered and uncovered due to external forcing. In addition, the total or partial mobility of wreck structures and associated artifacts can lead to archaeological objects acting as mobile nuclei for scour initiation, further complicating scour processes (McNinch et al. 2006; Quinn 2006).

Seabed scour also operates on a variety of spatial scales, from complete wreck sites to individual objects or artifacts. Controls on the spatial extent of scouring at wreck sites include a combination of the orientation, shape, and size of the causative object, the seafloor and sub-surface geology, the water depth, and the prevailing hydro- and sediment-dynamics (Caston 1979; Saunders 2005; Quinn 2006; Dix et al. 2007).

SCOUR SIGNATURES FORMED BY TIDAL CURRENTS

Tidal currents are the dominant mechanism for scour in most environments, including nearshore and inland environments such as bays, estuaries, and rivers, as well as in offshore environments where wave action has no significant or regular influence. Flows in tidal-dominated environments can be uni-directional or bi-directional, uni-directional being dominant in fluvial environments and bi-directional occurring in environments subject to daily tidal fluctuations. The most comprehensive field-based study on wreck-associated scour features formed under tidal currents is from the sand and gravel–dominated Outer Thames Estuary, United Kingdom (Caston 1979). In this side-scan sonar investigation, average scour lengths of 275 meters (902 feet) are reported, with some flow-parallel scour features extending up to 1 kilometer (0.62 mile) in the direction of flow of the stronger ebb or flood tidal current. Caston (1979) describes a gradational series of wreck-associated scour features, all of which parallel the peak flow. The orientation and width of the wreck, relative to the current flow, are determined as significant controls to the length of wreck-associated scour marks (Caston 1979).

The occurrence of double or single wreck marks is demonstrated to reflect the orientation of the wreck with respect to the peak tidal current flow (Caston 1979). Single scour marks emanate from wrecks that measure an average width of 13 m (43 feet) across the current, and the mean length of these scour shadows is 130 m (426 feet). Double scour marks, of mean length 400 m (1,312 feet), are generated by wrecks with an average width across the flow of 60 m (197 feet). The shortest and narrowest scour features were found associated with wrecks aligned with their long axis along the current, presenting streamlined shapes to the flow. The majority of scour depths recorded in the Thames Estuary was 1.5–2 m (~5–7 feet). Caston (1979) also demonstrates that wreck mark morphology is dependent on seabed lithology, with wreck marks on a sand floor being characterized by broad, shallow, longitudinally extensive troughs, whereas those on gravel floors are relatively narrow, deep, and less extensive.

In an attempt to quantify the relationships defined by Caston (1979) from the field data, Saunders (2005) constructed a laboratory-based scaled physical model in a uni-directional flume suitable for both flow visualization and movable bed scour experiments. Although this model operated at Reynolds numbers (dimensionless numbers that give a measure of the ratio of inertial forces to viscous forces) of 10^3 and 10^4 (whereas hydrodynamic processes at shipwreck sites typically operate at Reynolds numbers of 10^5 to 10^7), results from the experiment act as good proxies for field data (Saunders 2005). Subsequent experiments were undertaken by Lambkin and colleagues (2006) on both blocks. The experiments utilized variable width:height ratios, and scaled wreck models in a wind tunnel, which

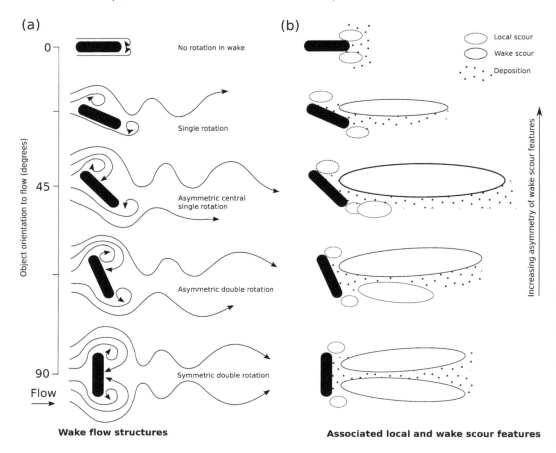

Figure 4.2. (a) Schematic representation of the postulated relationship between ship-wreck orientation and wake flow behavior. Where rotations in the wake are indicated, these can be considered to take the generalized form of a corkscrew with a rotation such that flow at the bed is directed inward (Saunders 2005). (b) Postulated relation-ship between shipwreck orientation and dominant wake scour and deposition features (Saunders 2005).

operated at Reynolds numbers of up to 10^6 and were thus comparable to the full wreck scale. The results suggested that these obstacle-derived flow features were independent of Reynolds when it exceeds 10^4.

Figure 4.2(a) summarizes the results of this study, illustrating the general behavior in the wake of an object at a progressively increasing angle to a uni-directional flow, as a wreck would encounter in fluvial environments and offshore environments with a single predominant current direction. At small angles, as flow is presented with a streamlined obstruction, a boundary layer develops along the sides of the object and separates from the object at the down-flow end. This separating boundary layer induces vorticity in the immediate lee of the object. In the model there is no evidence to support lee-wake vortex shedding; instead all fluid entrained in the vortex is ejected upward into the main oncoming flow.

As the angle increases, the vertical boundary layer flow at the vessel becomes detached at the up-flow end of the object and, in doing so, generates a pressure differential, leading to flow rotation in the immediate lee of the up-flow end. With increasing angles, lee wake flow rotation increases in magnitude, drawing in increasing amounts of overflow, resulting in the generation of a down-flow horizontal, flow-aligned vortex. Subsequently this horizontal flow rotation draws down higher velocity flow from the free stream, producing the wake scouring below it. As the angle to the flow increases further, through 45°, the vorticity in the lee of the down-flow end increases in magnitude until it also generates an opposing horizontal vortex in the wake. At 90° to the flow the lee wake vorticity at each end of the vessel is of similar magnitude, and it follows that the corresponding horizontal, flow-aligned rotations are also of similar magnitude.

Scour and depositional signatures resultant from these flow regimes are summarized in figure 4.2(b), where it is clear that as the object orientation to the flow varies, a distinct change in the lee wake scour patterning is observed. At an orientation of 0° to flow, the object presents only a very small projected aspect ratio, and minimal scour is observed. No evidence of wake scour is recorded at this orientation. The little scour that is observed is reminiscent of that developed around engineering structures such as bridge piers and can only be considered as local scour and hence determined by the processes of local scour.

At an orientation of 45°, wake scour is the dominant form of scouring recorded, developed down-flow as a central, flow-aligned scour depression for up to 18H (where H is the height of the object). Flow visualization techniques confirm that this forms directly under the wake's horizontal rotation, which draws down higher velocity flow, resulting in wake scouring. In some instances the resulting scour signatures suggest that a smaller horizontal rotation also develops in the lee of the down-flow end of the object, causing limited wake scouring below it. At an orientation of 90°, wake scour signatures again dominate. Twin symmetrical scour depressions form down-flow for up to 14H. Flow visualization confirms these forms directly under the counter-rotating vortex pair depicted in figure 4.2(a).

The generic flows identified from these experiments were used to design the field sampling strategy of Dix and colleagues (2007) for the investigation of scour at two shipwreck sites in the English Channel: an early twentieth-century unidentified wreck on Hastings shingle bank and the *Ariel* site on the Owers Bank. Using an array of eight seabed-mounted, upward- and sideways-looking Acoustic Doppler Current Profilers (ADCPs), these field deployments successfully captured the following elements of hydrodynamics in this tidally dominated environment: up-flow horseshoe vortex, flow acceleration at the margins of the wreck, lee-wake vortices, and areas of low flow velocity that could promote sediment accumulation.

As predicted from the precursor laboratory experiments by Saunders (2005) and Dix et al. (2007), regions of the wake where velocity locally increased at the bed (i.e., lee-wake vortices), were coincident with regions of scour. Conversely, regions associated with reduced velocity were coincident with sediment accumulation. Further, an extensive sediment shadow exists in regions of apparently reduced time mean flow, where ambient peak velocities are close to the threshold value for sediment transport and the direction of flow is well constrained.

This study also demonstrated that although the overall pattern of scour was an accumulative effect represented by net sediment transport over many tidal cycles, flow regimes changed significantly over a single tidal cycle, and so smaller scale objects with threshold of movement comparable to local sediments could be in semi-perpetual motion.

The processes and patterns observed in the flume experiments of Saunders (2005) depicted in figure 4.2 are further supported by multi-beam echo-sounder (MBES) data acquired over two World War I wreck sites in Belfast Lough (fig. 4.3) on the northeast coast of Ireland. These sites are located in a strongly bi-directional flow regime. The wreck of *Chirripo* is orientated at approximately 45° and *Tiberia* at approximately 90° to peak flow. The *Chirripo* site shows the classic transitional pattern between single and double scour signatures, with signatures extending up to 1,020 m (3,346 feet) from the wreck. The *Tiberia* site, located in deeper water, displays a classic double scour signature, with erosional and depositional features shorter and broader than those developed on the *Chirripo* site.

In contrast to shipwreck sites located in strong uni- or bi-directional flow regimes, at wreck sites under the influence of rotary tidal currents (with the direction changing through all points of the compass during the tidal period), local scour signatures dominate, while wake scour signatures are less developed or absent (fig. 4.4). The interaction of rotary tidal flow

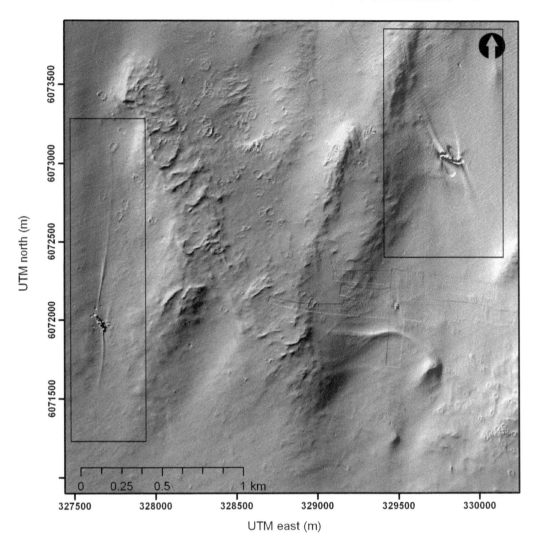

Figure 4.3. MBES data showing complex scour signatures formed around the *Chirripo* (west) and *Tiberia* (east) wreck sites in Belfast Lough under a bi-directional flow regime. The MBES data were acquired by the U.K. Royal Navy and the U.K. Hydrographic Office.

appears to cause the wreck to act as a stationary nucleus, promoting local scour around and under the wreck, causing gradual sinking of the wreck into the substrate. The MBES data in figure 4.4 demonstrate the almost complete burial of the wreck *City of Bristol* off the north coast of Ireland into a scour hollow formed under a rotary tidal current regime.

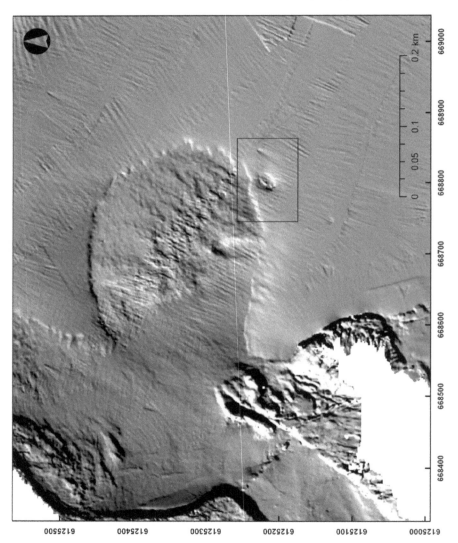

Figure 4.4. MBES data from the north coast of Ireland showing a well-developed local scour signature around the *City of Bristol* wreck site, developed under a rotary current. The MBES data were acquired by the JIBS project.

SCOUR SIGNATURES FORMED BY WAVES

In shallow water, high-energy environments, wave action (oscillatory flow) is typically the dominant process for scour. In the marine environment, as the wave boundary layer is much thinner than the current boundary layer, the shear stress exerted under a wave is much larger than for a tidal current of the same velocity (Whitehouse 1998). Therefore the dynamics and rate of degradation at energetic, shallow water wave-dominated wreck sites can be high in comparison to deeper water, current-dominated sites (Quinn 2006).

Model-based proxies for wreck site formation under dominant wave regimes exist in the form of physical models of scour around short horizontal cylinders under oscillatory flow conditions (Testik et al. 2005; Voropayev et al. 2003). Voropayev and colleagues (2003) describe four regimes of local (near-field) bed evolution based on heavy cylindrical objects under an increasing oscillating flow on a sandy bed: (i) no scour/burial, (ii) initial scour, (iii) expanded scour, and (iv) periodic burial. Figures 4.5(a) and 4.5(b) illustrate the transformation from initial scour to expanded scour pattern under higher energy conditions for a wreck under progressive shoaling waves. At scour initiation, a triple-scour signature is formed parallel to peak flow as shown in figure 4.5(a), with a central scour signature forming mid-ship and two shorter scour signatures nucleating at the bow and stern. In the majority of lab experiments conducted by Voropayev and colleagues (2003), the triple-scour signature formed at the onshore side of the cylinder due to the nonlinearity of the waves. However, for weakly nonlinear waves, similar (but weaker) signatures developed on the offshore side, analogous to paired double-scour features formed under bi-directional steady flows. With time, small sand waves develop at the bow and stern; they spread and initiate ripple formation in the onshore direction, decaying with distance from the site.

Under more energetic regimes, the scour initially develops as in figure 4.5(a) but becomes unstable and transforms into the expanded scour regime of figure 4.5(b) as the elongate triple-scour signatures merge into a semi-elliptical single-scour (Voropayev et al. 2003). Under continued forcing, if the amplitude of the bedforms increases to a level greater than the diameter of the cylinder, it may result in complete burial. Migration of bedforms can therefore cause periodic burial and exposure of the cylinder.

Figure 4.5(c) displays side-scan sonar data from the *Stypie* wreck site in Lough Foyle (Ireland), which supports the evolutionary regimes depicted

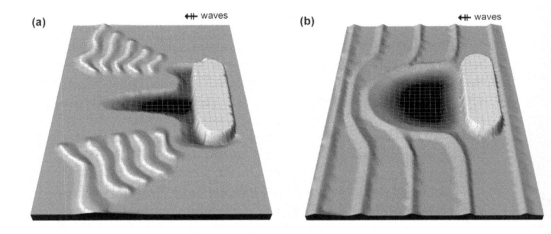

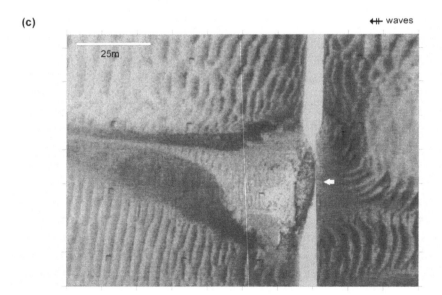

Figure 4.5. Idealized representations of the transformation from (a) initial scour pattern to (b) expanded scour pattern under higher energy conditions for a wreck under progressive shoaling waves. Models are based upon data and discussions presented in Voropayev et al. (2003). (c) Side-scan data acquired over the *Stypie* wreck site, Lough Foyle, Ireland (modified from McGettigan 2003).

in figures 4.5(a) and 4.5(b). The geometry and morphology of the scour patterns developed at the wreck site demonstrate strong correlation between the lab models and the field data, implying that the *Stypie* site currently lies in a formation state between the initial scour and expanded scour regimes in figure 4.5(a) and 4.5(b). This site therefore provides further justification for the use of lab-based scaled physical models for the interpretation of scour processes at shipwreck sites.

Discussion

The introduction of a shipwreck to the seafloor leads to an increase in flow velocity and turbulence intensity, culminating in scouring of seafloor sediment and ongoing site destabilization. Scour is therefore a threat to the stability of wreck sites and can contribute to the acceleration of physical, biological, and chemical degradation of sites, acting as a fundamental control in many aspects of site formation processes. Furthermore, information regarding the degradation and preservation of a wreck may be gleaned from the morphology and content of these material traps. The dimensions of the scour hollows indicate that these features may be more easily recognizable than partially degraded wrecks. In extreme cases, where a wooden wreck is so completely degraded that the majority of the superstructure is fragmented, the wreck may not provide the concentration of coherent material required to produce a strong acoustic signature, but the scour features may. This remains a poorly understood concept and represents an obvious future research area.

Seabed scour operates on a variety of spatial scales, from complete wreck sites to individual objects or artifacts. The total or partial mobility of wreck structures and associated artifacts can lead to archaeological objects acting as mobile nuclei for scour initiation, further complicating scour processes.

Scouring at shipwreck sites can operate under a variety of hydrodynamic regimes, under the influence of either waves or tides or a complex mix of both. Under uni-directional flow, typical for strong tidal environments where one flow dominates, shipwreck sites may display double or single flow-aligned scour signatures parallel to peak flow. Under bi-directional flow conditions, typical for tidal environments with strong flow in two directions, wrecks with their long axis aligned at 90° to the flow exhibit pairs of double-scour signatures, with relative scour lengths controlled by the magnitude of ebb and flood currents. Under the influence of strong rotary tidal currents, wrecks may act as stationary nuclei, promoting scour around

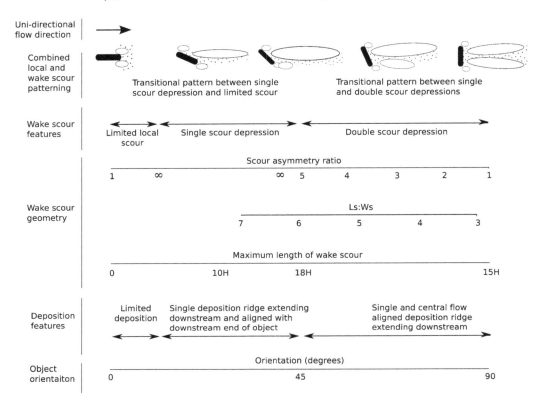

Figure 4.6. Constraints to wake scour chart, where Ls is scour length, Ws is scour width, H is object height, and LsN is scour length normalized to object height (Saunders 2005).

and under the wreck, possibly culminating in partial or complete burial of the wreck structure.

Under oscillatory flow conditions, typical for wave-dominated environments, scour initiates as a triple-scour signature, parallel to peak flow, at the onshore side of the wreck. Under higher energy conditions, the triple-scour signature becomes unstable and transforms into an expanded semi-elliptical single scour. Under continued forcing, an increase in bedform amplitude may cause complete burial of the wreck structure.

For nonperiodic, high-energy events (e.g., storm surges), it is possible that quasi-equilibrium scour signatures may be temporarily destroyed at wreck sites. However, over time, it is expected that a wreck site will return to pre-storm conditions, providing threshold conditions are not exceeded. Ultimately, site formation models for individual wreck sites must take account of periodic and nonperiodic forcing events. Failure to do so will lead to over-simplification of site formation models.

Controls on the spatial extent of scouring at wreck sites include a combination of the orientation, shape, and size of the causative object; the seafloor and sub-surface geology; the water depth; and the prevailing hydro- and sediment-dynamics. As a general guide, Saunders (2005) produced a chart depicting constraints to wake scour (fig. 4.6) based upon a simulation in which flow is uni-directional and has a depth averaged velocity of $0.4 \mathrm{ms}^{-1}$ and a substrate of medium sand. Although this simulation will not hold true for all wreck sites in all environments, it nonetheless provides some valuable constraints on the scales of scour signatures developed in response to external forcing. Once the dominant flow direction is established, it is possible to obtain relative wreck orientation information from the scour signatures by reading the chart from top to bottom (fig. 4.6).

First, the general nature of the overall scour is considered, which includes any evidence of local scour activity up-flow of any wake scour depressions. From observation, the wake scour patterning can initially be classed as exhibiting either a single or double depression. Single depressions are consistent with orientations less than 45° and double scour depressions are indicative of orientations between 45° and 90°. Second, the geometry of the wake scour features is considered. With double scour depressions, it is possible to obtain the asymmetry ratio, which can then give further indications as to the object orientation, the smaller scour depression emanating from the down-flow end of the object. Finally, any evidence of material deposition can also be considered. With a single scour depression any deposition ridges seen to extend down-flow to, or beyond, a distance consistent with the scour depression length will have emanated from the down-flow end of the object. Likewise, with information on object orientation and flow direction, any resulting scour patterning can also be predicted. In this instance the chart would be read from bottom to top.

In terms of future work, further research into the role of scour in shipwreck site formation processes is essential, with the disciplines of physical and numerical modeling representing some of the most attractive and obvious solutions. However, physical and numerical modeling of this strongly nonlinear process is still in its infancy, and further research is required in developing parameters for seabed and suspended sediment transport rates in the continuity equation for sediments (Voropayev et al. 2003).

ACKNOWLEDGMENTS

We thank the U.K. Maritime and Coastguard Agency and the Marine Institute of Ireland for the opportunity to work with the Joint Irish Bathymetric Survey (JIBS) MBES data. Funding for the €2.1 million project was provided from the EU INTERREG IIIA Programme, coordinated by the Department of the Environment for Northern Ireland. We thank the Agri-Food and Biosciences Institute, the U.K. Royal Navy and U.K. Hydrographic Office for the opportunity to work with the Belfast Lough MBES data.

REFERENCES CITED

Arnold, J. Barto, Thomas J. Oertling, and Andrew W. Hall.
1999   The *Denbigh* Project: Initial Observations on a Civil War Blockade-Runner and Its Wreck-Site. *International Journal of Nautical Archaeology* 28:126–144.
Ballard, R. D., A. M. McCann, D. Yoeger, L. Whitcomb, D. Mindell, J. Oleson, H. Singh, B. Foley, J. Adams, D. Piechota, and C. Giangrande
2000   The Discovery of Ancient History in the Deep Sea Using Advanced Deep Submergence Technology. *Deep Sea Research Part I* 47:1519–1620.
Ballard, Robert D., Lawrence E. Stager, Daniel Master, Dana Yoerger, David Mindell, Louis L. Whitcomb, Hanumant Singh, and Dennis Piechota
2002   Iron Age Shipwrecks in Deep Water off Ashkelon, Israel. *American Journal of Archaeology* 106:151–168.
Caston, G. F.
1979   Wreck Marks: Indicators of Net Sand Transport. *Marine Geology* 33:193–204.
Carreiras, J., J. Antunes do Carmo, and F. Seabra-Santos
2003   Settlement of Vertical Piles Exposed to Waves. *Coastal Engineering* 47:355–365.
Dix, J. K., D. O. Lambkin, M. D. Thomas, and P. M. Cazenave
2007   *Modelling Exclusion Zones for Marine Aggregate Dredging*. English Heritage Aggregate Levy Sustainability Fund Project 3365 Final Report.
Eckman, James E., and Arthur R. M. Nowell
1984   Boundary Skin Friction and Sediment Transport About an Animal-Tube Mimic. *Sedimentology* 31:851–862.
Gregory, David
1995   Experiments into the Deterioration Characteristics of Materials on the Duart Point Wreck Site: An Interim Report. *International Journal of Nautical Archaeology* 24:61–65.
Hatton, K. A., H. D. Smith, and D. L. Foster
2004   The Scour and Burial of Submerged Mines. *Eos Trans American Geophysical Union* 84(52). Ocean Science Meeting Suppl. Abstract OS52B-18.
Hay, Alex E., and Rachel Speller
2005   Naturally Occurring Scourpits in Nearshore Sands. *Journal of Geophysical Research* 110:F02004.

Kumar, A. Vijaya, S. Neelamani, and S. Narasimha Rao
2003   Wave Pressure and Uplift Forces on and Scour Around Submarine Pipeline in Clayey Soil. *Ocean Engineering* 30:271–295.

Lambkin, D. O., J. Dix, and S. R. Turnock
2006   Flow Patterning Associated with Three-dimensional Obstacles: A Proxy for Scour. In *Proceedings of the Third International Conference on Scour and Erosion*, 162–170. CURNET, Gouda, Netherlands.

McCann, A. M., and J. P. Oleson
2004   Deep Water Shipwrecks off Skerki Bank: The 1997 Survey. In *Deep-Water Shipwrecks off Skerki Bank: The 1997 Survey*, edited by A. M. McCann and J. P. Oleson. *Journal of Roman Archaeology* Supplementary Series no. 58.

McGettigan, John Joe
2003   Marine Archaeological Investigation of the Historic Shipwreck *Stypie* (Saint Bride). Unpublished thesis, University of Ulster.

McNinch, Jesse E., John T. Wells, and T. G. Drake
2001   The Fate of Artifacts in an Energetic, Shallow-water Environment: Scour and Burial at the Wreck Site of *Queen Anne's Revenge*. *Southeastern Geology* 40:19–27.

McNinch, Jesse E., John T. Wells, and Arthur C. Trembanis
2006   Predicting the Fate of Artefacts in Energetic, Shallow Marine Environments: An Approach to Site Management. *International Journal of Nautical Archaeology* 35(2):290–309.

Muckelroy, Keith
1978   *Maritime Archaeology*. Cambridge University Press, Cambridge.

O'Shea, John M.
2002   The Archaeology of Scattered Wreck-Sites: Formation Processes and Shallow Water Archaeology in Western Lake Huron. *International Journal of Nautical Archaeology* 31:211–227.

Quinn, Rory
2006   The Role of Scour in Shipwreck Site Formation Processes and the Preservation of Wreck-Associated Scour Signatures in the Sedimentary Record: Evidence from Seabed and Sub-Surface Data. *Journal of Archaeological Science* 33:1419–1432.

Quinn, R., J. M. Bull, J. K. Dix, and J. R. Adams
1997   The *Mary Rose* Site: Geophysical Evidence for Palaeo-Scour Marks. *International Journal of Nautical Archaeology* 26:3–16.

Richardson, Peter D.
1968   The Generation of Scour Marks Near Obstacles. *Journal of Sedimentary Petrology* 38:965–970.

Russell, Andrew J.
1993   Obstacle Marks Produced by Flow Around Stranded Ice Blocks during a Glacier Outburst Flood (Jökulhlaup) in West Greenland. *Sedimentology* 40:1091–1111.

Saunders, Robin
2005   *Seabed Scour Emanating from Submerged Three Dimensional Objects; Archaeological Case Studies*. Ph.D. Thesis, University of Southampton.

Sharpe, David R., and John Shaw
1989   Erosion of Bedrock by Subglacial Meltwater, Cantley, Quebec. *Geological Society of America Bulletin* 101:1011–1020.
Smith, H. D., D. L. Foster, S. I. Voropayev, and H.J.S. Fernando
2004   Modelling the Turbulent Processes Around a 3-D Cylinder. *Eos Trans. American Geophysical Union* 85 (47) Fall Meeting Suppl. Abstract OS21B-1217.
Soulsby, Richard
1997   *Dynamics of Marine Sands.* Thomas Telford, London.
Stewart, David J.
1999   Formation Processes Affecting Submerged Archaeological Sites: An Overview. *Geoarchaeology* 14:565–587.
Sumer, B. M., N. Christiansen, and J. Fredsoe
1997   The Horseshoe Vortex and Vortex Shedding Around a Vertical Wall-mounted Cylinder Exposed to Waves. *Journal of Fluid Mechanics* 332:41–70.
Sumer, B. M., and J. Fredsoe
1999   Wave Scour Around Structures. In *Advances in Coastal and Ocean Engineering,* edited by P.L.F. Liu, pp. 191–249. World Scientific, Singapore.
Sumer, B. M., R. Whitehouse, and A. Torum
2001   Scour Around Coastal Structures: A Summary of Recent Research. *Coastal Engineering* 44:153–190.
Testik, F. Y., S. I. Voropayev, and H.J.S. Fernando
2005   Flow Around a Short Horizontal Bottom Cylinder Under Steady and Oscillatory Flows. *Physics of Fluids* 17:47–103.
Trembanis, Arthur, and Jesse E. McNinch
2003   *Predicting Scour and Maximum Settling Depths of Shipwrecks: A Numeric Simulation of the Fate of Queen Anne's Revenge.* Proceedings of Coastal Sediments, Clearwater Beach, Florida.
Uchupi, Elazar, Maureen T. Muck, and Robert D. Ballard
1988   The Geology of the Titanic Site and Vicinity. *Deep Sea Research Part A. Oceanographic Research Papers* 35(7):1093–1110.
Voropayev, S. I., F. Y. Testik, H.J.S. Fernando, and D. L. Boyer
2003   Burial and Scour Around Short Cylinder Under Progressive Shoaling Waves. *Ocean Engineering* 30:1647–1667.
Ward, Ingrid A. K., Piers Larcombe, and P. Veth
1998   Towards New Process-Orientated Models for Describing Wreck Disintegration: An Example Using the *Pandora* Wreck. *Bulletin of the Australian Institute of Maritime Archaeology* 22:109–114.
Ward, Ingrid A. K., Piers Larcombe, and P. Veth
1999a   A New Process-Based Model for Wreck Site Formation. *Journal of Archaeological Science* 26:561–570.
Ward, Ingrid A. K., Piers Larcombe, Richard Brinkman, and Robert M. Carter
1999b   Sedimentary Processes and the *Pandora* Wreck, Great Barrier Reef, Australia. *Journal of Field Archaeology* 26(1):41–53.

Wheeler, A. J.
2002   Environmental Controls on Shipwreck Preservation: The Irish Context. *Journal of Archaeological Science* 29:1149–1159.

Whitehouse, R.
1998   *Scour at Marine Structures.* Thomas Telford, London.

Whitehouse, Richard, John Sutherland, and James M. Harris
2011   Evaluating Scour at Marine Gravity Structures. *Maritime Engineering* 164(MA4):143–157.

5

Corrosion Products and Site Formation Processes

IAN D. MACLEOD

Data on the nature of corrosion products found on metallic objects is often assigned to a series of unread appendixes that show the works have been done, but there is little to guide the reader, site manager, or project director as to the real value and meaning behind the observations. This lack of understanding of significance of the message of decay given to us by corroding objects has deep-seated roots. Very few graduates in archaeology have undertaken courses in electrochemistry and the complex processes involved in the build-up of corrosion products that lead to the precipitation of minerals on the surfaces of objects scattered by wave action across shipwreck sites. Since there is a dearth of information about such issues in the minds of those teaching the intimate details of materials conservation courses, it is understandable that many artifact reports state the facts about identification of corrosion products but provide no interpretation. This chapter introduces the nature of corrosion, and the impact of water movement on the kinetics of decay, and how the corrosion products can provide an exciting insight into the formation processes that present themselves like a newly discovered pristine wreck site to the maritime archaeologist. Case studies from wrecks examined by the author and colleagues in Australian waters are included throughout to provide concrete examples of these processes in action.

Corrosion of Metal

For metals found on historic shipwrecks, other than naturally occurring deposits of metallic copper, silver, and gold, the parent mineral ores have been heated and chemically processed to remove oxides, carbonates, sulfides, and sulfates to re-form the parent element. Corrosion is the electrochemical process taking place on a wreck site that reverses the processes used to create the metals. When different metals are combined they form a vast array of alloys, which have useful mechanical properties making them stronger or more malleable or ductile. This range of alloys has been exploited by shipbuilders over the centuries. For instance, the addition of tin to copper creates an array of hard-wearing bronzes, while adding zinc to copper results in a range of brasses used in sheathing and in rudder fittings. Iron alloys with 2.5–4.2% carbon result in strong cast irons, which are inherently brittle. Iron alloys with 0.02–0.18% carbon result in steels, which are more pliable. In order to understand what happens during corrosion of alloys in fresh and in salt water, knowledge of the microstructure of the metals is very helpful.

MICROSTRUCTURE OF ALLOYS

In a binary alloy (only two metals) the molten phases are mutually compatible but as the melt cools, solid material begins to fall out of solution. When molten metal solidifies the crystals grow in a branching formation; this is called a dendritic structure. The metal with the highest melting point crystallizes first, and this is called the alpha (α) phase. An example of a binary alloy is that of copper and silver, for which the simplified phase diagram is shown in figure 5.1. Silver coins on shipwrecks are prime examples of this type of alloy. The α phase is rich in copper, since this element has the higher melting point, but it also contains some of the lower melting point metal (silver), the proportion of which is dependent on their mutual solubility. As cooling progresses, the resultant liquid mixture becomes richer in the second component (silver), and the solidification temperature gradually falls until a common melting point is reached. This is called the eutectic point (see fig. 5.1), which contains both the α and the β phases. There is some silver dissolved in the copper-rich α phase and some copper in the silver-rich β phase.

The α phase reacts differently to changes in the microenvironment than the β phase. These subtle differences in composition result in different parts of the alloy fittings having different corrosion activity. Corrosion opens up the difference in the internal structures and this can lead to operational failure during the shipwrecking process.

Each metal has a differing desire for giving off electrons (corrosion) to dissolved oxygen. When the surface concentration of corrosion products exceeds the solubility of a mineral, then it will precipitate on the surface of the object and so record the chemical environment that led to its formation

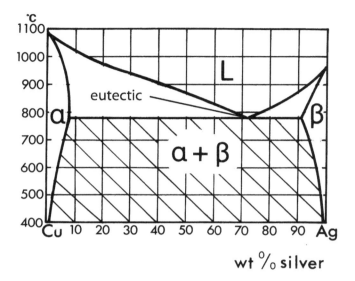

wt % silver

Figure 5.1. Phase diagram for copper and silver after *Metals Handbook, Metallography, Structures and Phase Diagrams*, 8, 253.

on the wreck site. Under a given set of conditions the α-phase components corrode preferentially, and then as the site changes, the β-phase components of the same alloy may become more corroded. It is not uncommon to find that metal degradation products have grown in layers that have widely different composition. The bands of decay reflect the changes in environment (fig. 5.2). Although this inherent susceptibility to corrosion can lead to materials failure under stress, it also provides archaeological evidence of the changes in microenvironment of the wreck site over time and leads to greater understanding of the site formation processes.

Aerobic and Anaerobic Corrosion

Water, an electrolyte, and an oxidizing agent are the three key components required for corrosion. Water is needed for the mobilization of metal corrosion products.

The electrolytes (in most cases dissolved salt) minimize the resistance for the transfer of electrons from the corroding metal to the oxidizing agent. Chloride ions are the most common and effective electrolyte in saline environments and are directly involved in the corrosion mechanism of copper, iron, and their alloys. In freshwater lakes where there is little salt in the form of chloride ions (e.g., Lake Huron, part of the Great Lakes, has $\frac{1}{5,000}$ the chloride concentration of seawater), other ions such as carbonate

Figure 5.2. Scanning electron micrograph of pewter corrosion products from the *Vergulde Draeck* (1656) shipwreck showing an anaerobic layer of lead sulfide (PbS) sandwiched between two layers of aerobic tin oxides. Full width of image 250 microns.

can serve as the electrolyte and carry the current for shipwreck corrosion. Brackish lakes are inherently more corrosive than freshwater lakes due to the higher chloride concentration.

Dissolved oxygen, a measure of the amount of oxygen that is dissolved in water, typically serves as the oxidizing agent. Oxygen solubility is higher in fresh than in salt water, so this tends to counteract the beneficial effects of lowered chloride levels. Corrosion in oxygenated fresh and salty water is called aerobic corrosion since the primary oxidizing material is dissolved oxygen. A summary of the impact of pH (acidity measured on a logarithmic scale 0–14, with neutral pH at 7), chloride concentration, and depth of a wreck site is shown in figure 5.3. The corrosion rates shown on the y-axis are those observed on shipwreck sites in the open ocean, while the effect of chloride ions is from experimental data on cast iron. The pH data were derived from measurements of cast iron from the wreck of the *Fujikawa Maru* (1944) in Chuuk Lagoon in the Federated States of Micronesia (MacLeod 2006). There is a logarithmic fall in corrosion rate with increasing depth and a logarithmic increase in corrosion rate with acidity. The corrosion rate increased linearly with each doubling of the salinity.

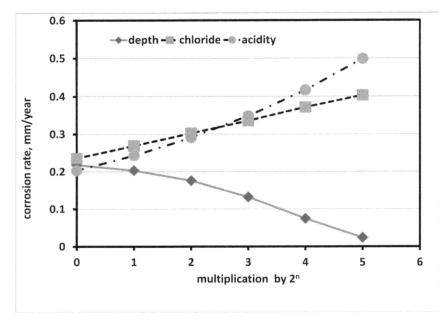

Figure 5.3. Schematic diagram showing how corrosion rates (mm/year) vary with depth, acidity (pH), and chloride concentration. Depth range 2–64 meters (6.6–210 feet), 5.5<pH>4.0, and chloride 4×10^{-3} to 1.23×10^{-2} molar.

Shipwrecks exposed to aerobic processes include wrecks and wreck components exposed in the water column in most of the word's submerged environments. Typically objects corroding in the first 20–50 centimeters (7.9–20 inches) of sediment are still under aerobic control, but when the objects are buried more deeply the decay mechanism changes to anaerobic. Anaerobic conditions are the antithesis of aerobic, as the word implies an absence of oxygen. For anaerobic sites the cathodic, or reduction reaction, processes involve reduction of water to produce hydrogen. In these situations water is the oxidizing agent. Anaerobic sites can occur in fresh, brackish, and salty water when an object is buried in the sand or other geological detritus. Wreck materials subject to anaerobic conditions include those buried in sediments as well as wrecks in the world's few anaerobic bodies of water (such as portions of the Black Sea). If the sediment is very fine, such as on the RMS *Titanic* site, anaerobic conditions can exist at a burial depth of a few centimeters. For example, a set of bath taps on the *Titanic* corroded in both aerobic and anaerobic conditions, with dramatic consequences. The brass pipes and connecting plumbing lying in the sediment were largely "eaten" away by anaerobic bacteria, while the handles and the faucet lying above the seabed were in good condition (MacLeod and Pennec 2004). Sections of a Swedish DC3 airplane recovered from the Baltic Sea in 2004 had been buried in anoxic mud since 1956, while the upper parts of the wreck had corroded in mildly aerobic conditions. The two burial environments resulted in totally different degradation mechanisms, which gave conservators many challenges (Tengnér 2014).

Effects of Temperature

The solubility of oxygen in water at a wreck site is dependent on the interplay of temperature and salinity. Just as increased dissolved salts decrease the amount of oxygen in solution, increased temperature also lowers the amount of oxygen. At 0°C (32°F) the freshwater concentration of dissolved oxygen falls 23% as the salinity increases to 40 parts per thousand. Over the same range of salinity the dissolved oxygen falls 19.7% as the temperature is increased from 0° to 30°C (32° to 86°F; Riley and Skirrow 1975, appendix 1, table 6, pp. 561–562). While an increase in temperature inherently increases corrosion rates, this factor is diminished by the lower amount of O_2 in solution and by the increased growth of any colonizing organisms, such as algae, sponges, and tunicates, and by calcareous deposits from coralline algae, sperpulids, bryozoans, and mollusks. Thicker marine growth is akin to an increased electrical resistance being placed in the corrosion circuit. Corrosion measurements on cast-iron cannon recovered off Western Australia, with mean annual temperatures of 29°–16°C (84°–61°F), indicate that the temperature effect is very much secondary in importance compared with the profile the gun has on the seabed, which controls the flux of corroding oxygen over the concreted surface (Carpenter and MacLeod 1993).

The impact of temperature on corrosion is perhaps greatest in influencing the differing amounts of colonization by marine organisms. Warm waters deposit much thicker layers of concretion than cold water. The presence of concretion results in the separation of the oxidation reactions, where metals lose electrons to become ionic species, and where oxygen is reduced at the interface of the concreted object and the surrounding water. This change is greatest with iron concretions in subtropical to equatorial seawater, where the pH can fall from 8.2 in seawater to 4.2 inside the concretion. The difference of four pH units equates to a 10,000 times greater acidity inside the concretion. The increase in acidity is due to the reactions of the initial corrosion products with water. The chloride ion concentration also increases to between 3 and 4 times the salinity of the surrounding water. Sudden removal of the protective concretion layer allows direct access of oxygen to the already corroded iron object sitting in a very high chloride solution. Corrosion rates are so high in such circumstances that cannon balls have been seen to steam.

CORROSION MECHANISMS

Corrosion products found on aerobically corroded metallic objects are dominated by oxides, hydroxides, chlorides, oxy-chlorides, carbonates, and some sulfates. Under anaerobic conditions a plethora of bacteria function in the marine and riverine environments, and their enzymes exert a major influence on the kinetics of corrosion as well as on the nature of the corrosion products. Deprived of oxygen for respiration and metabolic processing, the anaerobic bacteria utilize sulfate (SO_4^{2-}) ions as a source of energy, and sulfides are the by-product of these processes. All metals and alloys used in the construction and maintenance of ships produce insoluble metal sulfide corrosion products, so their presence is a sure sign that the artifacts have been buried at some stage in their site history (Machel et al. 1995). When reports show that a mixture of sulfides and oxides/hydroxides are found in the corrosion products, it is clear evidence that the objects have decayed in two different microenvironments and that there must have been a significant site disturbance to bring about such a change (fig. 5.2).

In any corrosion cell, current flows out of the anode where metals oxidize and into the cathode. The amount of current consumed at the cathode is therefore equal to and opposite of the amount given up by the anode. The voltage for the cathodic reaction falls with increasing current due to limits to the rate at which oxygen can diffuse to the corroding interface. Concomitantly the voltage of the oxidizing metal increases as the corrosion rate increases to the point where the currents and the voltages of the two halves of the corrosion cell match. This is a dynamic or kinetic voltage, and it is known as the corrosion potential or the E_{corr} for the system (Stern and Geary 1957).

Just as Galvani discovered that the current flowing from the voltaic pile of alternating sheets of copper and zinc could cause muscles from dead frogs to contract, so too the corrosion currents generated by preferential corrosion of different phases of the alloys used in ships' construction can produce some apparently unexpected results. Examples of such reactions include the redeposition of metallic silver from a silver chloride matrix covered with a layer of iron-stained marine concretion, which has acted as a barrier for oxygen reduction as the cathodic reaction (Kaneko et al. 1989). Under low oxygen conditions the copper-rich phases in the Ag-Cu alloy

Figure 5.4. Redeposited silver crystals grown out of a silver chloride matrix underneath an aerobic iron-stained concretion from a *schillingen* coin, 56% silver, 42% copper, from the *Zuytdorp* (1712) wreck site; full width 90μm.

Figure 5.5. Isomorphous redeposited silver on the surface of a *Zuytdorp* (1712) *schillingen*, 56% silver, 42% copper.

will corrode and give up electrons, which are consumed underneath the concretion layer by silver chloride to produce metallic silver crystals (Mac Leod 1982a). When the reaction rate is fast enough to produce very fine crystals of silver, it is possible to find pseudomorphs of the original surface deposited as a lustrous pure metallic silver layer on top of the corroded eutectic alloy of 56% Ag 42% Cu coins from the wreck of the *Zuytdorp* (1712). Discrete silver crystals are found on the surfaces of silver coins with silver contents greater than or equal to 92 weight per cent (figs. 5.4, 5.5; MacLeod 2013b).

Role of Microstructure in Corrosion Mechanisms

The underlying microstructure of metal, influenced by its manufacture and composition, determines the hardness of its surface and the physical properties that lead to the inclusion of the objects in the construction phase of a vessel. Analysis of the microstructure of a metal enables the conservator and archaeologist to discern the relevant technologies and how the mechanical working of the metal results in products of varying degrees of robustness, capacity to function, and avoidance of corrosion. These characteristics have resulted in different terminologies associated with certain metals such as wrought iron, steel, and cast iron. Wrought iron refers to the product of decarburized cast iron, which results in a material that is able to be hot worked or forged into shapes that define functional objects (Tylecote 1979). This process reduces the hardness of the cast iron and overcomes the susceptibility to brittle fracture. Steels are the product of blast furnace technologies and have similar composition to wrought iron but do not have the slag inclusions that decrease corrosion resistance (Tylecote 1979). Steels have well-defined and more uniform mechanical properties. Cast iron is a high carbon alloy that results from reducing iron ore with charcoal (Davis 1996). Cast iron is a hard, brittle, but readily cast alloy. Gray cast iron has ferrite (a pure iron phase), pearlite (a lamellar phase consisting of ferrite and cementite, iron carbide Fe_3C), with additional cementite and graphite phases. Because of their differences in reactivity, as reflected in the tables of standard oxidation/reduction potentials, the carbon phase of graphite remains unchanged by corrosion, and the iron-rich phases are preferentially corroded. When corroded concreted marine iron objects are sectioned during conservation, there is a very clear demarcation line at the corrosion front deep inside the once solid object (North 1982) (fig. 5.6). This dealloyed phase is called the graphitized zone as residual graphite is a major component along with cementite. The depth of graphitization provides the

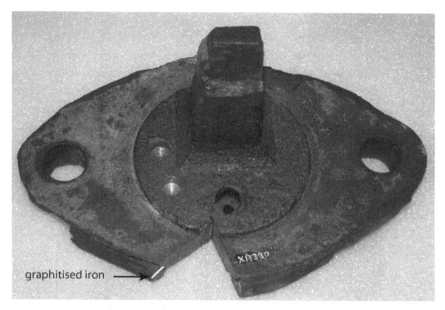

graphitised iron

Figure 5.6. Sectioned cast-iron flange from the SS *Xantho* (1872) engine showing depth of graphitization and the increased corrosion depth at sharp edges due to a combined corrosion front.

long-term measure of decay since the time the ship was wrecked. If the wreck site has exposed and buried elements, then it is not unusual to find up to a fourfold difference in the depths of graphitization of cannon (Carpenter and MacLeod 1993). A map of a wreck site showing the different depths of graphitization of cast-iron objects provides a valuable archaeological tool for practitioners (MacLeod and Viduka 2010; MacLeod 2013a).

Concretion Formation and Its Impact on Corrosion Products and Decay Mechanisms

A fundamental difference between ferrous and nonferrous metals lies in the interaction of their corrosion products with the marine biota. In the case of iron, all encrusting organisms are inherently limited in their growth rate by the availability of soluble iron, which is a principal inorganic component in the mitochondria that provide the power houses for oxidative respiration and the energy for growth and reproduction. The growth rate of marine organisms on iron artifacts on shipwreck sites is approximately double that on inert substrates such as bricks, stone, and low-fired earthenware (MacLeod 1988).

When colonized by organisms and thus encapsulated, the separation of the metallic elements from the direct impact of the dissolved oxygen in the surrounding seawater leads to the development of a corrosion microenvironment that is essentially free of oxygen at the metal-concretion interface. In this environment the pH is controlled by the hydrolysis of the primary corrosion products and the interaction of this acidic solution with the calcareous encapsulating organisms. The details of this interaction for ferrous materials are provided in the seminal work of North (North 1976), and the nonferrous concretions were also reported by the Western Australian Museum conservation laboratories (MacLeod 1982b). Anaerobic bacteria present in the entrained modified sea water, now rich in chloride ions, can convert iron phosphides into volatile phosphines, which have a direct effect on increasing the average rate of concretion growth on iron objects (Iverson and Olson 1983).

INTERPRETATION OF CORROSION PRODUCTS IN MARINE CONCRETIONS

Analysis of the proportions of nonferrous alloys found trapped inside the marine concretion shows that there is selective corrosion of different phases depending on the precise nature of the depositional environment. Cathodically protected copper-alloy objects occur when the copper-based artifacts are electrically connected with either iron objects or iron/steel structural elements of the vessel. This type of object is characterized by a tightly adherent and impervious thin layer of inorganic calcium carbonate, in the form of aragonite and calcite, which acts as an oxygen barrier. Physical contact of the copper-based material with an adjacent iron artifact will produce such protective coatings, as evidenced from the brass rudder gudgeon from the 1878 wreck of the *Lady Elizabeth* (fig. 5.7). Thus anaerobic copper corrosion products like chalcocite, Cu_2S, are found at the interface between the metal and the concretion layer (MacLeod 1985).

The ratio of calcium to magnesium for "cathodically protected concretions" is 22.4±3.4 compared with 10.8±3.0 for the concretions formed by marine organisms. Cathodically protected brass and bronze objects that have been studied indicate that associated iron objects protect the copper-rich phases of the alloys, but the zinc- and tin-rich phases in the brass and bronze objects, respectively, suffer from preferential corrosion (see table 1). Since the small amounts of antimony (Sb) in the alloys are soluble as a solid solution in the copper-rich α phase, this element is not selectively corroded and has been protected with the copper in which it is dissolved. In all anaerobic environments the degree to which alloying elements are selectively

Figure 5.7. Surface of a brass rudder gudgeon from the *Lady Elizabeth* (1878) that had been protected by a cathodically deposited calcareous layer. Note the Cu2S and Cu2O patina on the metal.

corroded is determined by the thermodynamic stability of the metal sulfide corrosion products. This is seen in the anaerobic microenvironmental data, where zinc is more strongly corroded out of the copper alloys than is antimony, followed by lead, then tin (see table 5.1).

The differences in the amount of oxygenation controlling the deterioration of materials on a site can be seen even on one artifact. A square brass capstan post support from the wreck of the *Cumberland* (1830) off Cape Leeuwin in Western Australia was found lying horizontally on the seabed with the outer face fully exposed to flowing seawater, while the underneath

Table 5.1. Selective corrosion indices for copper alloys

Site conditions	Cu	Zn	Sn	Pb	Fe	Sb
High O_2	1.16±0.13	0.47±0.11	0.21±0.19	0.7±0.5	2.6±1.7	2.0±0.6
Low O_2	0.7±0.2	1.01±0.18	3.6±1.4	2.4±1.2	4.8±3.4	-
Cathodically protected	0.75±0.25	44.5±23.7	6.2±3.4	2.9±1.6	21±13	0.7±0.5
Anaerobic copper[a]	0.997±0.003	4.1 ± 3.9	1.5±0.8	2.7±1.4		3.4±1.0

[a]Concretion analyses based on electron microprobe data on polished samples embedded in Araldite D.

Figure 5.8. Brass capstan pole protector from the *Cumberland* (1830) showing the lower concretion environment corresponding to corrosion with limited oxygenation.

side was naturally sheltered. Concretion samples were taken from four sites on each face of the object and analyzed for all metals, along with calcium and magnesium from the mixture of concretion and corrosion products. The tinned brass insert had an original composition of 13.9% zinc and 4.4% tin. As far as the microstructure of the metal was concerned it was in effect an 18.3% zinc brass, since tin mimics zinc, in terms of the microstructure of brasses, and thus the metal behaves as if it is a single phase brass (fig. 5.8). The as-cast brass has subtle differences in composition of the dendritic structure that become manifested in the two chemical environments to which the object was exposed. The results were consistent with different corrosion mechanisms controlling the decay on the upper (exposed) and lower (buried) sections of the object.

The highly oxygenated upper section of the object had selective corrosion of the copper and zinc α phase, while the tin-rich inter-dendritic zone was protected. The less oxygenated section of the fitting, lying against the seabed, had selective corrosion of the tin-rich areas of the alloy, which included lead and iron impurities (MacLeod 1985). The ratios of calcium to magnesium ($^{Ca}/_{Mg}$) in the concretions on the exposed and half-buried sides of the object changed in response to the different amounts of metal ions that corrosion had produced. The Sn^{4+}, Fe^{3+}, and Pb^{2+} ions present in much higher concentrations in the lower side of the concretion produced more acid through hydrolysis reactions, and this altered the calcium to magnesium ratio. Thus the *Cumberland* capstan insert demonstrates the sensitivity of nonferrous metals to subtle changes in the corrosion environment. It also provides archaeologists with proof of the need for careful documentation on the wreck site as to the orientation of the materials and the need to have detailed photos and descriptions of the layout of the wreck.

After either mechanical or chemical deconcretion, the surfaces of the cathodically protected alloyed copper objects are typically found to be in very fine condition. Although the amount of corrosion is very little, it is still wise to desalinate these objects, but the treatment times are one quarter of those for aerobically corroded artifacts (MacLeod 1987). The most significant thing to note is that since the concretion has been with the object throughout its life on the seabed, the concretion records the way in which the object has been responding to changes in the nature of the seabed.

A compelling example of the value of concretion analysis was found on the wreck site of the SS *Xantho* (1872) on a copper wire that once took lubricating oils to crankshaft journals on the steam engine. The remarkable history of the *Xantho* can be read at length in the classic work by McCarthy on the archaeology of iron shipwrecks (McCarthy 1988). When the concreted copper wire was sectioned it was found to contain sixteen bands of alternating precipitation of the copper sulfide chalcocite, Cu_2S, after being immersed in the coastal waters for 112 years, which averages out at seven-year cycles of burial and exposure. The fitting was attached to the cast-iron components of the engine, and so galvanic coupling with the brass oiler would have kept the object free of corrosion so long as the engine was exposed to flowing seawater. The site is characterized by periodic reburial phenomena in that the seabed rises by several meters roughly every seven years. Site inspections have shown that the whole engine complex could be buried under several meters of clay-rich sand in a matter of six months. Under these burial conditions the iron engine was no longer able to protect the copper fitting, and so the anaerobic environment, rich in sulfide ions,

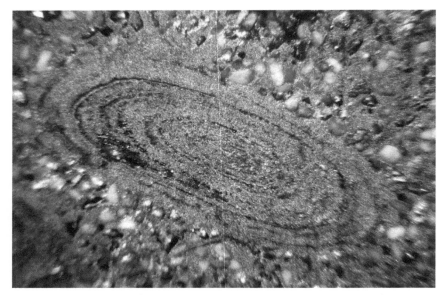

Figure 5.9. Cross section of corroded copper wire from the *Xantho* (1872) oil feed show-ing 16 corrosion bands over 112 years of immersion as the site was alternately buried and exposed.

produced the copper sulfides as corrosion products. Whenever the site was exposed, the protection from the engine would be turned on again (fig. 5.9; MacLeod 1992).

CASE STUDIES

ANAEROBIC CORROSION WITHIN A REEF STREWN WRECK

Lying 7 meters (23 feet) beneath the waters off Point Cloates, Western Australia, is the wreck of the American China trader *Rapid* (1811) which was the subject of three seasons of significant excavation and recovery of artifacts (Henderson 2007). Sediment depth profiles greater than 25 cm (9.8 inches) at 23.9±2.2°C (75±3.96°F) were sufficient to create anaerobic microenvironments for the copper fittings from the carpenter's store and for the massive copper drifts and bolts that were structural elements of this 1809 vessel built in Braintree, Massachusetts. The in situ temperatures in 1811–12 were determined through oxygen isotope analysis of a species of barnacle found growing on the ship's gripe (MacLeod and Killingley 1982). Under the same conditions the oak timbers were naturally waterlogged but relatively well preserved. The varying thickness of the ballast mound and coral sands created anaerobic microenvironments that were sufficiently oxidizing to precipitate the formation of the copper sulfide covellite as well as the sequential development of the transitional (non-stoichiometric) compounds digenite, djurelite, and finally chalcocite. The resulting chalcocite and covellite appear to be semi-passive, and therefore the metals were less likely to be subjected to further influence from the surrounding environment (MacLeod 1991). During the initial stages of the wreck formation process when the *Rapid* was stuck fast on the reef, aerobic corrosion would have mobilized the copper from the bolts into the cells of the surrounding oak timbers, which acted as a preservative, since aerobic copper corrosion products act as biocides. Following the impact of cyclones on the wreck site (MacLeod 1982a), which broke up the wreck, the copper-impregnated timbers became buried, and the aerobic corrosion products were transformed into the anaerobic sulfides (fig. 5.10).

From published thermodynamic data the voltages for formation of covellite cover the range of $-0.25 < E_H > -0.15$ volts, while for covellite the corresponding range is $-0.5 < E_H > -0.25$ volts vs. the normal hydrogen electrode (MacLeod and North 1987). From the $^{Ca}/_{Mg}$ ratios in the sulfide concretion matrices it is estimated that the pH had a mean value of 6.81 ± 0.49, which is characteristic of the microenvironment that is optimal for the reproduction

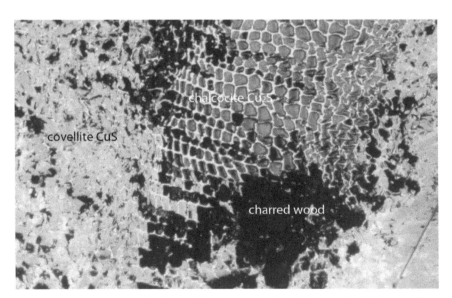

Figure 5.10. Cross section of oak wood from the *Rapid* (1811) showing both blue covellite (CuS) and dark gray chalcocite (Cu2S), illustrating a specific range of oxidation and reduction voltages.

of anaerobic sulfate-reducing bacteria such as *Desulfovibrio desuluricans*. The data from the microenvironment determined from concretion and corrosion product analysis provides fundamental information about the nature of the past site conditions and how this impacts the work of conservators and the interpretation by maritime archaeologists.

Corrosion of Lead and Site Mapping of Corrosion Products

Lead artifacts have generally been regarded as being of lower "value" to the maritime archaeologist than silver bullion, bronze, and brass objects. However, not only are lead artifacts extremely common on historic shipwreck sites, but they produce a vast array of corrosion products that are extremely sensitive to the corrosion microenvironment. Standard desalination treatments tend to show degrees of decay that roughly match the degree of oxygenation on the wreck site, with the most turbulent of the shallow sites producing decayed artifacts with a higher chloride content. Moreover, detailed analysis of lead corrosion products has shown that a large number of different minerals define the nature of the microenvironment from which the lead objects have come. The nature of the mineralogy has been found to be very sensitive to the kinetics of corrosion.

Corrosion products on pewters that had a lead content of 75±10% showed a remarkable similarity to the minerals found on corroded lead artifacts from a similar environment (MacLeod and Wozniak 1997). Analysis of lead artifacts from a number of shipwreck sites produced a total of seven major and seven minor corrosion products, whereas corrosion simulation experiments on 99±1% lead coupons in seawater produced four major and four minor corrosion products owing to the quiescent nature of the seawater used in the experiment. Despite the ubiquitous presence of lead artifacts in the form of sheathing, ballast pigs, musket balls, piping, and scuppers on nearly all shipwreck sites, there is relatively little information on their decay problems in the conservation literature (Campbell and Mills 1977).

Lead Corrosion in the Ocean and Laboratory

Electrochemical scanning on recast lead corrosion coupons from unregistered scrap lead objects that had been sectioned and embedded in casting resin showed that almost all the different corrosion products corresponded to a particular voltage that was identified by either SEM or X-ray diffraction. After exposure periods of up to ten weeks, five different corrosion products had been identified on the test coupons as $PbCl_2$, $PbCl(OH)$, $PbSO_4$, $Pb_3(CO_3)_2(OH)_2$, and $PbCO_3$, which transformed into $Pb_{10}(CO_3)_6O(OH)_6$.

The oxidation of lead is associated with either sequential or simultaneous precipitation of corrosion products containing various proportions of chloride, sulfate, oxide, hydroxide, and carbonate anions. The complexes $PbCl^+$ and $PbSO_4$ are known to be labile, whereas $PbCO_3$ and $PbOH^+$ are only partially labile in seawater (Beccaria et al. 1982). The availability of lead species at the corroding artifact surface is dependent on the surface pH, and for the neutral to near neutral pH range of 7<pH>6, $PbCl_2$ is the dominant species. For the more alkaline region defined by 9<pH>8, $PbCO_3$ predominates, but naturally lead continues to corrode under and through the patina (Turner and Whitfield 1979). Greater porosity of the corrosion products is associated with higher passive corrosion rates (Tranter 1976), as observed for hydrocerussite, $Pb_3(CO_3)_2(OH)_2$. The higher concentration of chloride ions (three times higher than normal seawater after 7 months) in crevice cells and the more acidic microenvironment than in seawater, pH 6.57, causes $PbCl_2$ to be the dominant corrosion product. Crevices can occur naturally when the wrecking process causes a lead artifact to be folded over onto itself, so it can be expected that the maritime archaeologist will find different corrosion products under folded-over lead sheet artifacts than on the surfaces fully exposed to flowing seawater.

The most compelling evidence of the ability to correlate in situ data from wreck sites with the laboratory-based identification of corrosion products was found when examining data from the wrecks of the *Hadda* (1877) and the *Lively* (ca. 1820), both of which were in high energy locations with an abundance of oxygenated seawater. The corrosion potentials were the same for both sets of lead artifacts and corresponded to the experimentally determined value for the anodic peak voltage of PbOHCl or laurionite. Apart from the effective concentrations of the hydroxide, chloride, sulfate, and carbonate anions, the voltage associated with the corrosion of lead will naturally depend on the solubility of the corrosion product. If the kinetics are rapid, then the voltage will be determined by the thermodynamics of solubility product; but if kinetic parameters, such as precipitation and hydrolysis reactions, are associated with energy barriers for their conversion or precipitation, there will be a discrepancy between observation and expectations based on thermodynamics.

Anglesite ($PbSO_4$) dominating the corrosion products on maritime lead artifacts is common to all the wreck sites examined by the author. Infra-red spectral studies on rolled lead exposed in air for more than 100 years confirms that the lead sulfate patina is protective (Tranter 1976). All containing the O^{2-} anion and found only on high energy sites are minerals such as

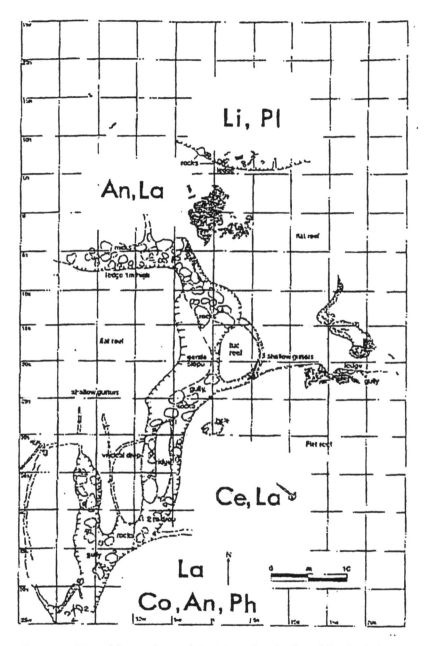

Figure 5.11. Map of the wreck site of HMS *Sirius* (1790) off Norfolk Island, showing distribution of lead corrosion products as a site energy mapping process (An Angelsite, Ce Cerussite, Co Cotunnite, La Laurionite, Li Litharge, Ph Phosgenite, Pl Plumonacrite).

the mixed lead (II) corrosion products oxide-sulfate lanarkite, Pb_2OSO_4; the oxide chloride mendipite, $Pb_3O_2Cl_2$; the oxide-hydroxy-carbonate plumbonacrite, $Pb_{10}(CO_3)_6O(OH)_6$; and red lead oxide in the form of litharge, PbO. Details of the nature of the varying degrees of turbulence on the wreck sites are found in the 1996 paper by MacLeod and Wozniak. The oxide-containing minerals found on the wreck of HMS *Sirius* came from the shallowest part of the site closest to shore, where the waves constantly tumble. Calculations of the localized current during the descent of a 4 m (13 foot) wave breaking over artifacts at 3 m (10 feet) has a velocity of 12 ms^{-1} at an angle a little steeper than 45° (Cresswell 1989). The massive flux of dissolved oxygen produces significant concentrations of oxide ions via reduction of oxygen to enable precipitates to form containing the O^{2-} anion rather than normal $PbCl_2$ or cotunnite (fig. 5.11; Barradas et al. 1975).

The *Sirius* (1790) wreck is located along the inner part of the reef at Kingston on Norfolk Island, Australian South Pacific. Portions of the site closest to the reef showed a greater dominance of cotunnite, $PbCl_2$, and the hydrolysis products of laurionite, PbOHCl, while 20 m (66 feet) away from the innermost parts of the wreck the mineral anglesite, $PbSO_4$, was dominant. In the most benign part of the site the hydroxy-carbonate mineral hydrocerussite, $Pb_3(CO_3)_2(OH)_2$, and the straight lead carbonate cerussite, $PbCO_3$, were also found. Phosgenite, $Pb_2(CO_3)Cl_2$, was found as a minor component on pieces of lead sheathing in this part of the site. Hydrocerussite was also found in the 7 m (23 foot) depth of the *Rapid* wreck site on the other side of Australia. By way of comparison, the even more turbulent site of the wreck of the Dutch East Indiaman *Zuytdorp* had the only reported example of the partly hydrolyzed lead chloride $Pb_2Cl_3(OH)$ or penfieldite.

On every wreck site there are a number of competing hydrolysis and precipitation reactions occurring during the corrosion of lead artifacts on the seabed. The presence of the double salts is consistent with the laboratory experiments, which show that these corrosion products dominate the patina in still seawater (Beccaria et al. 1982). A schematic representation of some of the complex equilibria involving lead is shown in figure 5.12.

Since each mineral containing the carbonate or hydroxide ions is sensitive to the prevailing pH, it is possible to calculate the pH at which multiple phases can be present in equilibrium. For the *Sirius* lead sheet (SI 66), which had anglesite, laurionite, and cotunnite as the major phases on the surface, the value of 5.2±0.2 is the calculated pH for co-existence of the

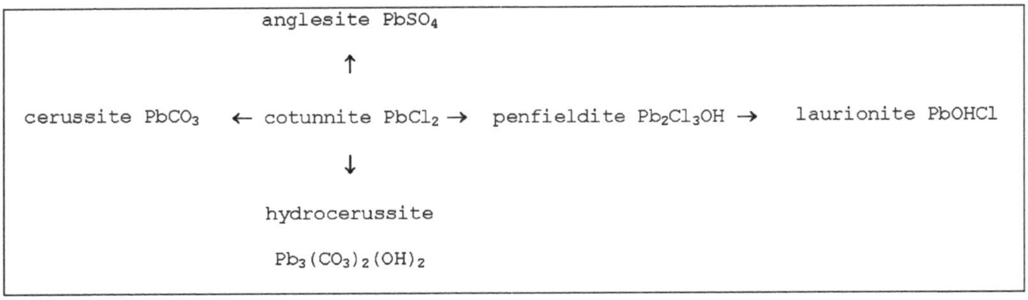

anglesite PbSO$_4$

↑

cerussite PbCO$_3$ ← cotunnite PbCl$_2$ →   penfieldite Pb$_2$Cl$_3$OH →   laurionite PbOHCl

↓

hydrocerussite

Pb$_3$(CO$_3$)$_2$(OH)$_2$

Figure 5.12. Schematic reaction scheme for transformation of lead corrosion products.

three minerals (Linke and Seidell 1965). Erosion phenomena from water-borne sand and grit can also exert influence on the formation of corrosion products.

At times unusual corrosion products can be found on lead artifacts that provide clues to the origin of the objects. A fine example of this was when the rare mineral pseudoboleite, Pb$_5$Cu$_4$Cl$_{10}$(OH)$_8$.2H$_2$O, along with the silver arsenic sulfide xanthoconite, Ag3AsS3, were found on a corroded lead ballast block(ZT 4179) from the wreck of the *Zuytdorp* (1712) along with the normal lead chloride and hydroxy chlorides found on the extremely well oxygenated wreck site. The presence of these minerals helped in tracking down the identification of the ore body as being of north English origin (van Duivenvoorde et al. 2013).

CONCLUSION

Analysis of the corrosion products formed on a number of Australian shipwrecks has shown that it is possible to reconstruct the physical and chemical environment that led to the formation of the suite of minerals that were found to be in an equilibrium state. From a detailed knowledge of the mineralogy and electrochemistry of corrosion it is possible to determine when the decay of wreck material is kinetically controlled or under thermodynamic control. It is vital to keep samples of concretion and corrosion products on recovered artifacts for future analysis since the ratios of alloying elements reporting to the concretion matrix provides very sensitive indicators of changes to the site and the burial conditions of wreck materials.

Since the marine growth has been living in a dynamic equilibrium on the artifacts from the time of colonization after the ship foundered, its analysis provides new and exciting paths of interpretation. Carefully unfolding crumpled nonferrous sheathing and fittings can reveal a wealth of information about the site formation processes that have survived the first round of conservation treatment and exhibition developments. Each decay product has a unique story to tell that enhances the value and meaning of the collection under control of the archaeologist.

It must be remembered that even in the absence of in situ corrosion data recorded at the time of excavations, or if it is either economically or socially inappropriate to return to a site, it is eminently feasible to reconstruct the past environments from a detailed analysis of the corrosion products and their site distribution.

REFERENCES CITED

Barradas R. G., K. Belinko, and E. Ghibaudi
1975   Effect of Dissolved Gases on the Pb/PbCl2 Electrode in Aqueous Chloride Electrolytes. In *Chemistry and Physics of Aqueous Gas Solutions*, edited by W. A. Adams, pp. 357–372. Electrochemical Society, Princeton, New Jersey.
Beccaria A. M., E. D. Mor, G. Bruno, and G. Poggi
1982   Corrosion of Lead in Sea Water. *British Corrosion Journal* 17:87–91.
Campbell H. S., and D. J. Mills
1977   A Marine Treasure Trove: Metallurgical Investigation. *The Metallurgist and Materials Technologists* October:551–557.
Carpenter, J., and Ian D. MacLeod
1993   Conservation of Corroded Iron Cannon and the Influence of Degradation on Treatment Times. *ICOM Committee for Conservation, Preprints, 10th Triennial Conference* II:759–766. Washington.
Cresswell, G.
1989   The Oceanography of the Norfolk Island Vicinity. 1988 Expedition Report on the Wreck of HMS *Sirius* (1790). In *Norfolk Island Government Project*, compiled by Graeme Henderson, pp. 46–70. Unpublished report.
Davis, J. R.
1996   *Classification and Basic Metallurgy of Cast Irons*. American Society of Metals Specialty Handbook.
Henderson, G. J. (editor)
2007   *Unfinished Voyages, Western Australian Shipwrecks 1622–1850*, volume 1. University of Western Australia Press, Crawley.
Iverson, W. P., and G. J. Olson
1983   *Microbial Corrosion*. Metals Society, London.
Kaneko, K., N. Inoue, and T. Ishikawa
1989   Electrical and Photoadsorptive Properties of Valence Controlled α FeOOH. *Journal of Physical Chemistry* 93:1988–1992.
Linke, William F., and Atherton Seidell
1965   *Solubilities of Inorganic and Metal Organic Compounds: A Compilation of Solubil-*

ity Data from the Periodical Literature, volume II. American Chemical Society, Washington.

Machel, H. G., H. R. Krouse, and R. Sassen
1995 Products and Distinguishing Criteria of Bacterial and Thermochemical Sulfate Reduction. *Applied Geochemistry* 10(4):373–389.

MacLeod, Ian D.
1982a Environmental Effects on Shipwreck Material from Analysis of Marine Concretions. In *Archaeometry: An Australasian Perspective*, edited by W. Ambrose and P. Duerden, pp. 361–367. ANU Press, Canberra.

1982b The Formation of Marine Concretions on Copper and Its Alloys. *International Journal of Nautical Archaeology* 11(4):267–275.

1985 The Effects of Concretion on the Corrosion of Non-Ferrous Metals. *Corrosion Australasia* 10(4):10–13.

1987 Stabilization of Corroded Copper Alloys: A Study of Corrosion and Desalination Mechanisms. *ICOM Committee for Conservation, 8th Triennial Meeting, Sydney*, edited by Kirsten Grimstad, pp. 1079–1085. Getty Conservation Institute, Marina del Rey.

1988 Conservation of Corroded Concreted Iron. *Proceedings of Conference 28, Australasian Corrosion Association, Perth*, 1:2–6.

1991 Identification of Corrosion Products on Non-Ferrous Metal Artifacts Recovered from Shipwrecks. *Studies in Conservation* 36(4):222–234.

1992 Conservation management of Iron Steamships: The SS *Xantho* (1872). *Multi-Disciplinary Engineering Transactions* GE(1):45–51.

2006 Corrosion and Conservation Management of Iron Shipwrecks in Chuuk Lagoon. *Conservation and Management of Archaeological Sites* 7:203–223.

2013a The Mechanism and Kinetics of In-Situ Conservation of Iron Cannon on Shipwreck Sites. *International Journal of Nautical Archaeology* 42(2):382–391.

2013b Corrosion Reversed: Deposition of Elemental Copper and Silver in Marine Concretions. *Corrosion and Materials* 38(6):48–53.

MacLeod, Ian D., and John S. Killingley
1982 The Use of Barnacles to Establish Past Temperatures on Historic Shipwrecks. *International Journal of Nautical Archaeology* 11(3):249–252.

MacLeod, Ian D., and N. A. North
1987 Corrosion of Metals. In *Conservation of Marine Archaeological Objects*, edited by C. Pearson, pp. 68–98. Butterworths, London.

MacLeod, Ian D., and S. Pennec
2004 Characterisation of Corrosion Products on Artifacts Recovered from the RMS *Titanic* (1912). In *Metal 2001: Proceedings of the International Conference on Metals Conservation, Santiago, Chile, April 2001*, edited by Ian D. MacLeod, J. M. Theile, and C. Degrigny, pp. 270–278.

MacLeod, Ian D., and A. Viduka
2010 Assessment of the Impact of Diving Tourism and Cyclones on the SS *Yongala* (1911) Shipwreck in the Great Barrier Reef from In-Situ Corrosion Data. *AICCM Bulletin* 32:134–143.

MacLeod, Ian D., and R. Wozniak
1996   Corrosion and Conservation of Lead in Sea Water. In *ICOM Committee for Conservation, Preprints, 11th Triennial Meeting, Edinburgh,* edited by Janet Bridgland, pp. 884–890. James and James, London.
1997   Corrosion and Conservation of Tin and Pewter from Seawater. In *Metals '95: Proceedings of the ICOM, Semur-en-Auxois,* pp. 118–123. James and James, London.
McCarthy, Michael
1988   SS *Xantho*: The Pre-disturbance, Assessment, Excavation and Management of an Iron Steam Shipwreck off the Coast of Western Australia. *International Journal of Nautical Archaeology* 17(4):339–347.
North, Neil A.
1976   Formation of Coral Concretions on Marine Iron. *International Journal of Nautical Archaeology* 5(3):253–258.
1982   Corrosion Products on Marine Iron. *Studies in Conservation* 27(2):75–83.
Riley, J. P., and G. Skirrow
1975   *Chemical Oceanography,* 2nd edition, volume 1. . Plenum Press, New York.
Stern, M., and A. L. Geary.
1957   Electrochemical Polarization I: A Theoretical Analysis of the Shape of Polarization Curves. *Journal of the Electrochemical Society* 104(1):56–63.
Tengnér, C.
2014   The Preservation of a Marine Archaeological DC-3 Aircraft. Conference paper, ICOM Committee for Conservation, Metals Working Group conference, Washington, D.C., April 7–9. In *Aluminum: History, Technology and Conservation,* edited by C. Chemello, P. Mardikian, and D. Hallam, in press.
Tranter, G. C.
1976   Patination of Lead: An Infrared Study. *British Corrosion Journal* 11(4):222–224.
Turner, D. R., and M. Whitfield
1979   The Reversible Electrodeposition of Trace Metal Ions from Multi-Ligand Systems Part II: Calculations on the Electrochemical Availability of Lead at Trace Levels in Seawater. *Journal of Electroanalytical Chemistry* 103:61–79.
Tylecote, R.
1979   *A History of Metallurgy.* 2nd edition. Metals Society, London.
van Duivenvoorde, Wendy, Jim Stedman, Kjell Billström, Zofia Anna Stos-Gale, and Michael McCarthy
2013   The Lead Ingots from the Wreck of the *Zuiddorp* (1712), Western Australia: A Report on Their Provenance and Manufacture. *International Journal of Nautical Archaeology* 42(1):150–166.

6

Degradation of Wood

DAVID GREGORY

The romantic view of a shipwreck is typically an almost intact ship sitting on the sea bed with its sails still attached to the rigging. In reality, what constitutes a shipwreck site are those parts and materials that have survived the wrecking process and, following a period of deterioration or stabilization, reached an equilibrium, albeit a dynamic one, with its new environment. Figure 6.1 shows an idealized view of a wooden shipwreck as it may appear after the wrecking process.

Effectively the wreck and its component parts are subjected to processes ongoing in two very differing environments; the open seawater and the sediments of the sea bed. The post-depositional formation processes operating on wooden parts of a shipwreck in these two environments differ drastically. This chapter focuses explicitly upon biological deterioration, which is the predominant deteriorative process of this particular material. However, it should be stressed that the biological processes act in suite with, and can be exacerbated by, many of the physical processes described in Chapters 2, 3, and 4 of this volume. The effects of biological processes leave their traces (products) on the wood, and through investigation in situ and in the laboratory post excavation, an understanding of the site's environment and its effect on the wood from sinking up until the point of archaeological intervention can be obtained. Taking these biological formation processes and their resultant products into account when carrying out any shipwreck investigation gives added insight when interpreting shipwreck assemblages.

The aims of this chapter are to give an overview of the deterioration processes of wood in the open seawater and burial environments. Brief introductions to wood boring organisms, the structure of wood, marine sediments, and the micromorphology of microbial wood degradation are

Open Seawater

Seabed

Figure 6.1. An idealized shipwreck on the seabed showing those parts which are exposed to the open seawater and those parts which are buried in the seabed. These two different environments will affect the deterioration processes acting upon the wood.

given. These are followed with a hypothetical discussion on how such information can be utilized to work backward in order to make inferences about the post-depositional site formation processes. The chapter is not meant as a practical "how to" laboratory guide, yet the bibliography contains relevant references on analysis of wood.

COLONIZATION AND DETERIORATION OF WOOD IN OPEN SEAWATER

When wood is exposed to seawater it is progressively colonized by a variety of biological organisms. Biocolonization is initiated by the attachment of bacteria to the surface, followed by other microorganisms including diatoms, fungi, microalgae, protozoa, and boring crustacea and mollusca. Bacteria and fungi produce extracellular enzymes that destroy the material on which they grow, while the crustaceans and mollusca bore into the wood, which they ingest and may subsequently utilize. Additionally, there are fouling organisms such as algae, polysoa, tunicata, and mollusca, which use the wood as a substrate to grow upon (Floodgate 1971; Jones et al. 1976; Cundell and Mitchell 1977; Zachary et al. 1978).

By far the most damaging of these organisms operating on shipwrecks in the open marine environment are the marine wood borers, which may cause damage and loss of archaeological information in a relatively short period of time. Wood borers can effectively be divided into two groups: the mollusca and the crustacea.

WOOD BORING MOLLUSCA: SHIPWORM

The wood boring mollusca are bivalves belonging to the suborder *Pholadina*, which contains the two related families *Teredinidae* and *Pholadidae*. The teredinids, usually called shipworms, are obligate wood borers, except for the mud boring genus *Kuphus* and seagrass-dwelling *Zachsia*. There are in total sixty-six species within this family (Turner 1966). The one most familiar to maritime archaeologists is the cosmopolite *Teredo navalis*, which is found worldwide. Infestation of wood by shipworms occurs during the free swimming, larval phase of their lifecycle. After about fourteen days in the water column, they settle on wood and develop from a juvenile to an adult that will never naturally leave the piece of wood; this is to say they do not move from one piece of wood to another. After settlement, shipworms bore into the wood and seldom along the wood's surface. The wood looks almost intact except for the small entrance holes (<1 millimeter [0.039 inch] in diameter). The damage is therefore hard to detect by the eye, especially

Figure 6.2. Section of pine wood exposed to shipworm-infested waters for three months. (a) Outside of the wood, where the presence of shipworm is attested only by small holes on the surface of the wood. (b) Inside of the wood, showing the extensive burrows created by the shipworm.

underwater. The devastation is often discovered late in the degradation process when the burrows are exposed (fig. 6.2).

Repeated rasping movements by the fine serrated shells at the anterior of the animal grind a perfectly circular hole within the wood. With help from unique endosymbiotic bacteria (*Teredinibacter turnerae*), which produce cellulolytic enzymes, *Teredo navalis* eats its way into wood. The small helmetlike shells cover only the anterior part of the adult animal, and when in the wood, a thin calcareous layer protects the rest of the elongated body. At the posterior end are situated a pair of retractable siphons and two species-specific pallets (fig. 6.3). By sealing their burrow with the pallets they can avoid unfavorable conditions from the surrounding water and survive for at least three weeks upon stored energy reserves. The tubelike siphons, the only part of the animal that is visible outside the wood (fig. 6.4), are used for filtration of plankton and obtaining an oxygen supply, which is ultimately the limiting factor for their survival. As the adults grow they follow the grain of the wood, avoid knots or joints, and seldom interfere with others or break into the burrows of their neighbors. Depending on age,

Figure 6.3. Shipworm removed from its burrow. To the right are the shells at the anterior of the animal. To the left are calcareous pallets that can seal the burrow.

Figure 6.4. Siphons of shipworm protruding from the wood surface.

population density, wood type, and the environment, the adult size of *Teredo navalis* ranges from a few millimeters up to one meter. With a growth rate of 0.5–1 mm (0.039 to 0.0197 inches) per day in temperate waters like those in Scandinavia, a 20 cm (7.87 inch) long piece of wood could be completely consumed by *Teredo navalis* within a year (see fig. 6.2).

Several environmental factors of seawater affect the physiological and ecological behavior of shipworms. However, the physical key parameters are salinity, temperature, dissolved oxygen, ocean currents, and the availability of wooden substrate (Turner 1966). A literature search of these key parameters can be found at the project Wreck Protect website (http://wreckprotect.eu/, National Museum of Denmark or Nationalmuseet 2013), and their effects on the growth of *Teredo navalis* are given in table 6.1. "Shipworm," not necessarily *Teredo navalis*, has been reported from wood dredged up from over 2 kilometers (1.2 miles) deep, and thus depth does not appear to be a limiting parameter. *Teredo navalis* are certainly ubiquitous in the littoral zone, given the optimal environmental parameters.

Table 6.1 Critical environmental parameters of *Teredo navalis* living in temperate waters

Parameter	Adults[a]	Larvae[b]
Temperature (°C)	>11	>12
Salinity (PSU)	>8	>8
Oxygen (mg O2/l)	>4	>4

[a]Reproduction possible by adults.
[b]Possible metamorphosis of larvae = risk of new attacks.

Currents also play a significant role in the dispersal of the larvae of the shipworm. The occurrence, abundance, and intensity of shipworm attacks are dependent on the aforementioned factors, which usually vary widely from year to year.

Wood Boring Crustacean: Gribble

The most common crustacean species are members of the genera *Limnoria, Sphaeroma,* and *Chelura* (Kuhne 1971). Unlike shipworm they have the ability to move by swimming or crawling to other adjacent pieces of wood and often do this as juveniles or young adults. In contrast to shipworms that penetrate wood, wood boring crustaceans (gribbles) mainly gnaw and

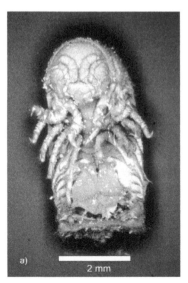

Figure 6.5. (a) A typical gribble (*Limnoria* spp.), which is a wood-boring crustacean. This individual was a mature adult and was 2–3 mm (0.079–0.118 inches) long. (b) A pine wood sample after 12 months' exposure showing typical attack by wood-boring crustaceans.

burrow at the surface, leaving many small galleries on the surface of the wood. Archaeologically speaking this may be more drastic than shipworm as the surface details of artifacts can be rapidly lost (fig. 6.5). As with the shipworms the gribbles have specific environmental requirements for their survival, but with broad requirements for salinity (ranging from 15 psu up to 40 psu) and temperature (from 10°C up to 40°C), they are relatively ubiquitous. However, as with the shipworm, it is the dissolved oxygen content of the surrounding sea water that is the limiting factor for their survival.

Deterioration in Sediments

Should a shipwreck come to be covered by sediment as a result of sediment accretion, or through the process of liquefaction, such as in the case of the wreck of the *Amsterdam* (Marsden 1985), the processes of wood deterioration are predominantly microbiological. Wood in such cases is not degraded by wood borers because the limited supply of dissolved oxygen within sediments prevents their respiration (Turner and Johnson 1971; Becker 1971). Instead, deterioration of wood is biologically mediated though the action of microorganisms (fungi and bacteria), which can survive in the low oxygen or even anoxic conditions typically found within marine sediments.

The Nature of Marine Sediments

Nearly all biogeochemical processes in young sediments (i.e., during early diagenesis) are directly or indirectly connected with the degradation of organic matter (Rullkötter 2000). Organic matter may be produced by algae and other organisms in open water, subsequently sinking to the seabed and becoming incorporated within the sediment. It may also be the remains of plant material such as eelgrass or seaweed, or ship wreck material deposited within the sediment.

The utilization of the organic matter by organisms within sediments involves oxidation reduction (Redox) reactions (Schulz 2000). These reactions follow a well-documented succession (fig. 6.6) with various chemical species (electron acceptors) being utilized based on the amount of energy they yield (Froelich et al. 1979).

From the pool of potential electron acceptors, the microbial community selects the one that maximizes energy yield from the available substrate. In marine sediments the sequence of electron acceptor utilization can be observed spatially in horizontal layers of increasing depth. In typical coastal

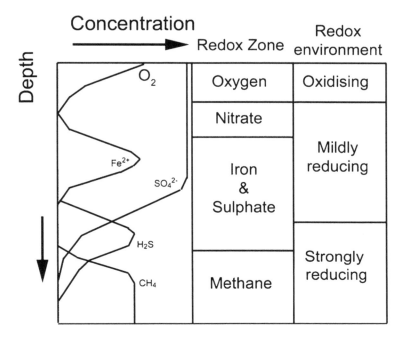

Figure 6.6. Diagram showing the various electron acceptors.

marine sediment, only the first few millimeters of the sediment are oxygenated. This is because oxygen yields the maximum amount of energy to microorganisms and is thus rapidly utilized by them. For a few centimeters under the oxygenated zone, nitrate serves as the electron acceptor, followed by manganese and iron oxides. Below this, sulphate is the principal electron acceptor, and sulphate reduction is often the dominant process in shallow marine sediments due to the high concentrations of sulphate in seawater and is the reason for the "bad egg" smell associated with muddy foreshores. Methanogenesis is usually confined to the sulphate-depleted deeper sediment layers, though the generated methane may diffuse upward into the zone of sulphate reduction. Thus the deterioration of organic matter still occurs in anoxic environments due to the activity of anaerobic organisms, albeit at a slower rate. Wooden shipwreck material is in effect just another type of organic matter, although much larger when compared with naturally deposited organic matter such as seaweed, and its deterioration in sediment will be dependent upon its depth in the sediment and the microorganisms and electron acceptors available.

Microbial Decay of Wood

Microbial wood decay can be seen using microscopic techniques. From the morphology of the decay pattern, the types of microorganisms causing decay can be ascertained. Knowing their environmental or ecological constraints means that the presence or absence of these organisms serves as a proxy indicator for the environment in which the wood is and has been lying (fig. 6.7). It is beyond the scope of this chapter to go into the structure of wood in depth, and the reader is referred to Björdal and Gregory (2012) for more information. This chapter is instead focused on the microstructure of wood and the morphology of microbial attack that can be seen with relatively simple tools such as light microscopy.

The wood cell wall (fig. 6.8) can be divided into a primary cell wall and a secondary cell wall. The primary cell wall is very thin, whereas the secondary cell wall can be subdivided into three different layers, referred to as the S1, S2, and S3 layers, with S2 being the thickest layer. The matrix between the fibers, called the middle lamella, bonds the individual cells together to form the wood tissue. The middle lamella and the two adjoining primary walls are often referred to as the compound middle lamella. In the center of a wood tracheid, or fiber, is a cavity called the cell lumen. The S2 layer in the late wood, the secondary cell wall, contains the majority of the wood's cellulose (ca. 80%), and it is this area that is most commonly degraded by microorganisms. The compound middle lamella, which consists primarily of lignin, is quite resistant to many types of microbial decay, and it is this fact, along with waterlogging, that prevents total loss of wood.

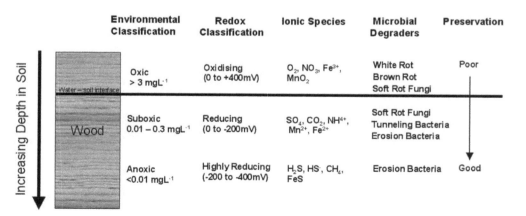

Figure 6.7. Microbial wood degraders and environmental conditions.

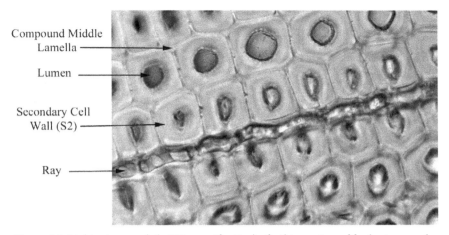

Compound Middle Lamella

Lumen

Secondary Cell Wall (S2)

Ray

Figure 6.8. Light micrograph (×450 magnification) of a thin section of fresh pine wood showing structure of the wood cell wall.

Thin cross sections with appropriate staining are extremely useful when considering the nature of microbial decay. Importantly, they reflect characteristic degradation patterns specific to the organisms causing them. The predominant microbial degraders of wood in marine sediments are soft rot fungi and what are termed tunneling and erosion bacteria.

Soft Rot

Soft rot is a type of decay caused by ascomycetes and fungi imperfecti. The term *soft rot* describes forms of fungal decay whereby characteristic chains of cavities with conical ends are produced within wood cell walls. Some soft rot fungi cause cell wall erosion in addition to forming cavities, but the term is commonly used to describe all forms of decay caused by ascomycetes and fungi imperfecti.

The most characteristic and best-known form of degradation by soft rot is expressed through cavities that are produced by enzymatic activity of hyphae growing parallel to the cellulose microfibrils within wood cell walls. The attack is mainly confined to the secondary cell walls and is confined to the vicinity of the hyphae, as shown in figure 6.9, and results in a series of small holes in the secondary cell wall. Erosion of the compound middle lamellae is rarely seen.

Soft rots are capable of decaying wood in waterlogged conditions and at oxygen levels that are too low for other wood decaying fungi. They are also tolerant of great fluctuations in moisture content. Attack can thus be found

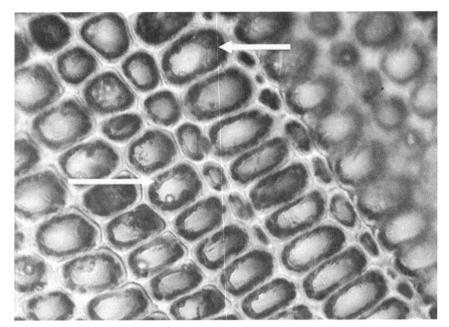

Figure 6.9. Light microscopy picture of soft rot attack in the secondary cell wall, in cross section (×450 magnification). Arrows indicate where soft rot hyphae have degraded the secondary cell wall.

in timber that remains dry for long periods and is wet only occasionally (or vice versa). On timbers that have lain exposed to water, or have been exposed prior to covering or burial with sediment, the typical softening of the outer regions of a timber are often caused by soft rot.

Tunneling Bacteria

Deterioration in sediments is predominantly caused by bacteria and is a very slow process; in the right circumstances archaeological wood can survive for tens of thousands of years (Björdal 2000). Tunneling bacteria are one kind of bacteria that have been seen to degrade the wood cell wall. As with the soft rot, it would appear that they require some dissolved oxygen to survive and certainly greater oxygen concentrations than erosion bacteria (Björdal 2000). They enter wood cells primarily through the cell lumen and have the ability to degrade lignin and the middle lamella region of the cell wall. Once the cell wall has been penetrated, the bacteria degrade all layers of the secondary wall, producing concentric bands of residual materials from degradation and extracellular slime, which are left behind and can characteristically be seen under the microscope (fig. 6.10).

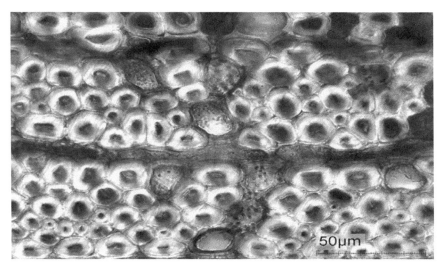

Figure 6.10. Light micrograph of longitudinal thin section (×450 magnification) with arrows showing deterioration of cells by tunneling bacteria—individual bacteria can be seen. Adjacent cells have been degraded where the bacteria have been able to degrade the lignin-rich compound middle lamella.

Erosion Bacteria

The predominant bacteria causing deterioration in waterlogged and anoxic environments have not been formally identified (Helms 2008) but are termed *erosion bacteria* due to the way they enter and erode the wood cell wall, leaving a distinct erosion pattern that can be identified through microscopy (Singh and Butcher 1991). Fortunately for archaeologists, erosion bacteria can only degrade the cellulose within the wood cell wall, and although they may modify the lignin in the compound middle lamella, they cannot completely degrade it. Hence the lignin-rich compound middle lamella survives, and its form is kept intact by the degraded parts of the cell being replaced by water. Very little is known about the actual bacteria that can degrade wood, and the classification of bacterial decay types is based on the micromorphology of attack. In the early phases of attack, erosion bacteria penetrate the wood surface through rays and pits, and from there they enter the cell lumen of the tracheids.

They attack the S3 layer and proceed into the cellulose-rich S2 layer, converting it into an amorphous mass consisting of residual cell wall material and bacteria that can be seen microscopically, as shown in figure 6.11. The middle lamella is not degraded even in later stages of decay but may be

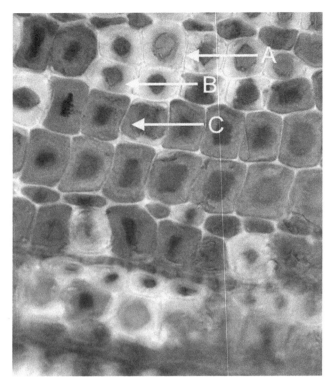

Figure 6.11. Cross section showing characteristic signs of attack from erosion bacteria (×450 magnification). Arrow A shows the compound middle lamella of the wood cell. Arrow B shows an undegraded cell wall. Arrow C indicates a degraded cell wall, whereby the cell lumen is filled with an amorphous mass of degraded cellulose and bacterial waste products.

somewhat modified. A further characteristic of this type of decay is the heterogeneous nature of decay, with sound tracheid fibers being found among heavily degraded ones (fig. 6.11). Decay of wood in waterlogged environments and with restricted oxygen levels is very often attributable to these bacteria.

ARCHAEOLOGICAL INTERPRETATION

Having discussed the processes of deterioration, how can we use this knowledge to help interpret wood from a shipwreck assemblage? As noted, the wood is a product of those processes acting upon it over time, and they will leave their mark on and in the wood. For example, let us consider a section of the top of an oak barrel probably used for storing liquid. When found on an unidentified sixteenth-century wreck in 5 m (16.4 feet) of water in northwest Ireland, it was totally buried in fine-grained sandy sediment (fig. 6.12). Figure 6.12(a) shows the top side of the barrel lid as found, revealing the remains of tool and maker's marks. However, the lower image shows the reverse side and, as can be seen, the remnant patterns and galleries of gribble. The fact that there were no signs of remnant gribble indicates that the barrel had been covered for some time. This interpretation was confirmed by microscopic analysis. As the tool marks show, the barrel is well preserved from an archaeological perspective, but the actual wood was very poorly preserved from a material perspective, hence the need for its subsequent conservation. When examined under the microscope the outer few millimeters showed signs of soft rot and some tunneling bacteria deterioration. This confirmed the remnants of gribble attack, and in combination these manifestations indicate that the barrel, or its lid at any

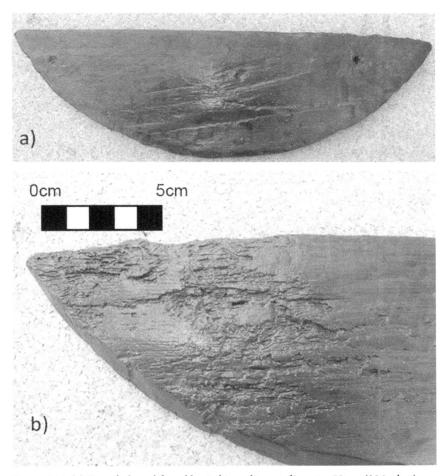

Figure 6.12. (a) Top of a barrel found buried in sediment, diameter 50 cm (20 inches). (b) The underside showed signs of attack by gribble, although no living specimens were observed.

rate, had been exposed to oxygenated seawater for a length of time before being covered by sediments. Below the outer few millimeters the wood was extensively degraded throughout by erosion bacteria, which survive best in anoxic conditions. This implies that for the majority of its time since sinking, the artifact had been buried.

The analysis conducted on the barrel highlights the wealth of information that can be gleaned from analysis of wooden artifacts and wreck components. Such analyses can be used as a way of identifying and limiting which parts of a wreck have been covered or uncovered since the time of wrecking, which can help archaeologists further their understanding of the depositional history of a shipwreck site.

REFERENCES CITED

Becker, G.
1971   On the Biology, Physiology and Ecology of Marine Wood-Boring Crustaceans. In *Marine Borers, Fungi and Fouling Organisms of Wood*, edited by E.B.G. Jones and S. K. Eltringham, pp. 303–326. Portsmouth.

Björdal, Charlotte
2000   *Waterlogged Archaeological Wood—Biodegradation and Its Implications for Conservation*. Acta Universitatis Agriculturae Sueciae, Silvestria 142. Ph.D. dissertation, Swedish University of Agricultural Sciences, Uppsala.

Björdal, Charlotte, and David Gregory
2012   *Wreck Protect: Decay and Protection of Archaeological Wooden Shipwrecks*. Archaeopress, Oxford.

Cundell, A. M., and R. Mitchell
1977   Microbial Succession on a Wooden Surface Exposed to the Sea. *International Biodeterioration Bulletin* 13:67–73.

Floodgate, G. D.
1971   Primary Fouling of Bacteria. In *Marine Borers, Fungi and Fouling Organisms of Wood*, edited by E.B.G. Jones and S. K. Eltringham, pp. 117–123. Portsmouth.

Froelich, P. N., G. P. Klinkhammer, M. L. Bender, N. A. Luedtke, G. R. Heath, D. Cullen, P. Dauphin, D. Hammond, B. Hartman, and V. Maynard
1979   Early Oxidation of Organic Matter in Pelagic Sediments of the Eastern Equatorial Atlantic: Suboxic Diagenesis. *Geochimica et Cosmochimica Acta* 43:1075–1090.

Gareth Jones, E. B., R. D. Turner, S.E.J. Furtado, and H. Kfihne
1976   Marine Biodeteriogenic Organisms: Lignicolous Fungi and Bacteria and the Wood Boring Mollusca and Crustacea. *International Biodeterioration Bulletin* 4:120–134.

Helms, Anne Christine
2008   *Bacterial Diversity in Waterlogged Archaeological Wood*. Ph.D. dissertation, Bio Centre, Danish Technical University, Kongens Lyngby, Denmark.

Kuhne, H.
1971   The Identification of Wood-Boring Crustaceans. In *Marine Borers, Fungi and Fouling Organisms of Wood*, edited by E.B.G. Jones and S. K. Eltringham, pp. 65–88. Portsmouth.

Marsden, Peter
1985   *The Wreck of the* Amsterdam. 2nd edition. Hutchinson, London.

Rullkötter, Jurgen
2000   Organic Matter: The Driving Force for Early Diagenesis. In *Marine Geochemistry*, edited by Schulz Horst and Zabel Matthias, pp. 129–153. Springer-Verlag, Berlin.

Singh, A. P., and J. A. Butcher
1991   Bacterial Degradation of Wood Cell Walls: A Review of Degradation Patterns. *Journal of the Institute of Wood Science* 12:143.

Schulz, Horst
2000   Redox Measurements in Marine Sediments. In *Redox: Fundamentals, Processes and Applications*, edited by J. Schüring, H. D. Schulz, W. R. Fischer, J. Böttcher, and W.H.N. Duijnisveld, pp. 235–246. Springer-Verlag, Berlin.

Turner, Ruth
1966   *A Survey and Illustrated Catalogue of the Teredinidae*. Harvard University, Cambridge.

Turner, Ruth, and A. C. Johnson
1971   Biology of Marine Wood Boring Molluscs. In *Marine Borers, Fungi and Fouling Organisms of Wood*, edited by E.B.G. Jones and S. K. Eltringham, pp. 259–296. Portsmouth.

Zachary, A., M. E. Taylor, F. E. Scott, and R. R. Colwell
1978   A Method for Rapid Evaluation of Materials for Susceptibility to Marine Biofouling. *International Biodeterioration Bulletin* 14:111–118.

II

Cultural Processes

7

Anthropogenic Impacts of Development-Led Archaeology in an Offshore Context

AMANDA M. EVANS AND ANTONY FIRTH

Anthropogenic activities have the potential to impact shipwreck sites in marine contexts both directly and indirectly. Anthropogenic processes of shipwreck site formation can occur during the wrecking event, such as through selective discard of materials during efforts to avert sinking. They can also occur as long-term, cumulative, or single-occurrence impacts at any time or for any duration after the wrecking event (Muckelroy 1978). Anthropogenic or cultural processes that can affect a site include fishing and trawling, salvage, the disposal of refuse, and, the focus of this discussion, development-led activities (Stewart 1999). Development-led impacts in an offshore context may result from a diversity of anthropogenic activities related to economic development, such as oil, gas, and renewable energies extraction; aggregates extraction; port and harbor development; and pipeline, transmission line, or cable installation (fig. 7.1).

This chapter is predominantly concerned with development-led activities occurring today and in the future; or, how development can affect sites by changing their character, coherence, and even their very survival. Archaeologists are commonly required to assess the effects of development on archaeological sites in advance of development taking place; much of this chapter focuses, therefore, on the likely effects of development activities based on the direct impacts of those activities on seabed features generally and on previous experience where archaeological sites have been impacted by development. Archaeologists must be familiar with development activities in order to anticipate their future impacts on archaeological sites. Thinking about development in terms of site formation can also aid the archaeologist in interpreting sites and assessing areas of seabed where development has already occurred. Intensive development of the seabed, in

	Physical Sampling	Construction	Operation	Decommissioning
Direct	Coring	Device/sub-station foundation	Setting of heritage assets	Device foundation/mooring removal
	Sampling	Device mooring	Landscape	Cable removal
	Sensor mooring	Cable trenches	Seascape	Vessel decommissioning
		Onshore cabling	Mooring/cable movement	Temporary works
		Construction vessels/vehicles	O&M vessels	
		Temporary works (e.g., access roads, hardstanding)		
Indirect		Construction-related erosion	Local scouring	
			Changes to bedforms	
			Coastal erosion	
			Changes in water table/salinity (tidal range schemes)	

Figure 7.1. The principal impacts on the historic environment from many offshore structures (in terms of visual effects) depend on their configuration with respect to the seabed and sea surface. This schematic illustrates the wide range of configurations that are being explored for placing wave and tidal energy devices (adapted from Firth 2013b).

addition to "clearing" old wrecks to facilitate navigation, has been occurring for well over a century in some places. Recognizing that development has affected these places through specific processes that can be identified and taken into account is an important aspect of the study of development in terms of formation processes.

A further reason for considering marine development as a formation process is that our overall understanding of the marine archaeological resource is driven to some degree by the opportunity to carry out investigations and by the discoveries that occur. Seabed development influences where archaeologists look, what types of site they are most concerned about, and what tools they are able to use; this in turn affects what is found and where, which then informs our knowledge of the archaeological resource as a whole. By way of illustration, the character of the marine archaeological resource around the United Kingdom was shaped, until recently, by the way in which sites were protected in law (Firth 1999). The emergence of development-led marine archaeology has changed our understanding. This should not be seen simply as removing the old bias but as introducing a new one. Patterns of development are driven by technical and economic imperatives that favor some things over others. Legislative authority, technology, and market demand drive development industries and therefore dictate areas under consideration for development. For example, archaeologists working in advance of oil and gas development are utilizing autonomous underwater vehicles (AUVs) at increasing water depths, while demand for shallow water assessments on certain continental shelves is decreasing. Hence the degree to which archaeological knowledge as a whole is being formed by engagement with marine development needs to be recognized and addressed.

Development-led activities are generally regulated at the state and/or national level, and are associated with archaeology that is conducted as part of regulatory compliance; this may be referred to by many names, depending on the region, and includes cultural resource management (CRM), commercial archaeology, and consultation archaeology. The primary concern of the regulatory agency in regard to development-led activities is to ensure that the activity has no adverse impacts on significant archaeological sites within the area of proposed effect. It is therefore essential to understand both the immediate and long-term impacts that are reasonably likely to occur as a result of the proposed activity.

OIL AND GAS EXTRACTION

Oil and gas operations have been impacting the offshore environment since the first offshore well was drilled out of sight of land, in the Gulf of Mexico in 1947 (National Commission 2011). In the United States, federal requirements for archaeological assessments have been in place for oil and gas permitting procedures since 1974. Over the last forty years it has become apparent that oil and gas operations have very specific seafloor impacts related to drilling and to structure and pipeline installation and removal. Regulatory responsibility and permitting authority for oil and gas operations depends on the project area. Using the United States as an example, oil and gas permits are issued for projects in federal waters by the Bureau of Ocean Energy Management (BOEM). Permitting regulations are published in the Code of Federal Regulations and issued to developers as Notices to Lessees (NTL). Archaeology NTLs require assessments based on geophysical surveys and/or visual inspections of the seafloor prior to permit approval for proposed development activities (e.g., drilling or pipeline installation). Assessments must detail seafloor conditions and identify any potentially significant archaeological sites present in the area of proposed effect. NTL-compliant assessments are prepared by qualified marine archaeologists and submitted to the permit applicant, who then submits them to BOEM as part of the permit process. Following the permit application review process, the activity is approved if everything meets compliance standards. Avoidance criteria or mitigation measures may be applied to certain magnetic anomalies, sonar targets, and subsurface features identified in the geophysical data that may represent potential archaeological resources. These avoidance criteria are included in the notification of approval issued to the operator. Operators typically prefer to adhere to avoidances; however, in some cases subsequent visual inspection of a target may be required if a potentially significant target is identified. The example given is specific to U.S. federal law but illustrates archaeology's role within the overall process of offshore development. The process varies among different nations and states, but universal to all development-led archaeology is the fact that mitigation and avoidance zones must be designed based on an accurate understanding of the seafloor impacts and potential effects of the proposed development activity.

The act of drilling is itself an obvious and immediate impact on the seafloor with the potential to cause significant damage to a shipwreck or other archaeological feature. Offshore, wells are drilled using depth-specific

Figure 7.2. Jack-up rigs at the Port of Galveston, 2009 (photograph by Amanda Evans).

techniques and equipment that have variable levels of impact on the sea-floor. In the United States there is a trend toward drilling in increasingly deeper waters. These deep-water wells are drilled with either moored (tethered) or dynamically positioned (untethered) drilling rigs and drill ships. Despite the perception of drilling as a major impact, the borehole itself is relatively small; it is the related activities and equipment associated with drilling operations that are more likely to cause significant seafloor disturbances.

In shallow water (less than 200 m [656 feet]), drilling operations are typically conducted using seafloor-mounted drill rigs, called jack-up rigs. Globally, seafloor-mounted jack-up rigs are the most common type of drilling rig utilized, representing 43% of the world's offshore rig fleet (Rigzone 2014). In the Gulf of Mexico, jack-ups and platform rigs account for two thirds of all rig types (Rigzone 2014). These rigs do not operate under their own propulsion and are towed into place by support vessels. The legs of

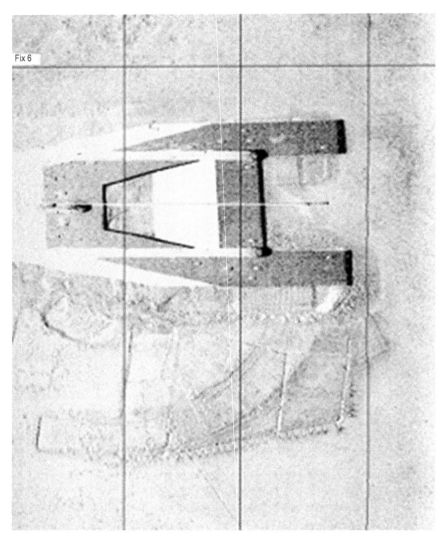

Fix 6

Figure 7.3. Sonar image of mat-supported rig on the seafloor (data courtesy Tesla Offshore).

this rig type are designed to be raised out of the water during towing and, once on location, lowered to the seafloor to bear the weight of the structure (figure 7.2). There are two basic styles of jack-up rigs; independent leg and mat-supported (fig. 7.3). Independent leg rigs typically have three stanchions (or legs) that support the rig. Each stanchion rests directly on the seafloor. Mat-supported rigs are similar to independent leg rigs except for the inclusion of a flat base connecting the stanchions and distributing the weight of the entire platform evenly over a broad footprint. In shallow water, historic shipwrecks and other cultural resources may be impacted by the physical borehole drilled for the well or by the placement of the rig's legs or mat.

Jack-up rigs are necessarily restricted to use in shallower water depths because of the limited length of their stanchions. Anchored or dynamically positioned semi-submersible rigs account for the majority of deep-water drilling (defined here as water depths up to 1,500 m [4,921 feet]) and ultradeep-water drilling (defined here as all water depths greater than 1,500 m [4,921 feet]) drilling. Drill ships are used for some applications but are far less common. The difference between anchored and dynamically positioned drill rigs is that the former are secured to the seafloor by anchors with mooring lines. In the northern Gulf of Mexico a typical anchor spread employs eight anchors; twelve anchors are required during hurricane season (June–November). A typical anchor radius is 2.5 times the water depth, therefore in 1,500 m (or approximately 5,000 feet) of water, the anchor spread can extend 3,750 m (or approximately 12,500 feet) beyond the proposed well borehole. Anchoring techniques for deep-water rigs include the use of both suction pile and gravity-installed anchors. Anchors range in size but must be sufficient to hold the platform in position under variable conditions. One type of anchor in use is the 84,000 lb OMNI-Max Anchor, which, at 9.7 m (32 feet) long and 3 m (10 feet) wide, "is a relatively small sized anchor when compared with a similar capacity suction pile anchor" (Shelton 2007; fig. 7.4).

Dynamically positioned rigs, also known as DP rigs, use advanced thrusters to maintain their position in the water during drilling operations. Bottom impacts for DP rigs are therefore limited to the borehole, transponder beacons set around the site for positioning, and associated drilling splay. The use of moored or anchored rigs causes an increased number of seafloor impacts due to the placement of an anchor array; its associated cables and chains, which can sweep across the seafloor; and any ancillary structures used during anchor deployment and recovery. Incidents of damage to historic shipwrecks have been documented in which the anchor chain or mooring line swept across the site.

Prior to 2011, archaeological assessments for drilling operations in the northern Gulf of Mexico were not required universally. Instead, a high probability model for shipwreck occurrence was used to identify areas where proposed permitted activities would require an archaeological assessment. The reliance on this high probability model was flawed in that it

Figure 7.4. Deep-water mooring anchor prior to installation in deep water (photograph by Amanda Evans).

was based on historic shipping routes and where wrecks had been previously found but did not take into account oceanographic conditions and ships that had deviated from common sailing routes, either intentionally or unintentionally (Lugo-Fernández et al. 2007). This resulted in limited survey requirements in deep-water areas that were increasingly favored by oil and gas developers. The high probability model included reported locations of known vessels, with varying degrees of probability. Unfortunately, in the case of the SS *Gulfstag*, 167 m (552 feet) long and 23 m (75 feet) wide, the steel-hulled tanker was in a different location than its reported position (NOAA 2013). The vessel was not identified during a pre-drilling hazards survey, due to the coarse survey parameters, and was impacted by mooring lines associated with the permitted drilling rig (fig. 7.5).

As noted, drilling creates a relatively small diameter borehole, but impacts caused by activities associated with drilling may require a larger mitigation to protect archaeological resources adequately. In addition to the direct bottom disturbances caused by setting or anchoring a rig on-site, the act of drilling produces cuttings, drilling mud or fluid, and produced water that may splay outward from the borehole during drilling operations

(Boesch et al. 1987:22). Drill cuttings are fragments of earth produced during drilling that are removed from the well borehole by flushing the shaft with drilling fluid or "mud." Water-based drilling muds are the only type legally allowed in United States waters; however, petroleum-based and synthetic-based fluids may be used elsewhere. Drilling mud is defined as a "freshwater or seawater slurry of clay (or natural organic polymer), barium sulfate, lignosulfonate, lignite, and sodium hydroxide, plus several minor additives" (Boesch et al. 1987:23). Drill cuttings consist of crushed rock and sediment produced by the grinding action of the drill bit as it penetrates through the well shaft toward the target depth (Boesch et al. 1987:23). Drilling fluid or mud is continually circulated through the well shaft to lubricate the drill bit, prevent the drill bit from overheating, and flush solids out of the well shaft (Neff et al. 1987:150). Operators often recirculate drilling fluids on the rig deck in order to separate out the drill cuttings, allowing them to reuse the drilling fluid (Neff et al. 1987:150). The separated drill cuttings, in some cases, are disposed of over the side of the rig. The dumped cuttings

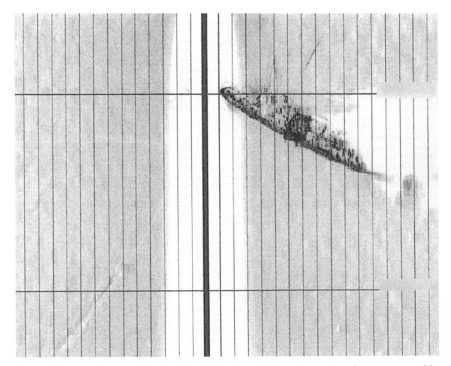

Figure 7.5. Sonar image of the steel-hulled tanker *Gulfstag*; the anchor drag scar is visible running from the bottom left, through the wreck, to the upper right (courtesy BOEM/BSEE; data acquired by C & C Technologies).

settle on the seafloor, creating a secondary disposal pile; drill cuttings and fluid splaying out from the borehole are the primary disposal pile (Neff et al. 1987:150).

According to Boesch and colleagues (1987:23), drilling of an exploratory (nonproducing) well can generate "5,000 to 30,000 barrels of drilling fluid (containing 200–2,000 metric tons of solids)" and "from 1,000 to 2,000 metric tons of drill cuttings." Development wells, added to the site of a successful exploratory well, are often shallower and have a smaller diameter than the exploratory well, resulting in less drilling fluid and cuttings. According to Neff and colleagues (2000:15), drill solids disposal piles located near platforms can be up to 26 m (85 feet) high; however, most are less than 10 m (33 feet) in height.

Regulatory agencies can protect identified or even potential archaeological resources from the direct impact of drilling activities by working with operators to move a proposed borehole, but it is harder to protect sites, especially unidentified resources, from the associated impacts related to drilling operations. It is possible that drilling splay or cuttings piles could accumulate around or over the top of archaeological resources in deep water. Observations have shown that drill cuttings and fluids are more likely to accumulate in deep-water settings. Drill cuttings typically do not collect on the seabed in shallow water. Instead, drill cuttings dissipate due to the effects of currents and waves (Zingula 1977:548; Neff et al. 2000:15). While numerous studies have been conducted analyzing the impact of cuttings on biological communities (NRC 1983; Boesch and Rabalais 1987; Neff et al. 2000; and UKOOA 2005), no known studies have been conducted that examine their impact on archaeological sites. It is unknown to what extent the introduction of post-depositional chemical compounds can alter the results of archaeological analyses. Preliminary research conducted in the wake of the *Exxon Valdez* oil spill focused on possible contamination of radiocarbon samples. Ten oil-impacted sites were examined, and preliminary results indicated that no adverse impacts to radiocarbon dating were identified (Reger et al. 1992). Without further study though, it is unknown to what degree, if any, petroleum-based drilling fluid or additives in water-based or synthetic-based fluids could contaminate a site and adversely impact artifact preservation, chemical sample testing, or data recovery. Certainly burial under drilling splay would obscure an archaeological site and make documentation more difficult and time-consuming.

Installation of a permanent (or semi-permanent) structure such as a platform or caisson often takes place at the site of a successfully drilled exploratory well. During drilling and subsequent platform operation phases, activities at a well site may include drilling additional wells with a different rig footprint or anchor array, the use of seafloor-mounted lift boats for maintenance or repair work, and anchoring associated with dive boats or other support vessels. Materials may be discarded from the rig, platform, or other service support vessels or introduced to the seafloor through accidental loss. In addition to ancillary activities associated with resource extraction, platforms and well caissons often become popular sites for fishermen and recreational divers, who may produce a different set of impacts to archaeological sites.

As demonstrated, a well site is part of a much larger system and cannot be considered in isolation. This is an important point to recognize when drilling a well location in proximity to a potential archaeological resource. Although the avoidance zone assigned to the resource may be adequate to ensure that drilling activities do not impact the site, the site may be subjected to greater development if the exploratory well is successful. The proximity of the resource to the construction area can complicate construction plans or result in inadvertent damage to the site. This issue can be alleviated by ensuring that future activities are considered when a well site is initially permitted near a significant archaeological resource.

Renewable Energy

Archaeologists' engagement with the offshore oil and gas industry in the United Kingdom is much less extensive than in the United States because of differences in regulatory regimes and the fact that marine archaeology does not feature strongly among "best practice" within that industry. In contrast, archaeology has had a relatively high profile in the emergence of renewable energies offshore; the potential effects on archaeological sites are an integral consideration in the course of obtaining consent for, and constructing, new renewable energy developments (Wessex Archaeology 2007; Gribble and Leather 2011; Firth 2013b).

Offshore wind farms (OWF) are the mainstay of the development of renewable energy in waters around the United Kingdom. As of January 2014 there were twenty-two offshore wind farms in operation, totaling 1,075 turbines with combined capacity of 3.6 gigawatts (GW). The operational wind farms vary in size from two turbines to 175 turbines (fig. 7.6). A further 12 projects totaling 856 turbines (capacity 3.8 GW) either have consent or are under construction (RenewableUK 2014). A series of much larger

Figure 7.6. An operational wind farm close inshore; recent schemes are typically much farther offshore (photo by Antony Firth).

"Round 3" projects is in preparation, with projects totaling 7.8 GW already progressing through the consenting process.

The principal source of impacts to archaeological sites arising from off-shore wind farms is the foundation. Offshore wind farms consist of large turbines that generate electricity from a massive three-bladed propeller. Each turbine is mounted at the top of a tall tower, which in turn is fitted to a foundation. The most favored form of foundation so far has been "monopiles." These are single, large diameter metal tubes that are driven or drilled many meters into the seabed. Meteorological stations (known as "met masts"), offshore substations, and other facilities have tended to be constructed in a similar way, on monopiles. Monopiles would penetrate an archaeological site that is buried in the vicinity of its footprint, including both ship and aircraft wrecks and prehistoric remains. Monopiles are usually driven all the way through the great depth of sediment that has been deposited within periods of archaeological interest on much of the U.K. continental shelf. Consequently, impacts to archaeological material could occur many meters beneath the surface of the seabed.

Although monopiles have been the favored foundation for many OWFs, other solutions are being considered to deal with the greater water depths encountered farther offshore. Borrowing concepts from offshore oil and gas, foundations consisting of steel lattice frameworks or "jackets" are being proposed, as are concrete gravity foundations that sit on the seabed and hold the turbine in place by their sheer mass (Reach et al. 2012). Options for floating turbines, moored using arrays of anchors, are also being considered. These different forms of foundation have different implications for the seabed and for any archaeological material that might be on or within the seabed.

Offshore wind farms require extensive networks of cables between the individual turbines, known as inter-array cabling, in addition to "export" cables that take the electricity back to the shore. The implications of cabling associated with offshore wind farms for archaeological sites are generally the same as cabling for other purposes and are discussed later in this chapter. In addition to the direct impacts of wind farms, as with other forms of development, the introduction of constructed features can interfere with hydrodynamic regimes, potentially causing scour that may expose archaeological material otherwise beyond the footprint of the foundations.

Although wind farms predominate among renewables offshore in the United Kingdom, three other forms of marine renewable energy are receiving serious attention, with test sites and demonstration sites already in operation: wave energy, tidal stream energy, and tidal range energy. In the case of wave energy, the intention is to convert the up-and-down motion of the surface of the sea into electricity. In tidal stream energy it is the tidal current that is captured as it flows back and forth. Tidal range energy is extracted by impounding an area of sea so that when the tide rises and falls, a difference in level or "head" is created; when the water is released it flows through turbines as it equalizes the levels. A wide range of different devices are being developed for wave and tidal energy; it is the way in which they are mounted relative to the seabed that is most important in terms of archaeological impacts, rather than how the devices work (fig. 7.7).

Some proposals require massive structures on the seabed, whereas others are moored and require extensive arrays of anchors. Impacts on archaeological sites depend on the way in which the device is held in place, the device's footprint, and the character of archaeological material that is or may be present. The need for inter-array and export cabling is similar to that in offshore wind farms. However, there are some important differences too. First, by extracting energy from the water, wave and tidal projects are interfering directly in flows of water and sediment, which may lead to alterations in the local geomorphology that could reveal once-buried sites to degradation or vice versa. Second, the complex hydrodynamics of a project

Tethered to the seabed

Floating on surface

Floating within water column

Built onto the seabed

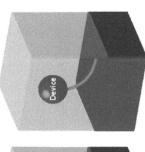

Major elements in water column

Major elements breaking surface

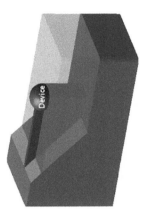

Major elements forming connection to coast

Supported from the seabed

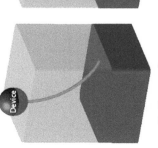

Mounted at surface

Mounted within water column

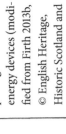

Figure 7.7. The principal impacts on the historic environment from many offshore structures (in terms of visual effects) depend on their configuration with respect to the seabed and sea surface. This schematic illustrates the wide range of configurations that are being explored for placing wave and tidal energy devices (modified from Firth 2013b, © English Heritage, Historic Scotland and Cadw).

may make it very difficult to change the planned position of turbines to avoid archaeological sites, requiring archaeological resources to be considered early in the planning process.

AGGREGATE EXTRACTION

The United Kingdom is heavily dependent on sand and gravel dredged from the sea for use in construction and to protect coastlines by "beach recharge." Dredging for aggregates is carried out using large specialist ships equipped with huge pumps (fig. 7.8). The suction from the pump is directed to a "drag head" that is pulled along the seabed on long tubes. As the drag head passes over the seabed, sand and gravel are sucked up the pipe into the hold of the ship (fig. 7.9). The ship returns to the wharf, where the cargo, typically 4,000–5,000 metric tonnes (4,409–5,512 U.S. tons), is discharged for processing. The passage of the drag head removes a strip of seabed about 20–30 centimeters (7.87–11.81 inches) deep across its width, which is typically a couple of meters.

Figure 7.8. An aggregate dredger in operation. On the port side a large suction drag-head is trailed along the seabed. A mix of aggregate and seawater is pumped up to the vessel and discharged into the hold through screens on the starboard side. Excess water and fine-grained material are discharged over the side (photograph courtesy of British Marine Aggregate Producers Association).

Figure 7.9. Trailer suction dredgers—used for both aggregates and navigational dredging—use a draghead that is lowered to the seabed as the vessel moves along. A mix of seabed material and seawater is pumped up to the vessel and discharged into the hold (image courtesy of British Marine Aggregate Producers Association).

Aggregate dredging has been shown to have an impact on archaeological material on numerous occasions. Known shipwrecks are avoided because of the risk they present to the dredging equipment, and indeed any "contamination" of the aggregate cargo with peat, for example (which may represent paleo–land surfaces), is also strongly avoided. Mindful of the possibility that aggregate dredging might be causing impacts to archaeological sites, the principal aggregate companies—working with their trade association, the British Marine Aggregate Producers Association (BMAPA)—developed its own guidance and introduced a protocol through which accidental discoveries could be quickly reported to an archaeologist (BMAPA 2003, 2005; Russell and Firth 2007). The operation of the protocol has resulted in hundreds of artifacts being recovered, all of which have passed through a dredger, demonstrating that archaeological material is definitely being impacted. In many cases the reported material is simply indicative of the centuries of human activity around the U.K. coast. In other cases the discovery of a large amount of material from one place or from repeated visits may indicate the presence of a more or less intact site. Examples include aircraft shot down during World War II and the amazing discovery of an assemblage of apparently in situ Paleolithic handaxes dating to over 200,000 years ago (Tizzard et al. 2011). Even in cases where there is a definite impact, the archaeological knowledge gained from industry-led assessment and reporting is a great boost, not only to understanding the possible effects of further aggregate dredging but also to assessing the potential impacts of other marine industries in the region (Firth 2013a).

Ports and Navigational Dredging

Ports and the navigation channels that serve them have an interesting relationship to the past. Often they are situated in places that have been ports for many centuries, so they have high potential for the presence of archaeological material underwater. Port construction and dredging can cause major impacts to archaeological sites, so significant effects can be anticipated (Adams et al. 1990). Ports have usually undergone construction and dredging in earlier phases of their existence, perhaps in relatively recent years but in some cases over many centuries. These earlier port activities have had consequences for material on the seabed, so one aspect of the study of formation processes in a port setting is to consider what damage might already have occurred, both with respect to individual ships that still warrant interpretation despite previous impacts and with respect to knowledge of the archaeological resource as a whole.

It is not unusual for port developers to take an extreme view of the implications for the archaeological record of previous phases of works, by suggesting that previous dredging will have removed completely anything that may once have been there. As a result, it may be claimed that there is no need even to look at the seabed (by commissioning a geophysical survey, for example) in areas where previous dredging is said to have taken place. However, several instances have shown that this line of argument is unsound (e.g., Parham 2011; Firth et al. 2012). It cannot be assumed that the archaeological record will have been erased if dredging has taken place historically; earlier dredging practices could be quite "patchy" in their effects, and dredging records, which might be used to demonstrate the "effectiveness" of earlier dredging, are often absent. Several important sites have been discovered in areas where dredging has occurred previously, and even sites that have been directly targeted for clearance (as a hazard to navigation) have been amenable to detailed analysis (Auer and Firth 2007).

The dredging techniques used in constructing ports and navigation channels are similar to aggregate dredging where trailer suction devices are employed. Other forms of dredging can take place, however, using large barge-mounted backhoes or cutter suction dredgers, for example. It is common also to use a "plough," which is a blade towed along the seabed to smooth out the ridges and troughs left by the principal dredgers. It should be noted that proposed dredging may not, in any case, affect the entire seabed within a proposed channel. Some areas may already be below the level that is being sought, so there is no need for dredging to take place. Certainly, understanding a proposal in terms of the intended dredge level, taking into account margins and any proposed overdeepening to allow for subsequent siltation, is important to the assessment of potential impacts.

As well as dredging, port construction can involve a variety of other processes that can have impacts on archaeological material. The construction of quay walls, reclamation, and piling for cranes are just a few examples that might have implications for any submerged archaeological material that is present.

Pipeline and Cable Installation

Oil, gas, or alternative energy that has been extracted/produced from an area offshore must be transported onshore for processing and consumption. The most common transmission method for these resources is through pipelines or cables, the construction of which represents a potential activity impacting submerged cultural resources. The installation and use of subsea pipelines and cables is the most common method for moving product to production or onshore transmission facilities. Regulations vary between jurisdictions, but pipelines in the U.S. Gulf of Mexico, for example, are required to be buried to a depth of at least 0.9 m (3 feet) below the seafloor in water depths of less than 61 m (200 feet); trenching is therefore a significant and direct seafloor impact. Pipeline and trench depths vary by region. In the U.S. Gulf of Mexico within shipping fairways, pipelines are required to be buried 3 m (10 feet) below the seafloor, and within anchorage areas 4.9 m (16 feet), to prevent accidental pipeline damage from anchoring activities, under regulation 30 CFR 250.1003(a)(1). The potential for damage to archaeological resources depends upon the method of pipeline installation, which is typically conducted using either anchored lay-barges or dynamically positioned reel-ships. Although dynamically positioned pipeline installation can occur in water depths as shallow as 33 m (100 feet), it is generally not used in less than 61 m (200 feet) of water (Cranswick 2001). Dynamically positioned reel-ships or barges do not require anchoring, limiting the seabed disturbance to the actual footprint of the pipeline and any associated trenching.

Anchored lay-barges are the most commonly used pipeline installation vessels in shallow water and have a significant area of potential effect. Operational procedures for anchored lay-barges restrict their use to areas where water depths are less than 300 m (1,000 feet) below sea level (Cranswick 2001); the amount of anchor cable available on an individual vessel may restrict the operating depth to even shallower waters. Pipeline burial, when required, is accomplished during installation through the use of a jet-sled or plow. The installation vessel deploys the pipe from the surface via a device called a stinger, which slides the pipe into the newly cut trench behind the jet-sled or plow. Jetting can cause substantial impacts to archaeological resources; however, historic shipwrecks, particularly large metal-hulled vessels, are relatively easy to avoid. Most operators are more than willing to route around a large metal-hulled vessel since the wreck could damage the highly specialized and expensive equipment used in pipeline installation, causing considerable construction delays. In deep-water areas, however, where vessel anchoring or trawling is not a concern, pipelines may be placed directly on the seabed without trenching.

In areas where pipeline burial is not required the pipeline itself may create impacts to historic resources (fig. 7.10). In the Gulf of Mexico, for example, the early nineteenth-century wooden-hulled vessel known as the Mica Wreck was bisected by a pipeline (Atauz et al. 2006; Jones 2004). The extant remains of the Mica Wreck are 19.8 m (65 feet) long with 2 to 3 m (7 to 10 feet) of relief located at a depth of 808 m (2,650 feet; Atauz et al. 2006:1). The wreck was not discovered until a pipeline post-installation inspection was conducted (Atauz et al 2006:1); at the time sonar surveys or archaeological assessments were not required in advance of drilling in the project area due to use of the aforementioned prediction model, and although a pipeline pre-lay survey was performed, requirements at the time did not ensure adequate sonar coverage over the portion of seabed impacted by the pipeline. Following the discovery of the Mica Wreck, an archaeological damage assessment was conducted, and it was determined that removal of the pipe would cause further damage to the two-masted schooner (Atauz et al. 2006:45). The pipeline was left in place, but the incident spurred regulatory changes designed to avoid similar incidents from occurring in the future.

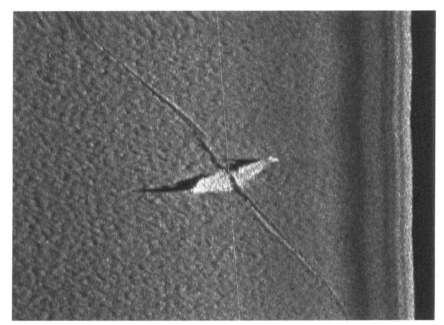

Figure 7.10. Sonar image of the Mica Wreck; pipeline is visible running from upper left, through the wreck, to the lower right (data courtesy BOEM/BSEE; acquired by U.S. Navy).

Vessel Anchoring

The process of installing pipelines, transmission lines, and cables offshore has the potential to impact archaeological resources, but as with drilling, impacts are more commonly attributed to vessel anchoring during installation. The example of the Mica Wreck, presented earlier, is an extreme incident that instigated regulatory changes. Anchors and anchor chain used by lay-barges during installation may cause substantial bottom-disturbing activities.

A standard pipeline lay-barge sets its anchors away from the ship equal to a distance of five times the water depth. An anchored barge typically requires 8–12 anchors, each weighing 30,000–50,000 lb (Cranswick 2001). The anchors are lifted onto anchor-handling support tugs, which are used to deploy the anchors along the route. Winches aboard the lay-barge are used to move the barge along the route by tightening up on the foreword anchors while simultaneously creating slack on the aft anchors. This action allows the barge to pull itself along a stable track. Generally, after the first anchors are set, they are repositioned every 610 m (2,000 feet) along the pipeline route (Cranswick 2001). Ground disturbance is not limited to the actual anchor touch-down points. As slack is placed on the stern lines (prior to pulling the vessel forward along the bow anchor lines), portions of the anchor chains rest or drag on the seafloor. The large diameter wire ropes and chains used to handle these massive anchors can cause substantial damage to archaeological resources, similar to the mooring lines and anchors used for drilling rigs.

Conclusions

Development-led impacts to archaeological resources may result from oil and gas operations, alternative energy production, port and harbor development, dredging, and installation of pipelines, transmission lines, or cables. Pipeline and cable installation may be the most significant threat to shipwreck sites associated with oil and gas development in the marine environment. The associated anchors and anchor chains can cause severe damage to shipwrecks in shallow water depths, and deep-water pipelines have been laid through or in close proximity to historic shipwrecks (Jones 2004; Ford et al. 2008). Often, an incident of damage to an archaeological resource results in changes to regulations to ensure that additional sites are not damaged in the same manner. Drilling is itself a relatively minor seabed impact, but the associated anchoring can cause significant impacts over a much wider area of the seafloor. Foundations and, again, cables are of greatest concern in respect of renewable energies of all forms. For both aggregate dredging and port and navigational dredging, it is the dredging itself that poses the risk, though the footprint and intensity of developments by these two industries may be quite different. Regulatory agencies must have an explicit understanding of the scope of the proposed undertaking in order to make an informed decision regarding required avoidances or potential mitigations on archaeological resources within the project area to safeguard submerged cultural resources from anthropogenic post-depositional site formation processes.

References Cited

Adams, Jonathan, A.F.L. Holk, and Thijs J. Maarleveld
1990   *Dredgers and Archaeology: Shipfinds from the* Slufter. Afdeling Archeologie Onder Water, Ministerie van Welzijn, Volksgezondheid en Cultuur, Alphen aan den Rijn.

Atauz, Ayse D., William Bryant, Toby Jones, and Brett Phaneuf
2006   *Mica Shipwreck Project: Deepwater Archaeological Investigation of a 19th Century Shipwreck in the Gulf of Mexico.* U.S. Department of the Interior, Minerals Management Service, Gulf of Mexico OCS Region, New Orleans.

Auer, Jens, and Antony Firth
2007   The "Gresham Ship": An Interim Report on a 16th-Century Wreck from Princes Channel, Thames Estuary. *Post-Medieval Archaeology* 41(2):222–241.

Boesch, Donald F., and Nancy N. Rabalais (editors)
1987   *Long-Term Environmental Effects of Offshore Oil and Gas Development.* Elsevier Applied Science, New York.

Boesch, Donald F., James N. Butler, David A. Cacchione, Joseph R. Geraci, Jerry M. Neff, James P. Ray, and John M. Teal
1987   An Assessment of the Long-Term Environmental Effects of US Offshore Oil and Gas Development Activities: Future Research Needs. In *Long-Term Environmental Effects of Offshore Oil and Gas Development*, edited by Donald F. Boesch and Nancy N. Rabalais, pp. 1–52. Elsevier Applied Science, New York.

British Marine Aggregate Producers Association (BMAPA) and English Heritage
2003   *Marine Aggregate Dredging and the Historic Environment: Guidance Note.* British Marine Aggregate Producers Association and English Heritage, London.

2005   *Protocol for Reporting Finds of Archaeological Interest.* British Marine Aggregate Producers Association and English Heritage, London.

Cranswick, Deborah
2001   *Brief Overview of Gulf of Mexico OCS Oil and Gas Pipelines: Installation, Potential Impacts, and Mitigation Measures.* U.S. Department of the Interior, Minerals Management Service, Gulf of Mexico OCS Region, New Orleans.

Firth, Antony
1999   Making Archaeology: The History of the Protection of Wrecks Act 1973 and the Constitution of an Archaeological Resource. *International Journal of Nautical Archaeology* 28(1):10–24.

2013a   Marine Archaeology. In *Aggregate Dredging and the Marine Environment: An Overview of Recent Research and Current Industry Practice*, edited by R. C. Newell and T. A. Woodcock, pp. 44–67. Crown Estate, London.

2013b   *Historic Environment Guidance for Wave and Tidal Energy.* Fjordr Ltd. on behalf of English Heritage, Historic Scotland and Cadw, Tisbury.

Firth, Antony, Niall Callan, Graham Scott, Toby Gane, and Stephanie Arnott
2012   *London Gateway: Maritime Archaeology in the Thames Estuary.* Wessex Archaeology, Salisbury.

Ford, Ben, Amy Borgens, William Bryant, Dawn Marshall, Peter Hitchcock, Cesar Arias, and Donny Hamilton
2008   *Archaeological Excavation of the Mardi Gras Shipwreck (16GM01), Gulf of Mexico Continental Slope.* U.S. Department of the Interior, Minerals Management Service, Gulf of Mexico OCS Region, New Orleans.

Gribble, John, and Stuart Leather
2011   *Offshore Geotechnical Investigations and Historic Environment Analysis: Guidance*

for the Renewable Energy Sector. Collaborative Offshore Wind Research into the Environment (COWRIE), Newbury, U.K.

Jones, Toby

2004 *The Mica Shipwreck: Deepwater Nautical Archaeology in the Gulf of Mexico*. Master's thesis, Department of Anthropology, Texas A&M University, College Station.

Lugo-Fernández, A., David A. Ball, M. Gravois, Christopher Horrell, and Jack B. Irion

2007 Analysis of the Gulf of Mexico's Veracruz-Havan Route of La Flota de la Nueva España. *Journal of Maritime Archaeology* 2(1):24–47.

Muckelroy, Keith

1978 *Maritime Archaeology*. Cambridge University Press, Cambridge.

National Commission on the BP Deepwater Horizon Oil Spill and Offshore Drilling (National Commission)

2011 *The History of Offshore Oil and Gas in the United States (Long Version)*. Staff Working Paper no. 22. Electronic document, http://www.oilspillcommission.gov/resources#staff-working-papers, accessed June 14, 2011.

National Oceanic and Atmospheric Administration (NOAA)

2013 Screening Level Risk Assessment Package, Gulfstag. Electronic document, http://sanctuaries.noaa.gov/protect/ppw/pdfs/gulfstag.pdf, accessed February 25, 2014.

National Research Council

1983 *Drilling Discharges in the Marine Environment*. National Academy Press, Washington, D.C.

Neff, Jerry M., Nancy N. Rabalais, and Donald F. Boesch

1987 Offshore Oil and Gas Development Activities Potentially Causing Long-Term Environmental Effects. In *Long-Term Environmental Effects of Offshore Oil and Gas Development*, edited by Donald F. Boesch and Nancy N. Rabalais, pp. 149–168. Elsevier Applied Science, New York.

Neff, Jerry M., S. McKelvie, and R. C. Ayers Jr.

2000 *Environmental Impacts of Synthetic Based Drilling Fluids*. U.S. Department of the Interior, Minerals Management Service, Gulf of Mexico OCS Region, New Orleans.

Parham, D.

2011 The Swash Channel Wreck. In *ACUA Underwater Archaeology Proceedings 2011*, edited by F. Castro and L. Thomas, pp. 103–106. Advisory Council on Underwater Archaeology.

Reach, I. S., W. S. Cooper, A. J. Firth, R. J. Langman, D. Lloyd Jones, S. A. Lowe, and I. C. Warner

2012 *A Review of Marine Environmental Considerations Associated with Concrete Gravity Base Foundations in Offshore Wind Developments*. A report for the Concrete Centre by Marine Space Limited.

Reger, Douglas R., J. David McMahan, and Charles E. Holmes

1992 *Effect of Crude Oil Contamination on Some Archaeological Sites in the Gulf of Alaska, 1991 Investigations*. Alaska Department of Natural Resources, Division of Parks and Outdoor Recreation, Office of History and Archaeology Report no. 30.

RenewableUK

2014   RenewableUK. Electronic document, http://www.renewableuk.com/en/renew able-energy/wind-energy/uk-wind-energy-database/, accessed January 22, 2014.

Rigzone

2014   Rig Report: Offshore Rig Fleet by Rig Type. Electronic document, http://www. rigzone.com/data/rig_report.asp?rpt=type, accessed January 4 2014.

Russell, Mark, and Antony Firth

2007   *Working Alongside the Marine Historic Environment: An Aggregate Dredging Industry Perspective*. CEDA Dredging Days 2007, Central Dredging Association, Rotterdam.

Shelton, John T.

2007   Omni-MAX Anchor Development and Technology. Electronic document, http:// www.delmarus.com/uploads/MTSOceans2007TechnicalPapermodified.pdf, accessed January 4, 2014.

Stewart, David J.

1999   Formation Processes Affecting Submerged Archaeological Sites: An Overview. *Geoarchaeology: An International Journal* 14(6):565–587.

Tizzard, Louise, Paul Baggaley, and Antony Firth

2011   Seabed Prehistory: Investigating Palaeolandsurfaces with Palaeolithic Remains from the Southern North Sea. In *Submerged Prehistory*, edited by J. Benjamin, C. Bonsall, C. Pickard, and A. Fischer, pp. 65–74. Oxbow Books, Oxford.

United Kingdom Offshore Operators Association (UKOOA)

2005   *UKOOA JIP: 2004*. Drill Cuttings Initiative-Phase III. 20132900.

Wessex Archaeology

2007   *Historic Environment Guidance for the Offshore Renewable Energy Sector*. COWRIE Project ARCH-11-05. COWRIE, Newbury, U.K.

Zingula, Richard

1977   Environmental Aspects of Drilling Fluid and Drill Cuttings Disposal. Paper at Oceans Conference, Los Angeles, 17–19 October. In *Oceans '77 Conference Record*, vol. 1, pp. 546–549. Marine Technology Society, Washington, D.C., and Institute of Electrical and Electronic Engineers, New York.

8

Quantifying Impacts of Trawling to Shipwrecks

MICHAEL L. BRENNAN

A ship that has sunk to the sea floor undergoes a variety of biological, physical, and chemical interactions with the marine environment. Over time, a shipwreck site comes into chemical and physical equilibrium with the surrounding environment as organic materials decompose, wood is consumed by borers, and metals corrode. In some cases, such as ancient shipwrecks with ceramic cargoes or wooden wrecks in anoxic waters, significant components of the ship can remain virtually indefinitely. The characterization of these conditions is part of the focus of archaeological oceanography (Brennan and Ballard 2014; Brennan et al. 2011). Despite the stable state of wreck sites on the seabed after centuries or millennia submerged, modern anthropogenic impacts now threaten to damage or eradicate these sites. In many parts of the world the most prevalent threat is mobile fishing gear. While the damaging effects of bottom trawling on benthic ecosystems has been a focal point of oceanographic and fisheries studies for decades, it has been generally overlooked by the underwater archaeological community. Only recently have efforts been made to classify (e.g., Kingsley 2012) or quantify (e.g., Brennan et al. 2012; 2013) the damage to shipwreck sites.

Archaeological discussions of trawling have focused primarily on observations and qualitative descriptions of damage. Damage to wrecks is wrought both by nets that snag and entangle modern steel and wooden-hulled wrecks, and by trawl doors, which destroy and scatter ceramic cargos and wooden components of ancient wrecks. In order to understand the impact of these activities on a larger regional scale and comparatively between sites, a quantification of the damage is necessary. This chapter provides a background on bottom trawl fishing and documented damage to shipwreck sites and a discussion of efforts to quantify the damage on ancient shipwrecks in the Aegean and Black Seas. There is a vast literature on

trawling gear and bottom trawl fishing and their effects on the benthic ecosystem; this chapter cites some essential publications in which the reader
will find additional bibliographies. Finally, efforts to protect shipwreck sites
threatened by trawling and to manage trawling effectively in areas of high
archaeological interest are discussed.

Mobile Fishing Gear

Weighted nets have been dragged across the seabed to catch benthic organisms for centuries. The earliest evidence for an awareness the damage this
activity does to the ecosystem comes from a petition to the British Parlia-
ment in 1376, when fishermen were concerned about effects to their fishery
(March 1953). The trouble with towing nets underwater comes from the
indiscriminate nature of this method for catching fish, including capture
of nontargeted species and juveniles or undersized fish. However, it was
not until the invention of the steam trawler in the 1900s that bottom trawling and the use of mobile fishing gear increased drastically in the size and
weight of the towed gear, as well as in the depths and areas of the continental shelf that could be reached (German 1984; Jones 1992). The 1950s saw
the introduction of synthetic fishing nets (Klust 1982), which do not break
as easily when snagged and also are dangers to marine life as they are not
biodegradable. These stronger nets thus allowed for higher-powered vessels and deeper trawling. While the size and expense of both the trawling
vessels and gear keep many fishermen in waters shallower than 1,000 meters (3,280 feet), overfishing and environmental degradation by this activity
have forced fishermen to look for new fishing grounds, thus expanding the
depths that can be reached by trawls to over 1,800 m (5,905 feet; Watling
and Norse 1998). Following a period of increasing concern in the 1990s
(Collie et al. 2000), bottom trawl fishing is now a heavily regulated activity in many coastal waters, and its effects on the benthic ecosystem are the
topic of much research. However, much more work in managing benthic
fisheries is ongoing in the form of federal regulations, restrictions in the
case of international waters, and the delineation of marine protected areas
(e.g., Arceo et al. 2013; Williams et al. 2011).

The first bottom trawls developed out of dredging technology and were
initially used by sailing ships before the invention of the steam trawl (NRC
2002). The nets are generally funnel shaped, with the top section equipped
with floats and the bottom with weights. The bottoms of the nets can sometimes be outfitted with rubber or steel rollers, or rockhoppers, to roll over

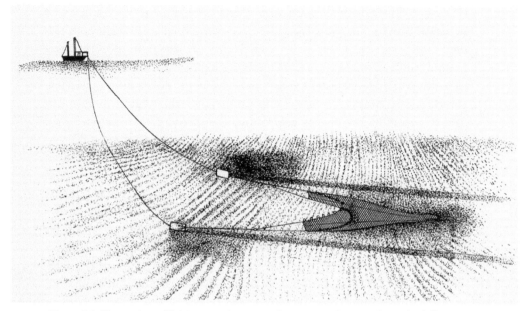

Figure 8.1. Illustration of fishing vessel towing a bottom trawl across the seabed (from DeAlteris et al. 1999; used with permission).

obstacles on the seabed, or with tickler chains, which drag into the sediment to draw fish from the sediment (NRC 2002; Watling and Norse 1998). The most common demersal mobile fishing gear in use today is the otter trawl (fig. 8.1). The motion of the vessel spreads apart a pair of otter boards, or doors, which weigh down the net and hold it open (NRC 2002; Watling and Norse 1998). Otter trawls were invented in the 1880s when fishermen wanted to hold their nets open without the rigid beam of the earlier beam trawler. Representing another common type of towed bottom fishing gear are dredges used for shellfish; these plow through the sediment with steel frames and metal ring bags, which carve deeper furrows into the seabed that intentionally dig up the sediment surface to dig out shellfish (Watling and Norse 1998). Most commonly for trawl gear, however, it is the otter doors and weighted bottom of the net opening that damage the seabed to the greatest extent.

These types of mobile fishing gear cause damage to the seabed in two ways: they carve furrows in the sediment with the otter doors or dredges, and they smooth over features on the seafloor with the weights, tickler chains, and rollers. Early observations of the size and morphology of trawl scars on the seabed were conducted from a submersible in the early 1970s

(Caddy 1973). Different fishing gear affects the seabed to varying extents depending on the weight of the gear, speed of the vessel, and seafloor lithology (DeAlteris et al. 1999; Ivanovic et al. 2011; O'Neill et al. 2009). Experimental studies by DeAlteris and colleagues have shown that trawl damage to rocky or sandy substrates in shallow, high-energy environments was less drastic and recovery time was almost immediate, while muddy bottoms in deeper waters in low-energy environments suffered greater damage with slow recovery. Substrate lithology is the primary factor in the duration of scars on the seabed (DeAlteris et al. 1999; Jones 1992; NRC 2002); trawl scars in high-energy environments have been shown to last between 2 and 7 months (Brylinsky et al. 1994), while scars in low-energy environments with low sedimentation are suggested to last for decades or longer (Brennan et al. 2012; Caddy 1973; Friedlander et al. 1999). In areas with high levels of trawl activity, scars discernible in side-scan sonar data appear to overprint each other. Older scars are slowly erased by sediment infilling, and new ones are scraped over, sometimes in the same direction, often in multiple directions. These marks show the intensity of trawling in a given area (Brennan et al. 2012; DeAlteris et al. 1999; Humborstad et al. 2004; Smith et al. 2003).

The rate at which trawl scars are erased by sedimentation or currents is different than the recovery time for the benthic ecosystem, which is more difficult to quantify. Much recent research has been conducted on the ecosystem response and recovery to trawl damage (de Juan and Demestre 2012; Kaiser et al. 2006; Rooper et al. 2011; Strain et al. 2012). As this type of research becomes more widespread, long-term studies are possible with the intent of repeated monitoring of communities to see how and at what rate they recover (Strain et al. 2012). Importantly, but perhaps not surprisingly, Strain and colleagues (2012) note that the conservation area off Ireland where they monitored the ecosystem changed to an alternative state due to trawling, where slow-moving or sessile organisms were replaced by highly mobile scavengers or predators due to the effects of repeated trawling. An additional effect is the lowering of the biomass and species populations in trawled areas where fishing catches heavily outweigh recovery of target species (see review by Jones 1992).

The scraping of the seabed surface to catch benthic organisms also causes damage by smoothing over features, increasing the roughness of the seabed but decreasing seabed complexity (Brennan et al. 2012; Humborstad et al. 2004). Bottom trawling crushes, buries, and exposes benthic organisms and structures on the seabed in way that has been likened to forest clear-cutting (Watling and Norse 1998). Deep-sea trawling today reworks continental shelf regions, modifying the submarine landscape by leveling it. A recent study likens this effect more to the disappearance of topography due to the spread of arable farmland than to forest clear-cutting (Puig et al. 2012). The threat to archaeological sites is clear, since shipwrecks on the modern submarine landscape are topographical features and are thus as susceptible as natural topography to damage by towed trawl gear (Brennan et al. 2012). Shipwrecks often act as artificial reefs by providing hiding places for fish, especially juveniles. The removal of such features threatens not only the cultural sites but also the ecosystem benefits provided by these habitats (Watling and Norse 1998; Krumholz and Brennan 2015). Therefore environmental management concerns for regulating bottom trawling should also take into consideration the presence and protection of archaeological sites in the area.

TRAWL DAMAGE TO SHIPWRECKS

The effects of trawl fishing on underwater cultural heritage (UCH) are difficult to quantify since these events are rarely observed directly and are difficult to measure indirectly. Artifacts such as amphoras, statues, wooden beams, and cannon have been dragged to the surface by fishing gear since the eighteenth century, and this occurrence is still commonplace today (Beltrame and Gaddi 2002; Kingsley 2012; Sakellariou et al. 2007). Trawls operate over large areas before hauling up their gear, so pinpointing the locations of trawled wrecks is difficult, especially in waters below diving depth. The damage done to wreck sites is dependent on a large number of factors that determine the extent to which a particular wreck is damaged. These include the prominence of the wreck on the seabed, sedimentation, amount of the hull preserved, and location near rocks or other features that may hinder trawling in that isolated area. Two wrecks sited near to each other can be trawled to very different degrees for such reasons. The type and amount of damage also depends on the type of gear used, power of the trawling vessel, and bathymetry of the surrounding area (Atkinson 2012).

A good overview of the variety of shipwreck sites that have had trawl damage observed and the types of damage is provided by Atkinson (2012). Trawls damage different types of shipwrecks differently. Ancient shipwrecks tend to consist of ship-shaped, convex piles of amphoras and other elements of the ship's cargo, the wooden structure of the ship having disintegrated around it. These sites present a very different topographical

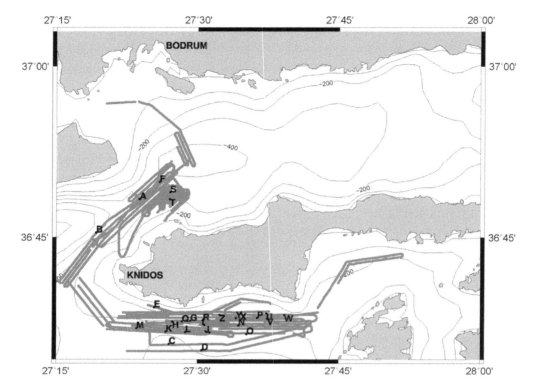

Figure 8.2. Map of Turkey highlighting the Bodrum and Datça peninsulas, and showing side-scan sonar coverage and ancient shipwreck locations (adapted from Brennan et al. 2012).

obstacle to towed trawl gear than do iron or steel hulls standing proud on the seabed. Trawls damage ancient wrecks either by dragging artifacts off-site or by breaking the ceramic artifacts; the weighted net either runs over them or the otter doors carve their way through. Early observations of trawl scars in deep water were made during expeditions to Skerki Bank, although no damage appeared to have been inflicted on the wrecks found there, except for some possible scattering of artifacts (Ballard et al. 2000; Foley 2008; Oleson and Adams 1997).

Direct observations of damage on ancient wreck sites are limited for wrecks in deep water, as trawling in this geographic region is generally prohibited nearshore due to restrictions on bottom trawling close to shore; for example, within 2.5 kilometers (1.55 miles) of Turkish coasts (KKGM 2006). Therefore such sites have only been investigated recently. Using side-scan sonar, Sakellariou et al. (2007) documented extensive trawl scarring in the Aegean Sea and identified a number of wrecks in the path of the trawl scars. Explorations by the RPM Nautical Foundation (Royal 2008, 2009, 2010) off Marmaris in southwestern Turkey, in the Adriatic Sea, and off Sicily noted substantial artifacts scattered and broken by drag nets, which scraped the tops off the amphora pile wreck sites. A more direct study of the damage trawls have inflicted on ancient wreck sites was conducted by the author (Brennan et al. 2012). Sixteen wrecks were located and examined off the Bodrum and Datça peninsulas in Turkey (fig. 8.2), some showing little evidence of trawl damage and others exhibiting severe damage, such as the Marmaris B wreck (fig. 8.3) (Brennan et al. 2012). This study also attempted to quantify the damage to these sites, as discussed later in this chapter.

More recent historic shipwrecks are typically greater obstacles to towed fishing gear, and fishermen often lose nets to them. The result of trawl encounters with wreck sites is often a tangle of nets and weights over sections of the site. This is very hazardous terrain for operations involving a diver, Remotely Operated Vehicle (ROV), or submersible while investigating the wrecks. Depending on the size, weight, and speed of the towed gear, trawls can also cause severe damage to the site itself and the integrity of the wreck structure. A few hits by trawl gear would likely cause nets to be entangled, but repeated strikes would begin to compromise the structure of the ship (Foley 2008). As in the case of ancient shipwrecks, discussions of the effects of trawling are a recent effort. Commonly, the presence of trawl nets entangled on a wreck site or of damage from trawling is mentioned as part of a site description, but there is no efforts to describe, characterize, or

Figure 8.3. Image of Marmaris B shipwreck site.

quantify the effects (Flecker 2002). Other studies discuss the damage and assess the impact of trawls but offer little comparison for how extensive the trawling damage is versus other processes or other sites (Beltrame and Gaddi 2002; Nœvstad 2007). More recent studies have focused on a series of wrecks that have been impacted by trawling and provide a more detailed examination of the damage to the sites, while also discussing options for site preservation.

A deep-water survey in the Gulf of Mexico examined six World War II shipwrecks. Three of these exhibited extensive damage from trawls, while the others, lying in waters deeper than 1,200 m (3,937 feet) where trawling is not practiced, were unthreatened (Church et al. 2009). The three tankers in depths shallower than 600 m (1,968 feet) exhibited numerous nets ensnared on parts of the wrecks, sections missing from the superstructures and pilothouses, and general damage to the hulls' integrity. Similarly, Marx (2010) shows that nearly every wreck in the Stellwagen Bank National Marine Sanctuary has been impacted by trawl gear, including the removal of upper structures and net entanglements. In this marine sanctuary, trawling is one of the few destructive activities still allowed, as it is considered incidental damage inflicted by approved activities (U.S. Department of Commerce 2010). On the U.S. mid-Atlantic outer continental shelf, bottom fishermen employ large metal scallop and clam dredges as well as trawl nets. Steinmetz's (2010) thesis on fishing gear derelicts and wreck damage includes SCUBA diver logs and observations from 52 shipwreck sites. The study documented entangled nets and/or scallop dredges on more than half of the sites. Her observations and discussions with fishermen showed that dredges can be snagged and lost on steel-hulled shipwrecks, but can easily rip through wooden wrecks, with no noticeable resistance to the dredging vessel. This work identified three modes of site formation by mobile fishing gear: deposition of gear on wreck sites, scrambling of artifacts and components of the wreck site, and extraction of artifacts and parts of the wreck by physically removing them by the force of the impact (Steinmetz 2010). This study also discusses the significant economic loss shipwrecks pose to operators' gear and proposes a joint effort between fishermen and archaeologists to minimize both cultural and financial loss.

The most comprehensive assessment of trawl damage to historic wrecks was performed by Kingsley (2010; 2012), who looked at 267 wrecks located in the English Channel. A total of 112 of the studied wrecks exhibited impacts from fishing gear, ranging in severity from tangled nets to furrows carved through wreck sites by dredges. The results of this study were used to make a justification of commercial salvage operations for profit. However, the collected data from Kingsley's work represent a large body of documented trawl damage to wreck sites. The study used Vessel Monitoring satellite data (VMS) aboard commercial fishing vessels to demonstrate that many shipwreck sites are located within frequently trawled territory. The HMS *Victory* wreck, one of the more significant sites in this survey, lies within an area of high activity (Kingsley 2010). The site itself has trawl and dredge scars nearby, and nets and cables litter the wreck. Cannon and other artifacts have been dragged off-site by trawl gear passes. Other sites in the English Channel have ceramic artifacts smashed and scattered across the wreck site and surrounding seabed, as is commonly observed for ancient wrecks. Kingsley (2010) concludes that until recently, trawl damage has been neglected by the archaeological community as a major cause of site destabilization, destruction, and loss of knowledge. Unlike ecosystems, this loss of knowledge can never be recovered.

QUANTIFICATION OF TRAWL DAMAGE

Observing the effects of bottom trawling on shipwreck sites is very different from understanding them. The latter requires documentation of the extent and intensity of trawling activities in a given area, both spatially and temporally, and ideally repeated monitoring of sites to assess the degree to which damage is occurring—a challenge for sites in deep water. The first step in compiling a broader understanding of the threat of trawling to underwater cultural heritage is ocean exploration and finding and documenting sites in deep water that are threatened. Quantifying the damage seen at any given shipwreck site is the second step. This is complicated by a variety of factors, including time, sedimentation, and the initial damage inflicted on the ship itself as a result of wrecking; this kind of damage may be difficult to distinguish from more recent damage to the ship's integrity caused by trawling. Additionally, wrecks in shallower waters, <100 m (328 feet), can be susceptible to damage from the effects of hurricanes and storm surges. Atkinson (2012) notes the difficulty that arises from the slow erasure of trawl scars over time around wreck sites, leaving little evidence of past trawling activity other than the damage to the wreck itself.

Effectively quantifying the trawl damage on shipwreck sites as well as the threat and potential for damage in a given area requires two stages. The first is to gauge the extent and intensity of trawling in the area; the second is to assess the actual damage to wreck sites themselves. Benthic ecology

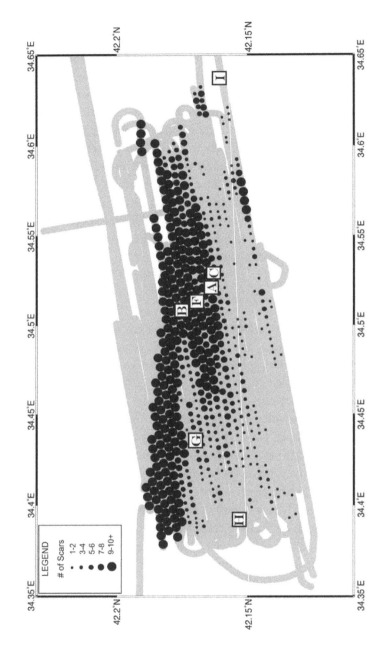

Figure 8.4. Trawl intensity map for survey area off Sinop, Turkey; letters show the locations of shipwrecks (from Brennan et al. 2013a).

studies have used side-scan sonar to document trawl intensity (DeAlteris et al. 1999; Humborstad et al. 2004; Smith et al. 2003), and a similar approach was applied to sonar data from the Aegean and Black Seas for areas in which a large number of shipwrecks were found (Brennan et al. 2012; 2013). Resulting intensity maps show the number of trawl scars visible on the seabed as differently sized points in relation to where shipwreck sites were found, for example off Sinop, Turkey in the Black Sea (fig. 8.4). Wrecks in areas of higher trawl intensities (Sinop A, B, C, and F) are much more heavily damaged than those in areas with few scars (Sinop G, H, and I). This, however, is only a measure of recent trawl activity, as is the VMS satellite data analysis by Kingsley (2010), but it provides a good measure for determining which wreck sites are more threatened by fishing activities and possible locales that need to be protected.

Damage to the wreck sites by trawls is the second part of this characterization, which is a direct measure of the impacts on each wreck. Quantifying damage to steel- or wooden-hulled historic wrecks is problematic, as differentiating between damage to the hull and superstructure caused by the act of wrecking and subsequent damage caused by trawls is difficult. In many cases entangled fishing nets, evidence of artifacts dragged off-site, and the presence of trawls scars nearby inform the researcher that a wreck was damaged by anthropogenic agents. Kingsley (2012) recognizes eight classes of damage but does not quantify them. Quantification of trawl damage to ancient shipwreck sites in the Aegean Sea (Brennan et al. 2012) was accomplished by determining a percentage of the visible surface artifacts that are broken at each wreck site. This step applies only to amphora wrecks, as this is not effective for some of the smaller sites consisting of ballast stones and a handful of artifacts, such as several that were discovered off Knidos, Turkey. Counts of broken and unbroken artifacts were made with photomosaics of each amphora wreck. Other ancient shipwrecks that were untrawled due to their location in depths below the reach of towed gear or near the anoxic waters of the Black Sea were included as controls in this study. Analysis of these wrecks indicated that <5% of broken artifacts should be expected from the wrecking event itself, and anything more may be attributed to trawling (Brennan et al. 2012).

Figure 8.5 shows a close-in look at the area southeast of Knidos, where numerous shipwrecks were located and documented by Nautilus expeditions from 2009–2012. A total of 36 ancient shipwrecks were located off the coasts of Bodrum, Knidos, and Marmaris, 26 of them around the headland of Knidos, and 21 within this area to the southeast, along the approach to

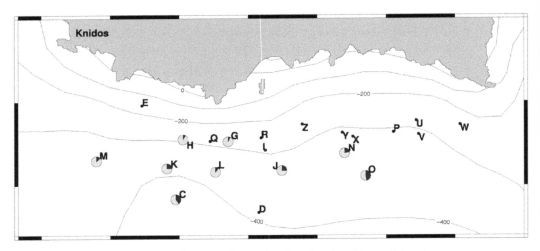

Figure 8.5. Close-in view of area southeast of Knidos showing shipwreck locations. Pie graphs represent in black the percentage of broken artifacts on some of the wrecks (adapted from Brennan et al. 2012).

the ancient haven (Brennan and Ballard 2013). Wrecks are represented in this figure by a point and associated Knidos wreck letter. The nine where frequency of broken artifacts could be quantified have the percentages illustrated with pie graphs. These wrecks show greater damage with distance from the coast of Turkey. This was published by Brennan and colleagues (2012), but the figures here include the additional wrecks documented in 2011 and 2012. Within 2.5 km (~1.6 miles) of the coastline, trawling is prohibited. Figure 8.6 plots the broken artifact percentages against distance from the coast, illustrating a step function. The three wrecks within the first 4 km (~2.5 miles) show a very low amount of damage, <10%, which is little more than that expected from the sinking event. The other six wrecks exhibit a much steeper trend with increasing distance from the coast, culminating with Knidos O, which has nearly half its artifacts broken and is over 7 km (~4.3 miles) from shore. This relationship was shown by Brennan et al. (2012) for just a few wrecks, but the inclusion of additional sites and data strengthens the case. The data statistically support the hypothesis that damage rate is at or near the level indicative of no trawling damage at wrecks within or immediately adjacent to the 2.5 km (~1.6 miles) reserve boundary and increase linearly from there. This illustrates that trawlers adhere to the restriction zone and trawl more heavily farther from the coast, in this way suggesting that other enforced restrictions could help preserve these wreck sites.

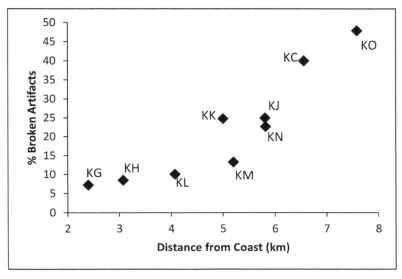

Figure 8.6. Bivariate plot showing percentage of broken artifacts and distance from shore (adapted from Brennan et al. 2012).

The relationship of trawl damage to ancient wreck sites with distance from shore is well illustrated by the group of wrecks southeast of Knidos because they are located on a relatively flat, featureless seabed, where trawling along the isobaths is easy. Areas of steeper topography, such as to the west and north of Knidos, where there are rocky slumps from the peninsula and large ridges of rock, complicate the submarine landscape and are generally avoided by trawlers. This is represented by the small amounts of damage visible on the Knidos B and F wreck sites (fig. 8.2) despite their location away from the coast. Trawl intensity is more varied in this area north of Knidos, and some wrecks are more affected than others. For example, Knidos S (fig. 8.7) is one of the most heavily damaged wreck sites, with nearly 65% of its artifacts broken, but Knidos F (fig. 8.8) and T, both within a few kilometers of S, are virtually undamaged. Knidos S, however, lies at the western edge of the Gulf of Gokova in flatter, more easily trawled terrain, while F and T are just outside, in areas of steeper slopes. This illustrates the importance of exploration and comprehensive surveys of potentially threatened areas to locate and document what UCH is there, and then to quantify the damage to sites in order to understand how best to manage and protect them.

While quantifying the damage to ancient shipwreck sites is a step forward, it does not allow for an evaluation of the threat posed by trawling

Figure 8.7. Image of Knidos S shipwreck site.

Figure 8.8. Image of Knidos F shipwreck site.

to the sites, as we lack an understanding of change over time, which will differ for every wreck site. Repeated surveys of wreck sites over time will greatly aid our understanding of the threat. *Nautilus* has returned to many of the wrecks off Knidos in subsequent years following their discovery, and little additional damage was observed. This is not the case, however, in the Black Sea. This suggests a more imminent, although no more serious, threat to wrecks in the coastal deep waters of the Turkish Black Sea coast. There are few areas suitable for trawling in the Black Sea, as the waters below ~150 m (492 feet) depth become anoxic (and therefore support no fish), but this makes the coastal areas more heavily trawled. The region is, in fact, one of Turkey's most important fishing grounds (Knudsen et al. 2010). Surveys conducted during *Nautilus* expeditions examined two wreck sites that showed evidence for substantial trawl damage during the intervening time since the sites' discovery. Sinop A is a Byzantine wreck found in 2000 and investigated in 2003 (Ward and Ballard 2004). In 2011 *Nautilus* returned to the site. Features noted in 2003, such as a pile of amphora that appeared to be in a stacked orientation, were gone, and trawl scars were evident throughout the site and seabed (Brennan et al. 2013). While no photomosaic was available from 2003 for comparison, a wreck found off Ereğli, Turkey, in 2011 was mapped a second time in 2012. Ereğli E was already a heavily damaged site in 2011, with 68% of its artifacts broken. Wooden timbers and what were identified as human bones had been upended by trawls and ripped to the surface of the seabed. A new photomosaic made upon returning in 2012 shows that eleven months later, nearly every artifact and identifiable feature had been moved or broken or was missing (Brennan and Ballard 2013). This site illustrates the importance of exploration and repeated surveys and also exemplifies the urgent need for management and protection of shipwreck sites in trawled waters.

Protecting Sites: Trawling Management

Published through Wreck Watch International's website, Kingsley's (2012) *Out of Sight, Out of Mind?* makes the point that trawl damage to shipwrecks is easy to ignore or underestimate because these threatened sites are not readily visible the way plowed rainforests or bulldozed Maya temples are. Kingsley (2012) takes a fairly pessimistic view on the preservation of shipwrecks in situ and the "moral maze" in which marine archaeology apparently wanders today. Additionally, he calls the recommendations for in situ preservation put forth by the United Nations Educational, Scientific and Cultural Organization (UNESCO) a poor all-encompassing managerial policy (Kingsley 2010). However, the UNESCO Annex does not claim in situ preservation as an all-encompassing policy but rather as the first option (Maarleveld 2011; UNESCO 2001). There may be cases when excavation of a shipwreck site threatened by trawling is warranted (Delgado 2009). However, it is this author's belief that trawling should not be used as a justification for commercial salvage of shipwrecks (Kingsley 2010; see Delgado 2010; Greene et al. 2011).

There are many factors to take into consideration when attempting to understand the threat of trawl fishing, including what UCH resources exist in a given area and how they are threatened. There are no easy answers. The reality of the time and expense of excavation and conservation, especially for deep-water sites, is harsh in today's financial climate. It must be recognized that the fishing industry is not a static entity with which to contend. Modern fishing activities are under intense pressure by fisheries biologists, marine ecologists, and environmentalists to limit and regulate trawl fishery damage to the benthic ecosystem and to curtail illegal trawling (Arceo et al. 2013; Cho 2012; Norse et al. 2012). Kingsley (2012:25) states: "To demand that the industry must tiptoe around the sunken past is a Utopian ideal that has no chance of becoming a reality." Yet archaeologists are not the only group fighting against trawling. As described earlier in this chapter, this method of scraping organisms off the seabed is highly destructive, raising ecological, biogeochemical, sedimentary, and archaeological concerns. There is much discussion at many governmental levels concerning restrictions on this activity, and there is every reason for underwater archaeologists to be at the table. Among the bodies that need to continue taking an active role, and making the argument that UCH is among the important elements to take into consideration when proposing restrictions on trawling, are organizations like UNESCO; the International Committee on the Underwater Heritage, an arm of the International Council on Monuments and Sites (ICOMOS); and the National Marine Sanctuaries division of the National Oceanic and Atmospheric Administration (NOAA).

Shipwrecks should not be viewed strictly within a historical or archaeological framework disconnected from the marine environment in which they lie (Brennan and Ballard 2014). Shipwreck sites come into equilibrium with the marine environment, which includes their position on the seabed as rocky substrates and their role as artificial reefs that attract fish, especially juveniles, as they provide hiding places and protection (Church et al. 2009; Watling and Norse 1998). Continued research by the author on the Knidos shipwrecks shows that lightly trawled ancient wrecks that still exhibit relief on the seabed have a higher fish population and biomass than heavily trawled wreck sites with scattered, broken artifacts and little relief remaining on the seabed, such as Marmaris B (fig. 8.3; Krumholz and Brennan 2015). If such sites are protected from trawling, especially in an area with numerous sites like south of Knidos, it could actually increase the fisheries and help the ecosystem and targeted species recover through a mechanism referred to as "spillover." There have been numerous studies documenting increases in fish populations and biomass within Marine Protected Areas (MPAs). Over time the increased density of individuals within a protected area causes increased competition for resources such as food and shelter, and fish tend to migrate outward, to areas outside the reserve. These mechanisms, while gradual, cause a net movement of individuals from MPAs into fished territory (Arceo et al. 2013; Forcada et al. 2009; Harmelin-Vivien et al. 2008; Molloy et al. 2009; Polunin and Roberts 1993).

Trawling and the use of other mobile fishing gear is one of the greatest anthropogenic threats to underwater cultural heritage. However, the underwater archaeology community is decades behind benthic ecologists and fisheries management in regulating these activities. The first step in such regulations is exploration and documenting what sites are out there and where, which can help determine what action to take. Areas of major maritime activity, such as approaches to historical harbors like Boston (represented by Stellwagen Bank sanctuary) and Knidos, Turkey, are those that would benefit most from trawl restrictions. The Stellwagen Bank sanctuary aims to preserve sites in situ, managing cultural resources while facilitating public and private use of the resource (U.S. Department of Commerce 2010). However, fishing operations, including trawling and dredging, are still allowed and the damaging effects are well documented by return visits to particular wreck sites, making the goal of in situ preservation difficult.

Enforcement of restrictions on the use of mobile fishing gear also has to contend with the realities of fishing lobbyists and the industry relying on these methods for their livelihood while providing for the large demand for fish on today's market. Preservation and protection of UCH faces an uphill battle in such a political environment. However, it is important to note that efforts to protect the UCH do not operate in isolation. These efforts can be combined with ongoing and parallel efforts to protect the marine ecosystem and improve fisheries. Restricting or banning mobile fishing gear in areas of high cultural importance such as those mentioned can both protect the multitude of sites in the area and improve the ecosystem and fishery through spillover by allowing species to take shelter among the artificial reefs of the wreck structures. Protecting wrecks within the confines of a reserve is a logical step that can maximize the impact of a protected area while minimizing its overall size and therefore the impact on the sustainable use of the ecosystem (e.g., fishing, boating, shipping, etc.). Trawling is being restricted in many coastal areas for the purposes of ecological recovery and fisheries management (Arceo et al. 2013), and including archaeologists and adding UCH to the discussions is a logical, and necessary, step to take.

Acknowledgments

The author wishes to thank Robert Ballard, Dan Davis, Joseph DeAlteris, James Delgado, Jason Krumholz, Chris Roman, Clara Smart, and Joyce Steinmetz for their help with this research and in preparing this manuscript.

References Cited

Arceo, Hazel O., Bertrand Cazalet, Porfirio M. Alino, Luisa Mangialajo, and Patrice Francour
2013   Moving Beyond a Top-Down Fisheries Management Approach in the Northwestern Mediterranean: Some Lessons from the Philippines. *Marine Policy* 39:29–42.
Atkinson, Christopher Michael
2012   *Impacts of Bottom Trawling on Underwater Cultural Heritage.* Master's thesis, Texas A&M University, College Station.
Ballard, R. D., A. M. McCann, D. Yoerger, L. Whitcomb, D. Mindell, J. Oleson, H. Singh, B. Foley, J. Adams, D. Piechota, and C. Giangrande
2000   The Discovery of Ancient History in the Deep Sea Using Advanced Deep Submergence Technology. *Deep-Sea Research I* 47:1591–1620.
Beltrame, C., and D. Gaddi
2002   Report on the First Research Campaign on the Napoleonic Brick, *Mercure*, Wrecked off Lignano, Udine, Italy in 1812. *International Journal of Nautical Archaeology* 31:60–73.
Brennan, M. L., R. D. Ballard, K. L. Croff Bell, and D. Piechota
2011   Archaeological Oceanography and Environmental Characterization of Shipwrecks in the Black Sea. In *Geology and Geoarchaeology of the Black Sea Region: Beyond the Flood Hypothesis*, edited by I. Buynevich, V. Yanko-Hombach, A. Gilbert, and R. E. Martin, pp. 179–188. Geological Society of America Special Paper 473.
Brennan, Michael L., Robert D. Ballard, Chris Roman, Katherine L. Croff Bell, Bridget Buxton, Dwight F. Coleman, Gabrielle Inglis, Orkan Koyagasioglu, and Tufan Turanli
2012   Evaluation of the Modern Submarine Landscape off Southwestern Turkey through the Documentation of Ancient Shipwreck Sites. *Continental Shelf Research* 43:55–70.
Brennan, Michael L., Dan Davis, Chris Roman, Ilya Buynevich, Alexis Catsambis, Meko Kofahl, Derya Ürkmez, J. Ian Vaughn, Maureen Merrigan, and Muhammet Duman
2013   Ocean Dynamics and Anthropogenic Impacts along the Southern Black Sea Shelf

Examined by the Preservation of Premodern Shipwrecks. *Continental Shelf Research* 53:89–101.

Brennan, Michael L., and Robert D. Ballard

2013   Deep-Water Ancient Shipwrecks of the Mediterranean, Aegean, and Black Seas: 1988–2012. In *New Frontiers in Ocean Exploration: The E/V Nautilus 2012 Field Season*, edited by K.L.C. Bell and M. L. Brennan, pp. 22–25. *Oceanography* 26(1:supplement).

2014   Archaeological Oceanography. In *Encyclopedia of Natural Resources*.

Brylinsky, M., J. Gibson, and D. C. Gordon

1994   Impacts of Flounder Trawls on the Intertidal Habitat and Community of the Minas Basin, Bay of Fundy. *Canadian Journal of Fisheries and Aquatic Sciences* 51:650–661.

Caddy, J. F.

1973   Underwater Observations on Tracks of Dredges and Trawls and Some Effects of Dredging on Scallop Ground. *Journal of the Fisheries Research Board of Canada* 30(2):173–180.

Cho, Dong-Oh

2012   Eliminating Illegal Bottom Trawl Fishing in the Coastal Waters of Korea. *Marine Policy* 36:321–326.

Church, Robert A., Daniel J. Warren, and Jack B. Irion

2009   Analysis of Deepwater Shipwrecks in the Gulf of Mexico: Artificial Reef Effect of Six World War II Shipwrecks. *Oceanography* 22(2):50–63.

Collie, J. S., G. A. Escanerol, and P. C. Valentine

2000   Photographic Evaluation of the Impacts of Bottom Fishing on Benthic Epifauna. *ICES Journal of Marine Science* 57:987–1001.

DeAlteris, J., L. Skrobe, and C. Lipsky

1999   The Significance of Seabed Disturbance by Mobile Fishing Gear Relative to Natural Processes: A Case Study in Narragansett Bay, Rhode Island. *American Fisheries Society Symposium* 22:224–237.

Delgado, James P.

2009   Inside INA: A Letter from the President. *INA Quarterly* 36(3):3.

2010   The Trouble with Treasure. *Naval History* 24:18–25.

de Juan, S., and M. Demestre

2012   A Trawl Disturbance Indicator to Quantify Large Scale Fishing Impact on Benthic Ecosystems. *Ecological Indicators* 18:183–190.

Flecker, Michael

2002   The Ethics, Politics, and Realities of Maritime Archaeology in Southeast Asia. *International Journal of Nautical Archaeology* 31:12–24.

Foley, B.

2008   Archaeology in Deep Water: Impact of Fishing on Shipwrecks. Electronic document, http://www.whoi.edu/sbl/liteSite.do?litesiteid=2740&articleId=4965, accessed December 2009.

Forcada, Aitor, Carlos Valle, Patrick Bonhomme, Geraldine Criquet, Gwenael Cadiou, Philippe Lenfant, and Jose L. Sanchez-Lizaso

2009   Effects of Habitat Spillover from Marine Protected Areas to Artisanal Fisheries. *Marine Ecology Progress Series* 379:197–211.

Friedlander, A. M., G. W. Boehlert, M. E. Field, J. E. Mason, J. V. Gardner, and P. Dartnell
1999   Sidescan-Sonar Mapping of Benthic Trawl Marks on the Shelf and Slope off Eureka, California. *Fishery Bulletin* 97:786–801.

German, Andrew W.
1984   Otter Trawling Comes to America: The Bay State Fishing Company 1905–1938. *American Neptune* 44(2):117–127.

Greene, E. S., J. Leidwanger, R. M. Leventhal, and B. I. Daniels
2011   *Mare nostrum?* Ethics and Archaeology in Mediterranean Waters. *American Journal of Archaeology* 115:311–319.

Harmelin-Vivien, Mireille, Laurence Le Direach, Just Bayle-Sempere, Eric Charbonnel, Jose Antonio Garcia-Charton, Denis Ody, Angel Perez-Ruzafa, Olga Renones, Pablo Sanchez-Jerez, and Carlos Valle
2008   Gradients of Abundance and Biomass Across Reserve Boundaries in Six Mediterranean Marine Protected Areas: Evidence of Fish Spillover? *Biological Conservation* 141:1829–1839.

Humborstad, O. B., L. Nottestad, S. Lokkeborg, and H. T. Rapp
2004   RoxAnn Bottom Classification System, Sidescan Sonar and Video-Sledge: Spatial Resolution and Their Use in Assessing Trawling Impacts. *ICES Journal of Marine Science* 61:53–63.

Ivanovic, Ana, Richard D. Neilson, and Finbarr G. O'Neill
2011   Modelling the Physical Impact of Trawl Components on the Seabed and Comparison with Sea Trials. *Ocean Engineering* 38:925–933.

Jones, J. B.
1992   Environmental Impact of Trawling on the Seabed: A Review. *New Zealand Journal of Marine and Freshwater Research* 26:59–67.

Kaiser, M. J., K. R. Clarke, H. Hinz, M.C.V. Austen, P. J. Somerfield, and I. Karakassis
2006   Global Analysis of Response and Recovery of Benthic Biota to Fishing. *Marine Ecology Progress Series* 311:1–14.

Kingsley, Sean A.
2010   Deep-Sea Fishing Impacts on the Shipwrecks of the English Channel and Western Approaches. In *Oceans Odyssey: Deep-Sea Shipwrecks in the English Channel, Straits of Gibraltar, and Atlantic Ocean,* edited by Greg Stemm and Sean Kingsley, pp. 191–233. Oxbow Books, Oxford.
2012   *Out of Sight, Out of Mind? Fishing and Shipwrecked Heritage.* Wreck Watch International, London.

Klust, Gerhard
1982   *Netting Materials for Fishing Gear.* FAO Fishing Manuals. Fishing News Books, Surrey, U.K.

Knudsen, Stale, Mustafa Zengin, and Mahmut Hakan Kocak
2010   Identifying Drivers for Fishing Pressure: A Multidisciplinary Study of Trawl and Sea Snail Fisheries in Samsun, Black Sea Coast of Turkey. *Ocean and Coastal Management* 53:252–269.

Koruma ve Kontrol Genel Müdürlüğü (KKGM)

2006   Circular no. 37/1 of 2006–2008 Fishing Year Regulating Commercial Fishing in Seas and Inland Waters. Electronic document, http://www.kkgm.gov.tr/regulation/circular/37-1.html, accessed December, 2009.

Krumholz, Jason, and Michael L. Brennan

2015   Fishing for Common Ground: Investigations of the Impact of Trawling on Ancient Shipwreck Sites Uncovers a Potential for Management Synergy. In *Marine Policy* 61:127–133.

Maarleveld, Thijs J.

2011   Open Letter to Dr. Sean Kingsley, Wreck Watch International, Regarding his Questionnaire on In Situ Preservation. *Journal of Maritime Archaeology* 6(2):107–111.

March, Edgar J.

1953   *Sailing Trawlers: The Story of Deep-Sea Fishing with Long Line and Trawl.* David and Charles, Camden, Maine.

Marx, Deborah

2010   Fishing Threatens Historic Shipwrecks. *INA Quarterly* 36(4):8.

Molloy, Philip P., Ian B. McLean, and Isabelle M. Cote

2009   Effects of Marine Reserve Age on Fish Populations: A Global Meta-analysis. *Journal of Applied Ecology* 46:743–751.

National Research Council (NRC)

2002   *Effects of Trawling* and *Dredging on Seafloor Habitat.* National Academy Press, Washington, D.C.

Nœvstad, Dag

2007   Cultural Heritage in Arctic Waters. In *Bottom Trawling and Scallop Dredging in the Arctic: Impacts of Fishing on Non-target Species, Vulnerable Habitats and Cultural Heritage,* edited by Elena Guijarro Garcia, pp. 287–335. Nordic Council of Ministers, Copenhagen.

Norse, Elliott A., Sandra Brooke, William W. L. Cheung, Malcolm R. Clark, Ivar Ekeland, Rainer Froese, Kristina M. Gjerde, Richard L. Haedrich, Selina S. Heppell, Telmo Morato, Lance E. Morgan, Daniel Pauly, Rashid Sumaila, and Reg Watson

2012   Sustainability of Deep-Sea Fisheries. *Marine Policy* 36:307–320.

Oleson, J. P., and J. Adams

1997   Formation, Survey, and Sampling of the Wreck Sites. In *Deep-Water Shipwrecks off Skerki Bank: The 1997 Survey,* edited by A. M. McCann and J. P. Oleson. *Journal of Roman Archaeology* Supplementary Series no. 58.

O'Neill, F. G., K. Summerbell, and M. Breen

2009   An Underwater Laser Stripe Seabed Profiler to Measure the Physical Impact of Towed Gear Components on the Seabed. *Fisheries Research* 99:234–238.

Polunin, N.V.C., and C. M. Roberts

1993   Greater Biomass and Value of Target Coral-Reef Fishes in Two Small Caribbean Marine Reserves. *Marine Ecology Progress Series* 100:167–176.

Puig, Pere, Miquel Canals, Joan B. Company, Jacobo Martin, David Amblas, Galderic Lastras, Albert Palanques, and Antoni M. Calafat

2012   Ploughing the Deep Sea Floor. *Nature* 489:286–289.

Rooper, Christopher N., Mark E. Wilkins, Craig S. Rose, and Catherine Coon
2011   Modeling the Impacts of Bottom Trawling and the Subsequent Recovery Rates of Sponges and Corals in the Aleutian Islands, Alaska. *Continental Shelf Research* 31:1827–1834.

Royal, Jeffrey G.
2008   Description and Analysis of Finds from the 2006 Turkish Coastal Survey: Marmaris and Bodrum. *International Journal of Nautical Archaeology* 37: 88–97.
2009   Albanian Coastal Survey Project: 2008 Field Season. *INA Annual 2008*, 21–25.
2010   In Distress: Rescuing a Roman Merchantman 1700 Years Later. *INA Quarterly* 36(4):9.

Sakellariou, D., P. Georgiou, A. Mallios, V. Kapsimalis, D. Kourkoumelis, P. Micha, T, Theodoulou, K. Dellaporta
2007   Searching for Ancient Shipwrecks in the Aegean Sea: The Discovery of Chios and Kythnos Hellenistic Wrecks with the Use of Marine Geological-Geophysical Methods. *International Journal of Nautical Archaeology* 36:365–381.

Smith, C. J., H. Rumohr, I. Karakassis, and K.-N. Papadopoulou
2003   Analysing the Impact of Bottom Trawls on Sedimentary Seabeds with Sediment Profile Imagery. *Journal of Experimental Marine Biology and Ecology* 285–286:479–496.

Steinmetz, Joyce Holmes
2010   *Examining Mid-Atlantic Ocean Shipwrecks and Commercial Fish Trawling and Dredging.* Master's thesis, East Carolina University, Greenville.

Strain, E.M.A., A. L. Allcock, C. E. Goodwin, C. A. Maggs, B. E. Picton, and D. Roberts
2012   The Long-term Impacts of Fisheries on Epifaunal Assemblage Function and Structure, in a Special Area of Conservation. *Journal of Sea Research* 67:58–68.

UNESCO
2001   Convention on the Protection of the Underwater Cultural Heritage 2001. Electronic document, http://portal.unesco.org/en/ev.php-URL_ID=13520&URL_DO=DO_TOPIC&URL_SECTION=201.html, accessed December, 2009.

U.S. Department of Commerce, National Oceanic and Atmospheric Administration
2010   *Stellwagen Bank National Marine Sanctuary Final Management Plan and Environmental Assessment.* NOAA, Office of National Marine Sanctuaries, Silver Spring, Maryland.

Ward, Cheryl, and Robert Ballard
2004   Black Sea Shipwreck Survey 2000. *International Journal of Nautical Archaeology* 33:2–13.

Watling, Les, and Elliott A. Norse
1998   Disturbance of the Seabed by Mobile Fishing Gear: A Comparison to Forest Clearcutting. *Conservation Biology* 12:1180–1197.

Williams, A., J. Dowdney, A.D.M. Smith, A. J. Hobdat, and M. Fuller
2011   Evaluating Impacts of Fishing on Benthic Habitats: A Risk Assessment Framework Applied to Australian Fisheries. *Fisheries Research* 112:154–167.

9

Cultural Site Formation Processes Affecting Shipwrecks and Shipping Mishap Sites

MARTIN GIBBS AND BRAD DUNCAN

Most studies of maritime site formation processes have concentrated upon the various natural and to a lesser extent cultural processes physically impacting the remnants of the vessel (the shipwreck) and closely associated artifacts, while ignoring wider influences that have resulted in the current archaeological record. This chapter explores how cultural processes not only affect the transformation of a ship into a shipwreck site but also how continuing human interactions can produce other archaeological sites that are equally important for understanding the archaeology of shipwrecks. In addition, we consider how wider cultural practices, systems, and ideologies also warrant investigation when researching behavioral aspects of shipwreck site formation processes.

MARITIME CULTURAL SITE FORMATION PROCESSES

In his seminal 1976 paper Muckelroy introduced the notion of applying a specifically maritime-oriented model of site formation processes as a means of understanding the apparent loss and dispersal of structural components and relics from a shipwreck site, resulting in the current archaeological signature (Muckelroy 1976). Muckelroy's original schema considered both natural and cultural processes that worked toward transforming a ship's structure and contents from an organized but dynamic (systemic) state to a disorganized but stable (archaeological) context (Muckelroy 1976:158). To use Muckelroy's (1976, 1980) terms, these processes can be conceived of either as *filters*, which extract material from the assemblage, or as *scrambling devices*, which rearrange patterns. They might also result in additional material being added to the site (such as discarded, abandoned, or lost salvage gear, structures, or even vessels as well as impacts on the environment and landscape). These effects are eventually seen by archaeologists, who then further contribute to the site transformations by their own invasive activities.

Many authors have sought to improve on Muckelroy's original concept, although most have focused on natural processes (e.g., McCarthy 1998; Ward et al. 1999; Stewart 1999; Martin 2011; and see section 1 of this volume). Despite Gould's (1983) *Shipwreck Anthropology* highlighting a number of potential paths for studying cultural processes surrounding ships and shipwrecks, prior to the 1990s only a few studies appear to have engaged with these concerns (Keith and Simmons 1985; Lenihan 1987; Hardy 1990). However, since the late 1990s there has been renewed interest in cultural transformations affecting wreck sites, such as Souza's (1998) work on post-depositional factors, Simpson's (1999) discussion of historic salvage, Richards's works (2008, 2011) on abandonment, and Stammers's (2004) overview of ship breaking. Recent interest in maritime cultural landscapes has also seen increasing attention given to associated cultural processes and sites extending beyond the immediate wreck environment (Duncan 2006a; Ford 2011).

Our discussion begins by drawing a distinction between natural and cultural site formation processes evident at *shipping mishap* sites. We use the term *shipping mishap sites* as advocated by Duncan (2000) to include all sites and ancillary places associated with the loss, stranding, grounding, or collision of a vessel. Natural processes can be defined as nonhuman factors affecting the archaeological integrity of the wreck; for instance, chemical and physical processes such as wind, waves, corrosion, heat, and the interaction of organisms with the wreck (Martin 2011). Anthropogenic impacts include activities such as fishing or dredging damage, which, while humanly produced, are unintentional or without direct knowledge that there is an impact upon a wreck site. Some of these aspects are addressed elsewhere in this volume. For the purposes of this chapter a cultural site formation process is therefore considered to be one in which there is intentional human interaction with the wreck site and its associated components. Cultural site formation studies should include not only what people bring in and take out of a wreck site, but where they take it from and to, and why they undertake these actions. As we discuss, sometimes the evidence of these cultural processes may be visible on the surviving structure of the ships, in the distribution of materials and relics around or beyond the wreck, or in artifacts, sites, environmental modifications, and landscapes associated with other activities linked to the use of the wreck, even in situations where the structure of the vessel is no longer present. It is therefore necessary to consider not only the action that led to the wreck event and its immediate aftermath, but also the long-term behaviors surrounding the site. It is only by achieving an understanding of both natural *and* cultural processes that we can fully comprehend how and why the site exists in its present form, or how and why it may change in the future. From understanding the archaeological signatures of analogous sites, we may be able to derive behavioral influences that were taking place at other shipwrecks in similar circumstances and environments.

While this chapter is not an exhaustive review of all the potential cultural processes acting upon shipwrecks, we consider a range of behaviors, processes, and associated sites and archaeological signatures that might manifest in the archaeological record. Similar types of processes could happen at very different scales, from a small wooden boat through to an aircraft carrier. Processes could also happen at varying intensity and over different time scales. Some of the processes we discuss later were sequential as a consequence of their relationship to the progression of a wreck event, while others could happen in varying order, be concurrent, or not happen at all, depending on environmental, social, economic, or legal circumstances. As noted, many are equally applicable to wrecked, intentionally deposited, or abandoned vessels. Over time, or depending on perspective, one type of site could also transform into another, resulting in different responses and processes taking place. This chapter does not attempt to provide examples or specific detail for the different transformations described; instead, the emphasis is on encouraging archaeologists to look more broadly at wrecks, sites, and signatures. A more detailed study is presented in a forthcoming book by the authors, exploring how communities responded to shipwreck, including salvage operations (Duncan and Gibbs 2015).

For the sake of simplicity we refer to many of the cultural processes acting upon shipping mishap sites via the portfolio term *salvage*. The archaeological study of salvage is therefore inclusive of not only the processes and signatures associated with the recovery of a ship/derelict/wreck structure and the materials aboard but also the evidence of associated off-site salvage operations, structures, and materials.

In order to understand the cultural site formation processes that have acted upon a wreck site, we must first understand what constituted the ship. Every vessel has a life history. Its construction and form are in a constant state of transformation as repairs and replacements are made to the structure and fittings, as new technologies (and especially modes of propulsion) supersede and replace old, as its type of utility varies, and as cargoes, passengers/crew, and their belongings aboard change (see Lenihan 1987; Auer 2004). Knowing as much about the architecture, the unique life history, and biographical archaeology of the (as yet) unwrecked vessel is an important first step in understanding what changes have occurred within the site following the wreck or deposition event. For example, Murphy's "one last voyage" hypothesis proposes that "the more economically stressed a ship-producing and/or vessel using group becomes, the more extensive are the repairs performed on a vessel, ultimately extending the ship's use-life beyond sensible retirement" (Murphy 1983:75). These factors may present significant contributions to the wrecking event and subsequent site formation processes and might be incorrectly interpreted as the result of postwreck processes. We therefore need to consider at what point in its life a vessel becomes a wreck and what subsequently happens to turn it into the current archaeological site.

In a series of papers, Gibbs (2002; 2003; 2005; 2006) explored shipwreck cultural site formation processes by adopting a framework used by Leach (1994) in the analysis of disaster response. This framework suggested some of the cultural factors that might influence the occurrence of a shipwreck and the nature of a shipwreck site, including successive salvage processes (fig 9.1).

Duncan's (2000, 2004a) research has traced how risk avoidance and risk taking behavior played roles in determining shipping routes and wreck locations. He postulated that mariners' recognition of hazards (and potential hazards) and their consequent reactions to the risks posed (i.e., risk mitigation) were a significant factor that determined the occurrence of shipwrecks' patterning and their subsequent cultural landscapes. Picking up on this latter point, he has also explored the role that shipwrecks and wreck material played within the social, economic, and symbolic maritime cultural landscapes of both mariners and landlubbers alike. In particular, the use of wrecks as economic resources well after the wrecking event has been demonstrated to contribute markedly to the final archaeological signatures of wreck sites (Duncan 2006a:213–282). An important underpinning for these works is the understanding that shipwrecks are not "time capsules" (see Muckelroy 1976:56–57; Dean et al. 1992:32; Gould 2000:12–13) but that the wreck sites were, and are, constantly being utilized and accessed well after the wrecking event and hence are transformed on a regular basis.

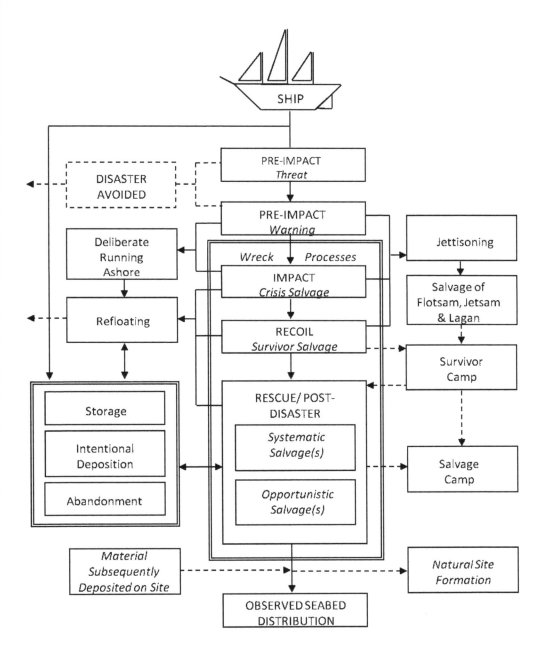

Figure 9.1. Cultural site formation factors in shipping mishaps (adapted from Muckelroy 1978 and Ward et al. 1999).

The Influence of Marine Underwriting on Shipping Mishap Behaviors

If we accept Duncan's (2000, 2004a) premise that risk was a major factor affecting the incidence of vessel mishaps, then the group perhaps most focused on the avoidance of financial risk associated with shipwrecks is marine underwriters. Marine insurance underwriters and marine insurance law therefore provide a useful benchmark for the definition of what actually constitutes a shipwreck. However, the popular definition of a shipwreck is more a loose historical usage than a legal one in terms of marine insurance. Marine underwriters tended to define shipping mishaps not in terms of shipwrecks but in degrees of loss (Broxham and Nash 2000:x). Shipping mishaps were divided into categories dependent on the extent of the loss incurred in the incident (table 9.1). Modern legal definitions stipulate that a wreck is "any part of vessels or their cargoes cast upon land or sea" (De Kerchove 1961:925). Hardy Ivamy (1974:209, 599) specified that a vessel becomes a wreck when it is no longer salvageable.

Table 9.1. Vessel incidents and loss

Collisions	Where the vessel collides with another vessel or structure.
Groundings	Where the vessel collides with the seabed causing damage to its hull/associated fittings.
Strandings	Where the vessel runs aground but remains partly or wholly above water. There are two types of strandings:
Accidental Stranding	Where the vessel collides with the seabed.
Deliberate Stranding	Where the vessel is deliberately steered ashore into shallow water to avoid becoming an **Actual or Total or Constructive Loss**.
Constructive Total Loss	Vessel is in imminent danger of becoming an actual loss, and is abandoned accordingly.
Actual Total Loss/General Average Loss	Vessel is destroyed and ceases to be recognizable as its original function as a ship or boat. Jettisoned material was also considered a **General Average Loss**.
Abandonment	Could only take place under stipulated conditions where it was recognized that the ship, cargo, and lives of those onboard were under imminent threat.

Note: After de Kerchove 1961.

The processes of wreck avoidance, abandonment, and subsequent salvage have (for at least the last several thousand years) been surrounded by a web of legalities, customs, and rights that have dictated acceptable behavior of mariners in times of shipping mishaps. These legalities and policies have specified who can (or should) undertake vessel abandonment and salvage; how and to what extent it should be done dependent on the circumstances; and as a result, who benefits materially and financially (usually via a maritime *lien*). For instance, the surviving fragments of the *Lex Rhodia de Jactu*, formulated ca. 900–800 BC and considered the ancestor of Western maritime legal codes, outline the contractual obligations pertaining to the jettisoning (*jactu*) of cargo to avoid wrecking (Britannica 1911). This remnant text from a larger document on maritime law describes relevant actions and lien under specific circumstances (such as the implications of cutting down masts, or using divers to salvage) and gives details of the resulting financial relationships. There are numerous successor laws and treatises on relevant precedents (e.g., Molloy 1677; Abbott 1802), as well as modern analyses of these (e.g., Melikan 1990), through which the evolution of these practices can be traced into the modern era.

Marine insurance is obviously another descendant of the *Lex Rhodia* (Roover 1945). Insurance codes provide extensive definition and delineation of risk and liability; detail appropriate priorities, actions, and expectations with regard to salvage of structure and cargo in particular circumstances; and include directives for the disbursement of profits from sale of salvaged structure and goods (e.g., Hopkins 1867; Gow 1917; Hardy Ivamy 1974). These in turn are linked to international and local codes surrounding salvage rights, in particular the Law of Salvage, which balances ownership of the vessel and cargo against the risk and real danger experienced by the salvors (due to environment, weather, or circumstances) and the service provided in the recovery of property (such as technologies and labor used and efficiency of recovery; Brice 2003; Mandaraka-Sheppard 2007; see table 9.2).

It is notable that the actions of mariners during shipwrecks and strandings were often driven by the stipulations of marine underwriter law and codes. Consequently, it must be considered that behaviors during and after wreck events were not simply to secure the safety of vessel, cargo, and people but may also have been attempts to work within or around various laws or insurance codes. Official reports and even autobiographical accounts of actions during and after wreck events would also have been sensitive to the implications of how these events were represented. Activities such as

Table 9.2. Shipwreck materials

Wreck	Anything without an apparent owner, afloat upon, sunk in, or cast ashore by the sea . . . includes jetsam, flotsam, lagan and derelict.
Derelict	1. Goods or any other commodity (especially vessels) abandoned or relinquished by its owner, either by consent, compulsion or stress of weather—usually with the owner indicating they intend to make no further claim (abandonment).
Jettison	The act of throwing goods overboard to lighten a ship or improve stability in stress of weather or in any other cases of necessity or emergency.
Wreckage	Goods cast ashore after a wreck.
Flotsam	Cargo which floats after jettison.
Jetsam	Cargo which sinks after being jettisoned.
Lagan	Goods cast overboard from a sinking vessel and buoyed as to be subsequently recovered, or large articles which sink with the ship in wreck.
Salvage	The property which has been recovered from a wrecked vessel, or the recovery of the vessel herself.

Note: After de Kerchove 1961.

abandonment, deliberate strandings, responses to particular environmental circumstances, or accepting or refusing assistance could significantly alter culpability of the captain and resulting claims upon the vessel and contents by salvors. It is therefore postulated that insurance underwriting companies essentially dictated (where possible) a major part of the process of the wrecking event and eventual salvage that took place at many wreck sites. Consequently, understanding the logic behind certain decisions in vessel operation and use, or the behaviors undertaken during the wrecking event and salvage, may require an appreciation of the specific laws and obligations imposed upon mariners under specified circumstances. For instance, the vessel may also demonstrate forms of risk taking, such as deliberate insurance fraud or ship owners and operators choosing to employ worn or unseaworthy vessels, hedging the expense of the loss of cargo against benefits from possible insurance claims (cf. Murphy 1983).

SALVAGE AS SITE FORMATION PROCESS

In order to understand salvage as a cultural site formation process, we must first explore the extent of activities that salvage entails. Some of the most basic potential questions regarding the study of salvage as both a site formation process and a cultural activity were posed in a short paper by Simpson (1999:4, 6).

> What is missing? What is present? Is the position of this artifact or cluster a product of pre-depositional choices, the wrecking process itself, or the product of salvors grouping salvageable items for recovery at a later time? Are these timbers from the ship or are they left over from a salvage operation. . . . What materials were salvaged and what materials were not? How was the wreck salvaged? Why were certain objects recovered over other objects? Is there a staging area associated with the wreck site?

Simpson (1999:8) also noted that maritime archaeology should not just look at who the salvors were but should also consider any economic and social effects the salvaged material had on surrounding communities (including indigenous groups), the trajectories of artifacts after salvage, and how the meanings of these objects changed over time. All these factors should be borne in mind in the following discussion.

Maritime archaeology has long recognized the need to consider the different forms of salvage across time and different circumstances. Muckelroy (1976, 1980) noted salvage process in his flowchart, while Keith and Simmons (1985) suggested differentiating the impacts of "salvage in antiquity" from those of "modern salvage." McCarthy (2001:93) proposed a distinction between "primary salvage" and "secondary salvage," primary salvage being the recovery of materials by their owners, operators, or agents, presumably close to the time of wrecking, while secondary salvage is the modern recovery of materials by professional salvors or sports divers.

We have previously suggested (Gibbs 2006) that the concepts of primary and secondary salvage might be supplemented by making the following distinctions:

1. Pre-impact actions
2. Crisis salvage
3. Survivor salvage
4. Systematic salvage
5. Opportunistic salvage

These distinctions are discussed in detail later in this chapter, as are several other major processes, including hulks, abandonment, strandings/groundings, and ship breaking. In addition to the wreck and associated

Table 9.3. Categories of material making up a ship

Category	Materials
Cargo and Contents	Non-fixed items not associated with the mechanical operation of the ship and which were meant to be removable, including the ship's boats and life-rafts.
Fixtures and Fittings	Minor fixed items, fittings, yards, chains, ropes, anchors and cannon, minor mechanical items, and equipment.
Minor Structural	Items not normally removed, but the removal of which would not compromise the integrity of the hull, such as bulkheads, decks, masts, superstructure, major mechanical items, and equipment.
Major Structural	Elements of the ship for which removal would affect the integrity of the vessel, including hull planking, ribs, and other structural items.

Note: Data from Gibbs 2006:3.

materials, the distinctions can also be applied to off-site materials (flotsam, jetsam, and lagan), as considerable quantities of material could float away from a wreck (or be separated from it as a result of the associated salvage operation). Some coastal communities have their own formal and informal codes and rights for accessing wreck materials that wash ashore. This could mean that protection was required, such as by police or customs officials, until the legal owners or agents could organize collection (see later discussion).

There are many potential sources for studying how people responded to shipping mishaps, undertook salvage, or related to wreck sites and derelict vessels as part of their cultural landscapes, including government, legal and commercial documents, corporate or institutional histories, nontechnical historical accounts, and ethnographic studies. The most detailed and readily available are explanations of twentieth-century principles, techniques, procedures, and equipment for responding to various types of shipping mishaps, including numerous technical manuals (e.g., Bartholomew et al. 2006; Wilkins 2006), descriptive contemporary accounts (Young 1933; Meier 1943; Wheeler 1958; Bartholomew and Milwee 2009), and written oral histories (e.g., Benham 1980). However, there are also ancient and historical descriptions of early salvage attempts and technologies (e.g., White 2005:191), historical studies and analyses (e.g., Bevan 1996; Ahlström 1997; Driver and Martins 2006), and many images and photographs that illustrate these processes and uses.

To simplify discussion regarding salvage or other cultural processes that extracted from, scrambled, or added to material associated with a wreck site, we have previously used a simple hierarchy of a ship's structure and contents (table 9.3). This is based in broad terms on the relative difficulty of removing materials and how they relate to the structural integrity of the vessel (table 9.1). These categories are flexible and not strictly hierarchical, as a large or heavy cargo item, or one situated in the lower hold of the ship, might be substantially more difficult to access and remove than lighter fittings or structural elements situated elsewhere (Gibbs 2006:4).

1. Pre-Impact—Saving the Ship

The captain or person(s) in command of a vessel in peril (including the potential salvor) was faced with decisions that were not only to ensure the preservation of human life but also meant to serve best the long-term interests of the vessel and its cargo. The removal of material from a vessel might occur soon after the realization that it was in peril, prior to the actual wreck event (i.e., "pre-impact"), starting the sequence of decisions and actions that alter the ship and its contents and ultimately manifest in the archaeological site. When a commander was faced with an impending collision or a potentially avoidable catastrophe, deliberate jettisoning of cargo, fittings, and even structural material might have been used to lighten the ship and make maneuverability easier, resulting in jetsam or lagan (Gibbs 2006). A leaking vessel might also have been subject to emergency repairs to maintain buoyancy, such by as plugging holes or pumping.

In some instances a ship in peril might be able to get external assistance from another vessel, including from professional wreckers who patrolled high risk areas (e.g., the Florida Keys; see Viele 2001). Attempts might be made to undertake *afloat salvage*, either through offloading cargo or through trying to save the vessel by various means such as towing or securing it in place. In some instances a shore-based lifeboat service might be able to make it to the ship or, in heavy seas, send a line from shore via a rocket system. If a line could make it aboard, a hawser arrangement would then be rigged from shipwreck to shore, usually fixed between the mast and an A-frame on the shore (or on a hill, dune, or cliff above it). Passengers could then be hauled ashore in a bosun's chair, and even cargo could be winched over if necessary. In later Western European cultural contexts the rescue of human lives was considered a humanitarian "good shepherd" action with no or low salvage value, although failure to prioritize this over material salvage would often have severe repercussions for the rights the salvors might have over any property or value (Benham 1986). This was a critical period, as accepting assistance would initiate salvage laws, leaving the captain and ship owners liable to claims. Even when in imminent peril, the captain was expected to negotiate the terms of assistance prior to relinquishing command (i.e., "abandoning" the ship).

2. Crisis Salvage

In the absence of immediate external assistance or salvation before, during, or immediately after a wreck event, a ship's crew and passengers might engage in "crisis" salvage. This form of salvage focused on recovering survival necessities, usually within the more accessible cargo, fittings, or minor structural materials, depending on circumstances and time available (Gibbs 2003). During this period, items might be thrown overboard to facilitate refloating or to aid survival of people in the water (i.e., floatable items were thrown overboard). These processes were often specified by insurance underwriters as precursor actions that must take place before a vessel could be abandoned and therefore declared a constructive total loss (Hardy Ivamy 1974:383). Items thrown overboard might be considered for later salvage and include those materials known as flotsam, jetsam, and lagan (Duncan 2006a:247).

Rescue services in the form of lifeboat sheds and rocket stations have their own archaeological visibility. Lifeboat rescues would often strategically use kedging anchors to control their drift back to a wreck, which would then be abandoned after rescuing survivors. Rocket lines often left rocket shells on the wreck site, and sometimes lifeboats sank during the rescue. There was also a whole range of infrastructure associated with the lifeboat service itself. This included features located in isolated areas known for repeated shipping mishaps, such as rocket sheds and purpose-made tracks, as well as lifeboat sheds, piers, and wreck bells located within local settlements (see Duncan 2006a:262).

Another form of crisis salvage dictated by risk management during crisis periods was to run the vessel aground deliberately in an area where it would not sink completely or be subjected to further physical damage from the elements. In marine insurance there are various nuances regarding whether a wreck is a stranding or grounding (see table 9.1). While accidental stranding was common, deliberate stranding was also used as a strategy for ships that were leaking or otherwise facing the prospect of actual/constructive total loss. Deliberate stranding was therefore used as a strategy to prevent sinking, preserve the structure of the vessel, and increase opportunities for repair, refloating, or salvage operations. If propulsion/mobility/steerage and control of the vessel were possible, the desirable type of site would be one where the seafloor was sufficiently soft to reduce damage to the keel and hull when the vessel was driven up and was preferably in an area outside dangerous swell or other hazards. Local knowledge of an area often included insight into which places (such as sand banks) afforded the best opportunities for deliberate stranding should it be necessary (Duncan 2006a:219). This aspect is discussed further in the section on systematic salvage.

3. Survivor Salvage

Following the main wreck event, should the situation of the wreck allow this (such as if stranded on a reef), survivors might engage in more complex forms of salvage ("survivor salvage") before formal rescue took place. Materials might be dispersed in lifeboats or to a survivor camp if land was available. The survivor camp offers a complementary assemblage of the ship's materials and if close enough to the wreck site might also become the base for salvage operations by rescuers or subsequent salvors. This aspect has been dealt with in detail in a previous paper by Gibbs (2003).

4. Systematic Salvage

Systematic salvage is usually conducted by professional salvors with the time, workforce, and technology to undertake an intensive and sustained effort to remove all or some of the cargo, fittings, and minor and major structural elements. Systematic salvage was most likely carried out by the owners of the vessel or their authorized agents (akin to McCarthy's "primary" salvage).

The extent of a systematic salvage of a wreck (in whole or part) was determined by a number of factors. These factors include the amount of available salvage equipment and manpower close to the site; allocated time; time window (e.g., weather); threat to life; and the real, perceived, or supposed economic, strategic, or social (including symbolic or religious) benefits of successful recovery of material (Gibbs 2006:14). These considerations dictated salvage priorities regarding what to take; the order in which it was taken (and to what extent); and conversely, what to leave behind. Decisions not to salvage, to perform only limited salvage, or to abandon a wreck completely presumably came when the structural remains or the materials within fell below a predetermined threshold.

Salvage priorities, processes, and techniques were dependent upon multiple inter-related factors, some of which are indicated in table 9.4. Shipwreck salvage literature (e.g., Ward 1956; Bartholomew et al. 2006) embodies some of these considerations in the terminology of several different types of salvage, each implying environmental conditions and/or different types or levels of technical activity (table 9.5). Other forms of salvage and wreck-related activities discussed later, such as refloating, breaking, placement, or abandonment, might arise as a consequence of these.

Systematic salvage might also commence minutes or years after a wreck event, depending upon legal, logistical, and environmental conditions. As already described, a strategy would be formulated based on the condition of the vessel, its circumstances, and the capabilities of the salvors. If the wreck were close to shore, salvage might take place at low tide when access was available across tidal flats. If the vessel was stranded and undamaged rather than derelict, then efforts might focus on the refloating process (discussed later). A salvage camp might be established on shore, to house salvors and possibly officials and to act as a base for salvage gear and storage of recovered materials. Depending upon the activities being carried out, the salvage camp would presumably be in the nearest possible proximity to the wreck.

Various forms of infrastructure might be constructed to formulate transfer of goods from the wreck site. These types of infrastructure might include a corduroy road of logs or tramway, over which vehicles or carts could transport materials; shore-based winches/engines and/or flying foxes (and their associated supporting beds) to haul material ashore; causeways, jetties, or piers from shore to wreck; or breakwaters or coffer dams to shield the site from prevailing weather, seas, and tidal changes. Anchors or structures (e.g., piles/dolphins) were sometimes used to prevent further movement of the derelict. Other environmental modifications could include removal of reef or digging trenches into beaches to facilitate access or removal (e.g., Duncan 2006a:267). Extensive ship breaking in situ and abandonment of all or part of the residual structure were also practiced (discussed later).

For a vessel that had sunk but was still accessible from the surface, one or several salvage vessels such as tugs, lighters, barges, and pontoons were generally used as work platforms. Some of these might be modified or specialized salvage craft, capable of housing the various types of equipment required to access the vessel and its interior and recover goods. Such equipment might include diving gear, cranes, winches, and underwater lifting

Table 9.4. Factors affecting salvage priorities, processes, and techniques

Size, type and construction of the vessel

Purpose of the vessel (e.g., naval, commercial, passenger)

Type of cargo being carried (size, composition)

Structural integrity of the vessel (or derelict) and potential for recovery

The extent to which the vessel (or derelict) remains above water (grounded/stranded) or submerged

Short- and long-term environmental conditions (weather, swell, currents, bottom composition)

Logistical constraints (e.g., proximity to shore, distance from settlements, and/or transport networks and suitable places for salvage camps/storage)

Technologies and labor force(s) available locally and regionally, including specialist knowledge and experience

Cultural dangers (such as during war, indigenous attack, and contested ownership)

Perceived values of removing different components, which prioritized the order and intensity of removal (e.g., the removal of the vessel's structure in whole or part vs. cargo and contents)

Consideration of hazards, risk, and expense of salvage versus potential profit

Processes and procedures stipulated by legal, insurance, corporate, institutional, or other policies, codes, and guidelines

Other cultural factors (e.g., social, superstitious, or symbolic significance encouraging or discouraging removal of material)

Time since the original wreck event, and the progress of these factors (e.g., primary or secondary salvage)

Table 9.5. Major salvage types

Salvage Type	Explanation
Afloat	Salvage of a vessel still afloat (and potentially damaged). Assistance provided to ships that are afire, flooding, battle damaged, or victims of other misfortunes at sea.
Offshore	Salvage of a stranded vessel or derelict in exposed conditions.
Harbor	Salvage of a stranded vessel or derelict in sheltered waters.
Stranded	Refloating of grounded ships to restrict damage to the ship or the environment, return a valuable ship to service, remove it for disposal or breaking, or to save cargo.
Cargo and equipment	Salvage of cargo and fixtures prioritized, meaning structure may be destroyed or dismantled to facilitate removal.
Wreck removal	Removal of a derelict without necessarily undertaking salvage (low or no value).
Clearance	Removal or salvage of vessels (sometimes multiple vessels), typically after a catastrophic event such as a war or natural disaster, to ensure a harbor or waterway remains open.
Deep-ocean	Operations, objects are located, investigated, and recovered from the ocean floor, sometimes at great depths.

Note: After Bartholomew et al. 2006:2–1; Bartholomew and Milwee 2009:33.

devices. These vessels might also require their own mooring systems. There are instances where hazardous circumstances resulted in spillage of the salvage materials and the loss of the salvage vessel(s) and/or equipment (e.g., Love 2006:79).

An episode of systematic salvage would continue until the desired value had been extracted and salvage operations were abandoned either temporarily or permanently. A vessel or site might be subjected to successive periods of systematic salvage depending on whether the values of the wreck shifted, the salvage technologies or labor force improved, or environmental circumstances and conditions influenced hazard, effort, or access to the site. Surrounding these cycles of systematic salvage might be numerous episodes from opportunistic salvors, potentially operating with different intentions and values (discussed later).

5. Strandings and Groundings

Stranding sites, where vessels have been completely removed, represent an under-explored archaeological resource (Duncan 2006a: 218). Despite absence of a hull, there may be substantial evidence of significant activity associated with the nature of the wreck event and the processes of removing the vessel (see Duncan 2000:142; 2006a:259). In effect these are "phantom" wreck sites (Duncan 2000:142; Gibbs 2006), but nonetheless the places at which these events occurred are quite possibly as common as catastrophic wreck sites or even more so.

The difference between deliberate and accidental stranding has already been noted. In either scenario, if a stranded vessel was undamaged, then the simplest response would be to try to refloat it on the rising tide or if necessary wait for a spring tide or seasonal change. This process might entail lightening the ship by careful offloading (and eventual reloading) of ballast, cargo, or heavy fixtures and fittings (such as anchors and cannon). However, for the sake of expediency and safety, these items were sometimes jettisoned without any likelihood of immediate recovery (Benham 1986). Consequently, while the vessel itself would be successfully refloated and removed, the site of the stranding might be marked by considerable quantities of ballast and other material, which in some instances can look much like the signature of a shipwreck (Duncan 2006a:218; 2006b:253, 393, 434, 520).

Depending on bottom conditions, a vessel stranded on a beach might need to be freed from sediment, either manually or through mechanically digging or dredging. Many of the structures used to salvage wrecks had similar applicability for stranding sites. Structures to access the vessel (such as plankways or corduroy roads), and to undertake the excavation, remove the sediment, and then try to prevent refilling of the hole between tides (shoring and retaining walls), could result in considerable short-term environmental modification. The use of more elaborate structures such as coffer dams and structures placed above and below water could provide placement assurance and/or stabilize the vessel and prevent further slippage into deeper water. Explosives could be used to blast through obstructing reef or rock, while the process of removal might itself damage reef surfaces and seafloors in archaeologically visible ways (such as by gouging from the keel scraping over the bottom). If the tide or the vessel's own power was not sufficient to lift it off the obstruction, then other vessels (such as tugs) could assist in hauling it off. In the absence of other vessels, shore-based structures could be used, such as carefully placed arrangements of underwater anchors, or land-based winching systems known as beach gear, which might include using existing strong points or burying anchors.

A vessel might require repair before an attempt was made to refloat it, such as careening, in which the vessel is rolled onto its side to allow access to the lower hull and keel. In order to careen a vessel, cargo and heavy fixtures and fittings might need to be shifted or offloaded to allow the vessel to list, sometimes aided by rigging block and tackle to hoist the vessel over, with the hawser fixed to another vessel, to anchors, or to points ashore (such as trees or even a buried anchor). In some instances severe damage might require removal of major structural elements (e.g., crushed bow, stern, or masts) to regain hydrodynamic qualities and allow recovery to another location for later repair, salvage, or abandonment.

Righting a fully capsized or severely heeled over vessel was a complex operation. Depending upon whether the intention was to try to save the structure or simply to remove it, the options might be to bring the vessel back onto its own keel or even refloat it and remove it upside down or on its side. Depending upon environmental circumstances, rotating a capsized vessel could be assisted by tidal changes, careful placement of weight internally, and by the use of buoyancy devices or external winching systems on shore, on salvage vessels, or on the seafloor, although this was also dependent upon the shape of the vessel (cf. Benham 1986:56). To gain sufficient leverage to roll it upright, a headframe or shearlegs might be constructed on the hull.

In attempting to refloat a partially or wholly sunken vessel the main aim was to recover some level of positive buoyancy, which might be achieved in various ways. Getting wires or hawsers beneath a wreck and winching it up, using external pontoons or flotation devices (such as lift bags), repairing and sealing the hull and expelling the water by pumping or introducing air, placing buoyant objects inside (e.g., empty drums, float bags, or a collection of smaller buoyant objects), or a combination of these were some of the means of achieving this. Modified vessels such as "wreck-raising" hulks, or specialized vessels of various kinds, such as those equipped with cranes, might be used. In order to pass a line beneath a sunken vessel, tunneling beneath the hull might be required. Structural recovery and refloating might also involve sections of a vessel rather than the complete hull.

Recovery of the hull structure was dependent not only on the conditions, technology, labor, and expertise available but also on the structural integrity of the hull and its ability to withstand the strains of being pulled, dragged, or lifted. A failed attempt to save the hull might, at best, leave the derelict where it was and, at worst, result in structural failure and breakage of the hull into parts, negating some or all of its salvage value. The salvage gear itself, including pontoons and flotation devices, wires, ropes, and dive gear, might not be recoverable, or worth the effort of recovery, thus entering the archaeological record. Even after successful refloating, the various structures used to assist the process might remain in place, while the environmental modifications might remain visible or have other long-term consequences.

6. Opportunistic Salvage

Opportunistic salvage is the nonsystematic removal of structure and contents, likely to be undertaken by people without the legal right to remove material (cf. McCarthy's "secondary" salvage). Opportunistic salvage could and often would commence almost immediately after a wreck event, especially if a ship was breaking up and material was being dispersed close to shore. Many of the priorities for salvage outlined so far also applied in these circumstances, although from a different perspective and with the added necessity in many cases of undertaking such activities while avoiding official attention. Local maritime communities often had their own traditions and codes regarding their priorities, practices, and rights to wreck salvage, especially flotsam and jetsam washed ashore on their beaches, regardless of formal legalities. Intimate knowledge of currents and the likely places for material to wash ashore (flotsam/jetsam traps) meant that they could target the best areas for collection, preferably before legal owners or authorities arrived to deny them access (Duncan and Gibbs 2015).

Opportunistic salvage could be undertaken at various levels, from small-scale plundering of materials washed ashore from a wreck to large-scale looting of the ship's cargo and structure. Assuming that circumstances allowed, opportunistic salvors (also known as looters and sometimes wreckers) might even board the derelict itself and undertake larger-scale removal of cargo or breaking of the structure. Illicit removal of wreck material included a variety of actions with potential archaeological visibility. These include caching of goods (such as in holes, caves, beneath collapsed sand dunes, or in specially constructed lined pits or barrels) and removal and concealment of materials at residences or in more distant and often isolated storage facilities. Salvaged objects might be distributed around the community in various ways for local use, including structural materials and fittings being incorporated into houses, buildings, and fences or reused in local watercraft. Proximity to areas susceptible to wreckings also led to both legal and illicit trading networks, where shipwreck items were further spread throughout the community.

Looters might attempt to distract authorized salvors or guards or employ various means of extending the opportunity to remove wreck materials, including employing drastic actions such as setting a derelict vessel alight to prevent its removal or to conceal previous theft. Most opportunistic and illicit looting was short in duration, and sporadic, but potentially repeated by different parties over an extended period of time. Collection could be a short-term activity or a long term and even cross-generational action as communities waited for seasonal changes in currents and storm events to wash ashore new material, including material from older wrecks (Duncan 2006).

Although often disorganized in nature, opportunistic salvage potentially removed vast amounts of wreckage, cargo, and other items from the wreck site, as it was often undertaken by whole communities within a short space of time. Secondary sites associated with maintaining civil obedience were often constructed close to wreck sites (e.g., police and customs camps), which in turn were subjected to further criminal behavior (Duncan 2006a: 240–246). The study of opportunistic salvage presents important insights into the removal and deposition of materials in and out of wrecks sites.

7. HULKS

Vessels considered unseaworthy, technologically redundant, or otherwise not worth retaining for transport purposes, yet still structurally sound, might continue to exist as a hulk. Although not a shipping mishap, hulks are considered here for their potential to generate archaeological signatures that might be confused for a shipwreck site, while aspects of their structural modification might be misleading if the hull is subsequently found by archaeologists (see Delgado 2009). In general, vessels to be used as hulks were derigged and moored, sometimes permanently, in a harbor or roadstead and modified for further use. Given the long-term static sheltered position, structural modifications to interior and exterior could be extensive and dramatic, with some of the characteristic hallmarks of a hulk being the accretion of new structural elements on the upper works and deck. In some instances rigging might be retained for use in sail training or as a crane. Some potential uses for hulks are listed here, each with implications for the types of structural modifications this might require and artifact deposits in and around the site.

- Exclusion or isolation—prison, defense, quarantine, reformatory, valuable or dangerous goods (e.g., powder magazine)
- Storage—including coal hulks
- Accommodation and services—housing, military barracks
- Services—stores, chapel, hospital, school, offices, sail training, blacksmith shop
- Recreational—bathing enclosure, playground
- Barge or lighter—often with a cut-down superstructure
- Landing stage, floating crane, loading, base for other equipment
- Wreck raising or dry dock (floating or fixed ashore) for other vessels
- Fire-ship (offensive weapon)

Hulks often became long-term and important components of harbor landscapes (see Duncan 2006b). Nearshore hulks were sometimes connected to land by jetties or other structures, although in some cases it was the potential to keep the hulk floating away from shore and isolated that made them desirable (such as for prisons, quarantine, explosives, or storage of valuables; Williams 2005; Menzies 2010). While hulks might rest on tidal flats, many remained floating and in some cases would be moved as required to new locations. At the end of their useful lives most were removed for breaking or disposal elsewhere, incorporated into landfills (sometimes in situ at their mooring), although some were broken in place or allowed to disintegrate (Duncan at al. 2013). Some were even converted back into vessels. Archaeologically, hulks may be visible through surviving associated structures or mooring anchors (Duncan 2006b:255). Also, given the extended occupation of one area, many of these uses potentially generated significant quantities of refuse, which would invariably be discarded overboard onto the adjacent seafloor (Adams and Davis 1998; Williams 2005). Duncan has observed similar scatters under long-term anchorages for naval, fishing, and pilot vessels (2006a:125, 181, 191).

8. Abandonment and Intentional Deposition

Richards (2008, 2011) has provided an extensive consideration of maritime site formation processes deriving from vessel abandonment: catastrophic (desertion during a wreck event), consequential (ruining a ship to save lives), and deliberate (intentional deposition). This deliberate abandonment category is the most relevant here, with various potential trajectories for vessels outlined.

- Ritualistic discard (e.g., ships use as graves)
- Structural adaptation for use as buildings or foundations or as reclamation structures (e.g., retaining walls, cribbing, breakwaters, training walls, piers)
- Salvage and recycling—stored for recycling of materials (see breaking, below)
- Ship graveyards and breakers' yards—deliberate abandonment in a particular locale (strategic scuttling—sometimes in a single event—as a blockade device or to deny vessels to an enemy vs. discard as refuse in one area over an extended period)
- Strategic modification—(e.g., as fireships)
- Fish aggregation devices, dive destination

The processes of abandonment might include placement or deposition above or below water as well as above and below ground (Delgado 2009; Richards 2011; Duncan 2006a:111, 124: App. D, 1–26). For placement below water, measures might be needed to ensure that discarded wrecks did not move, such as scuttling by mechanical or explosive means, driving piles adjacent to or through hulls, or other forms of structural modification by demolition or burning, all potentially visible archaeologically. Clusters of scuttled ships were referred to as ship graveyards and were often viewed by the community as shipwrecks, despite their intentional placement (see Duncan 1994; Duncan 2006a:214).

9. Shipbreaking and Destruction

The most drastic form of salvage is ship breaking, the systematic demolition of a vessel for recycling or complete destruction, sometimes also referred to as "shipwrecking" (see Stammers 2004:83). Although a site where a single vessel is dismantled, including in situ salvage of the majority of structure from a wreck, might be considered a breaking site, there were often areas suitable for ships to be broken easily (by virtue of being able to drive them onto tidal flats), or formal yards where multiple vessels could be processed, consecutively or concurrently. In some instances these were related to shipyards. Proximity to where salvaged materials might be processed or transported away, or where contaminants might be removed or disposed of, might also affect the location of a breaking yard (Pastron and Delgado 1991). Infrastructure such as breakwaters or stone jetties was sometime constructed, both to allow access to deep water and to provide shelter from prevailing weather conditions (Duncan 2004b; 2008a; 2008b).

Archaeologically this might be visible in various ways: by moorings, dolphins, or other structures for placement assurance during operations; infrastructure such as wharfs or jetties, winches and winding gear or cables to remove structure, salvage pontoons or barges, and areas for salvaged or ship components or unsalvaged hulks (e.g., Pastron and Delgado 1991; Duncan 2004b; 2008a, 2008b). Many ship breaking yards were located on the periphery of major settlements in marginal coastal areas or in rivers. In some instances breaking yards were closely related to storage areas for defunct vessels, being kept until economic conditions make breaking worthwhile, as well as to abandonment and dumping areas for remnant structure and materials. There are several basic intentions behind breaking:

- To remove structural components for use elsewhere (such as incorporation into another vessel).
- To remove structural materials for recycling (e.g., smelting).
- To reduce the structure to reduce the bulk substantially prior to abandonment or to free up space occupied by the vessel.
- To destroy the vessel completely.

Depending upon circumstances and the intention behind the salvage strategy (i.e., whether to recover structure or other components in an intact state or not), manual cutting, mechanical demolition, or explosives might all be used. Burning was another means of reducing a wreck for discard or to facilitate recovery of noncombustible fixtures and fittings without the time and expense of dismantling (Pastron and Delgado 1991). Setting a derelict afire might also happen in accidental or negligent ways (vandalism, for firewood, etc.). Finally, there might be destruction of a vessel, derelict, or hulk for experimental purposes (weapons or structural testing), including through use as a target. Furthermore, as ship breaking methods were often very similar to the methods employed by salvors, investigations of the archaeological remains of former ship breaking yards (Duncan 2004b, 2008a, 2008b) and other current research being undertaken by the authors also offers insights into the potential techniques used by salvage crews in breaking and salvaging wrecks.

Social Aspects of Salvage

Although the focus of this chapter is necessarily on the mechanics of maritime cultural site formation processes, we should briefly pick up on Simpson's (1999:4–6) questions regarding the "who" and "why" of salvage and stress that these activities were embedded in real social, economic, and symbolic worlds. It is important to try to determine the motivations and capabilities of those undertaking activities related to shipping mishaps, including prevention, rescue, and the different forms of salvage and re-use of materials over the short and long term. Many coastal communities integrated these activities into their daily lives, ranging from formal government, institutional, or commercial groups providing services to occasional participation in mishap-related activities, such as opportunistic beachcombing or even the secondary purchase or use of salvaged materials. Accessing wreck sites or beachcombing for seasonally deposited wreck materials could also become cross-generational pursuits, for example with the same wreck or stranding site being revisited over an extended period. Such activities sometimes became effectively "traditional" practice and subject to formal and informal codes of conduct within the community (Knowles 1997; Duncan 2006a). There is also increasing interest in the biography of objects salvaged from mishap sites, their symbolic significance, and how they move through communities (Steinberg 2008; Hosty 2010; Gregson et al. 2011). Some of these aspects will be dealt with in detail in the authors' forthcoming book (Duncan and Gibbs 2015).

We also need to consider that salvage processes, especially breaking, required considerable skill and experience. There have long been individuals and groups specializing in these sorts of activities, presumably with traditions of technology and practice, as well as associations with wrecks in particular areas or repeated use of certain locations for activities such as ship breaking. Associations with particular communities, ethnic/caste/ social groups, or socioeconomic strata should also be considered. For instance, Pastron and Delgado (1991:65) found that much of the labor force working in the San Francisco breaking yards consisted of low-paid Chinese laborers. In the modern context the Alang (India) ship breaking yards actively exploit low socioeconomic and caste groups (Langewiesche 2000; Kot 2004). However, the fact that salvors were seen as benefiting from the misfortunes of others sometimes led to incorrect perceptions regarding their legality and morality (e.g., Viele 2001; Seal 2003; Bathurst 2005).

CONCLUSION

The cultural site formation processes surrounding shipping mishaps, and the salvage, modification for reuse, intentional placement, and abandonment of vessels are undoubtedly the causes of some of the most dramatic transformations seen on maritime mishap ("shipwreck") sites. There is greater complexity in the archaeology of vessel mishaps and the technologies and processes of salvage than has traditionally been allowed within maritime archaeological research. In the preceding sections we have attempted to illustrate some of the possible behaviors and actions surrounding vessel mishaps and the continuing uses and transformations in the later stages in the life of a vessel.

While there has not been the scope to discuss specific historical or archaeological examples, our intention has been to stress that the evidence of these processes is frequently legible within the archaeological record. Evidence of salvage is often very discernible on sites, even if through the absence of the vessel itself. In some instances the mechanisms of salvage (ropes and wires, structures, jettisoned material, and environmental modifications) on land and sea are still obvious. As we have suggested, these processes are worthy subjects for intensive investigation in their own right, especially as salvage processes were the subject of considerable innovation and experimentation, which should be detectable in the archaeological record. Greater understanding is needed of the social, economic, and symbolic significance of many of these actions, as well as their place within a wider landscape of human activity, as is understanding of changes over time. There is a wealth of modern, historical, and ancient documentary, image, ethnographic, and archaeological resources available for the study of maritime cultural site formation processes, and we hope that these sorts of investigations will become more common as part of the broadening of interest in maritime archaeology.

REFERENCES CITED

Abbott, Charles
1802   *A Treatise of the Law Relative to Merchant Ships and Seamen.* London.
Adams, Chris, and Mike Davis
1998   *Convict Establishment Bermuda.* Electronic document, http://convicthulks.com/, accessed January 31, 2013.
Ahlström, Christian
1997   *Looking for Leads: Shipwrecks of the Past Revealed by Contemporary Documents and the Archaeological Record.* Finnish Academy of Science and Letters, Helsinki.
Auer, Jens
2004   *Fregatten Mynden*: A 17th-century Danish Frigate Found in Northern Germany. *International Journal of Nautical Archaeology* 33(3):264–280.
Bartholomew, Charles, Bert Marsh, and Richard Hooper
2006   *U.S. Navy Salvage Engineer's Handbook,* volume 1. Naval Sea Systems Command, Department of the Navy, Washington, D.C.
Bartholomew, Charles, and William Milwee
2009   *Mud, Muscles and Miracles: Marine Salvage in the United States Navy.* 2nd edition. Naval History and Heritage Command, Naval Sea Systems Command, Department of the Navy, Washington, D.C.
Bathurst, Bella
2005   *The Wreckers.* Harper Collins, London.
Benham, Hervey
1980   *The Salvagers.* Essex County Newspapers, Colchester.
1986   *Once Upon a Tide.* Harrap, London.
Bevan, John
1996   *The Infernal Diver: The Lives of John and Charles Deane, Their Invention of the Diving Helmet and Its First Application.* Submex, London.
Brice, Geoffrey
2003   *Maritime Law of Salvage.* Sweet and Maxwell, London.
Britannica
1911   *Encyclopedia Britannica.* Electronic document, http://www.1911encyclopedia.org/, accessed November 20, 2004.
Broxham, Graeme, and Mike Nash
2000   *Tasmanian Shipwrecks: Volume Two 1900–1999.* Navarine Publishing, Hobart.
Dean, Martin, Ben Ferrari, Ian Oxley, Mark Redknap, and Kit Watson (editors)
1992   *Archaeology Underwater: The NAS Guide to Principles and Practice.* Henry Ling, Dorset.
De Kerchove, Rene
1961   *International Maritime Dictionary.* Reinhold, New York.

Delgado, James
2009   *Gold Rush Port: The Maritime Archaeology of San Francisco's Waterfront.* University of California Press, Berkeley.
Driver, Felix, and Luciana Martins
2006   Shipwreck and Salvage in the Tropics: The Case of HMS *Thetis*, 1830–1854. *Journal of Historical Geography* 32:539–562.
Duncan, Brad
1994   *The Ships' Graveyard Area Wrecks—A Case for Declaration as a Historic Shipwrecks Area.* Internal report, Maritime Heritage Unit, Heritage Victoria, Melbourne.
2000   Signposts in the Sea: An Investigation of the Shipwreck Patterning and Maritime Cultural Landscapes/Seascapes of the Gippsland Region, Victoria. Unpublished honours thesis, James Cook University, Townsville.
2004a   Risky Business: An Investigation of the Role of Risk in the Development of the Cultural Seascape of the Gippsland Region of Victoria. *Bulletin of the Australasian Institute for Maritime Archaeology* 28:11–23.
2004b   *Maritime Infrastructure Heritage Project, Stage Two: Geelong.* Heritage Victoria, Melbourne.
2006a   *The Maritime Archaeology and Maritime Cultural Landscapes of Queenscliffe: A Nineteenth Century Australian Coastal Community.* Ph.D. dissertation, James Cook University, Townsville.
2006b   *Maritime Infrastructure Heritage Project, Stage One: Melbourne.* Internal Report, Heritage Victoria, Melbourne.
2008a   Coch's/Koke's Shipbreaking Yard Survey. *Australasian Institute of Maritime Archaeology Newsletter* (December 2008) 27(4):15–16.
2008b   Coch's/Koke's Shipbreaking Yard Survey. *Australasian Society for Historical Archaeology Newsletter* 38(4):23–25.
Duncan, Brad, Martin Gibbs, and Till Sonnemann
2013   Searching for the Yellow Fleet: An Archaeological and Remote Sensing Investigation of the Prison Hulk Wrecks *Deborah* and *Sacramento. Bulletin of the Australian Institute for Maritime Archaeology* 37:66–75.
Duncan, Brad, and Martin Gibbs
2015   *Please God Send Me a Wreck: Responses to Shipwreck in a 19th Century Australian Community.* Springer, Dordrecht.
Ford, Ben (editor)
2011   *The Archaeology of Maritime Landscapes.* Springer, Dordrecht.
Gibbs, Martin
2002   Behavioural Models of Crisis Response as a Tool for Archaeological Interpretation—A Case Study of the 1629 Wreck of the V.O.C. Ship *Batavia* on the Houtman Abrolhos Islands, Western Australia. In *Natural Disasters, Catastrophism and Cultural Change*, edited by John Grattan and Robin Torrence, pp. 66–86. One World Archaeology Series. Routledge, New York.
2003   The Archaeology of Crisis: Shipwreck Survivor Camps in Australasia. *Historical Archaeology* 37(1):128–145.
2005   Watery Graves: When Ships Become Places. In *Object Lessons: Archaeology and*

Heritage in Australia, edited by Jane Lydon and Tracey Ireland, pp. 50–70. Australian Scholarly Press, Melbourne.

2006 Cultural Site Formation Processes in Maritime Archaeology: Disaster Response, Salvage and Muckelroy 30 Years On. *International Journal of Nautical Archaeology* 35:4–19.

Gould, Richard (editor)

1983 *Shipwreck Anthropology*. Albuquerque.

Gould, Richard

2000 *Archaeology and the Social History of Ships*. Cambridge University Press, Cambridge.

Gow, William

1917 *Marine Insurance: A Handbook*. MacMillan, London.

Gregson, Nicky, Mike Crang, and Helen Watkins

2011 Souvenir Salvage and the Death of Great Naval Ships. *Journal of Material Culture* 16:301–324.

Hardy, Debbie

1990 A Century on the Sea-Bed: The *Centurion*. *Bulletin of the Australian Institute for Maritime Archaeology* 14(2):23–34.

Hardy Ivamy, Edward

1974 *Marine Insurance*. 2nd edition. Butterworths, London.

Hopkins, Manley

1867 *A Manual of Marine Insurance*. Smith and Sons, London.

Hosty, Kieran

2010 The *Dunbar*: A Melancholy Obsession. *Bulletin of the Australasian Institute for Maritime Archaeology* 34:57–66.

Keith, Donald H., and Joe Simmons

1985 Analysis of Hull Remains, Ballast and Artefact Distribution of a 16th-Century Shipwreck, Molasses Reef, British West Indies. *Journal of Field Archaeology* 12(4):411–424.

Knowles, Joan

1997 *Traditional Practices in the Tasmanian World Heritage Area: A Study of Five Communities and their Attachment to Place*. Report for the Steering Committee of the Traditional Practices in the World Heritage Area Project. Hobart.

Kot, Michael (director)

2004 *Shipbreakers* (documentary film). National Film Board of Canada with Storyline Entertainment.

Langewiesche, William

2000 The Shipbreakers. *Atlantic Monthly* (August 2000), 286(2):31–49.

Leach, John

1994 *Survival Psychology*. Palgrave Macmillan, Sydney.

Lenihan, Daniel J. (editor)

1987 *Submerged Cultural Resources Study: Isle Royal National Park*. Southwest Cultural Resources Center Professional Papers no. 8. Submerged Cultural Resources Unit, National Park Service, Santa Fe.

Love, Don
2006   *Shipwrecks around Port Phillip Heads.* Roebuck Society, Victoria.
Mandaraka-Sheppard, Aleka
2007   *Modern Maritime Law and Risk Management.* Taylor and Francis, London.
Martin, Colin
2011   Wreck Site Formation Processes. In *The Oxford Handbook of Maritime Archaeology*, edited by Alexis Catsambis, Ben Ford, and Donny Hamilton, pp. 47–67. Oxford University Press, London.
McCarthy, Michael
1996   *SS* Xantho, *an Iron Steamship Wreck: Towards a New Perspective in Maritime Archaeology.* Ph.D. dissertation, James Cook University, Townsville.
1998   Australian Maritime Archaeology: Changes, Their Antecedents and the Path Ahead. *Australian Archaeology* 47:33–38.
2001   *Iron and Steamship Archaeology: Success and Failure on the SS* Xantho. Springer-Kluwer, New York.
Meier, Frank
1943   *Fathoms Below: Under-Sea Salvage from Sailing Ships to the* Normandie. Dutton, New York.
Melikan, Rose
1990   Shippers, Salvors, and Sovereigns: Competing Interests in the Medieval Law of Shipwreck. *Journal of Legal History* 11(2):163–182.
Menzies, Jennifer
2010   Utilized Hulks in Sydney Harbour's Maritime Cultural Landscape 1788–1938: An Archaeological Consideration. Unpublished honours thesis, University of Sydney.
Molloy, Charles
1677   *De Jure Maritimo et Navali, or, A Treatise of Affairs Maritime and of Commerce in Three Books.* London.
Muckelroy, Keith
1976   The Integration of Historical and Archaeological Data Concerning an Historic Wreck Site: The "Kennemerland." *World Archaeology* 7(3):280–289.
1980   *Maritime Archaeology.* Cambridge University Press, Cambridge.
Murphy, Larry
1983   Shipwrecks as Database for Human Behavioral Studies. In *Shipwreck Anthropology*, edited by R. Gould, pp. 65–90. SAR Press, Albuquerque.
Pastron, Allen, and James Delgado
1991   Archaeological Investigations of a Mid-19th-Century Shipbreaking Yard, San Francisco, California. *Historical Archaeology* 25(3):61–77.
Richards, Nathan
2008   *Ships' Graveyards: Abandoned Watercraft and the Archaeological Site Formation Process.* University Press of Florida, Gainesville.
2011   Ship Abandonment. In *The Oxford Handbook of Maritime Archaeology*, edited by Alexis Catsambis, Ben Ford, and Donny Hamilton, pp. 856–878. Oxford University Press, London.

Roover, Florence
1945   Early Examples of Marine Insurance. *Journal of Economic History* 5(2):172–200
Seal, Jeremy
2003   *The Wreck at Sharpnose Point*. Picador, London.
Simpson, Glenn
1999   Historical Salvage and Maritime Archaeology. In *Underwater Archaeology*, edited by Adrianne Askins Neidinger and Matthew A. Russell, pp. 3–10. Society for Historic Archaeology, Salt Lake City.
Souza, Donna
1998   *The Persistence of Sail in the Age of Steam*. Springer, New York.
Stammers, Michael
2004   *End of Voyages: The Afterlife of a Ship*. Tempus Publishing, London.
Steinberg, David
2008   *Shipwreck Salvage in the Northern Territory: The Wreck of the Brisbane as a Case Study in Site Salvage and Material Culture Reuse*. Australasian Institute for Maritime Archaeology, Special Publication no. 14.
Stewart, David
1999   Formation Processes Affecting Submerged Archaeological Sites: An Overview. *Geoarchaeology: An International Journal* 14(6):565–587.
Viele, John
2001   *The Florida Keys: The Wreckers*. Pineapple Press, Florida.
Ward, James
1956   *Use of Explosives in Underwater Salvage*. Ordnance Pamphlet 2081. Bureau of Ordnance, Department of the Navy, Washington. Electronic document, http://www.eugeneleeslover.com/ENGINEERING/OP2081/OP2081.pdf.
Ward, Ingrid, Peter Larcombe, and Peter Veth
1999   A New Process-Based Model for Wreck Site Formation. *Journal of Archaeological Science* 26:561–570.
Wheeler, George James
1958   *Ship Salvage*. George Philip and Son, London.
White, J. (editor)
2005   *Translation of Biondo Flavio (1474) Italy Illuminated,* Volume 1. Harvard University Press, Cambridge.
Wilkins, J. K.
2006   *US Navy Salvage Manual,* Volume 1: *Strandings and Harbour Clearance*. S0300-A6-Man-010. United States Navy Sea Systems Command. Electronic document, http://www.rancd-association.com/DIVERS_DOWNLOADS_COMMERCIAL_DIVING_files/MANUAL-U.S.%20NAVY%20SALVAGE%20MANUAL%20VOLUME%201%20STRANDINGS%20AND%20HARBOR%20CLEARANCE.pdf.
Williams, Brad
2005   The Archaeological Potential of Colonial Prison Hulks: The Tasmanian Case Study. *Bulletin of the Australasian Institute for Maritime Archaeology* 29:77–86.
Young, Desmond
1933   *Ship Ashore: Adventures in Salvage*. J. Cape, London.

III

Site Formation
and Heritage Management

10

English Heritage and Shipwreck Site Formation Processes

IAN OXLEY

The history of shipwreck site formation studies is a brief one spanning around four decades (Oxley 1998, 1992). In that time a few voices have attempted to define common strands to what is clearly a vastly complex relationship between the multitude of material types contained in the hundreds of thousands of wrecks that have occurred over the thousands of years of humankind's interaction with the sea, and their subsequent transformation in their burial environments. The formal management of any country's marine historic environment is an even more recent development, dating to the late 1990s, leading to the emergence of marine heritage management as a discipline in its own right.

In this chapter I aim to describe initiatives and trends that highlight the origins and development of a national heritage agency's involvement in, and use of, wreck site formation theory and research (figure 10.1). Framed in the interim policy developed before English Heritage assumed formal responsibilities for the marine historic environment (Roberts and Trow 2002), the approach was taken forward following the author's appointment in 2002 as head of maritime archaeology for English Heritage. This approach acknowledged that the marine historic environment does not exist in isolation because it is an integral part of the wider marine environment, surrounded by and often firmly embedded in what may be termed the *natural* marine environment. That wider marine environment is of great economic importance for society, which has stimulated developments that not only generate new discoveries but also give rise to threats and impacts on existing known sites.

Even over the short period since its formal involvement, English Heritage has taken a series of evolutionary steps to develop its own expert capacity,

Figure 10.1. *Designation Selection Guide: Ships and Boats, Prehistory to Present* (English Heritage 2012b).

tools, systems, and structures, together with building knowledge and understanding of the surviving heritage. However, today resource managers are more often customers of services and the procurers of research, rather than carrying out all functions in their own right. As curators responsible for managing heritage resources responsibly, these managers must ensure that research is well founded; and procurers must demonstrate value for money, in the interests of all stakeholders; and decision makers must have good quality information, readily to hand.

Although not codified as a specific or core heritage agency objective, site formation theory, understanding, and research run throughout English Heritage's programs and projects for particular heritage assets. The agency fosters wider awareness, appreciation, and planning, as it increasingly recognizes and understands its relatively new marine responsibilities.

This chapter reviews marine historic environment management initiatives that English Heritage has undertaken and how the consideration of site formation processes has played, and currently plays, an integral part in the management of submerged shipwreck sites in England's waters. It also gives examples of the organization's sustained, long-term interest in and support for in situ management.

ENGLISH HERITAGE

English Heritage, the U.K. government's advisor on all aspects of the historic environment in England, land and sea, is an executive nondepartmental public body sponsored by the Department for Culture, Media, and Sport. The organization has four main aims: identifying and protecting England's heritage, championing England's heritage, helping others look after our common heritage, and helping people to enjoy our heritage. An important part of English Heritage's approach is to engage in partnership work with central government departments, local authorities, voluntary bodies, and the private sector to conserve and enhance the historic environment, broaden public access to heritage, and increase people's understanding of the past.

With the introduction of the National Heritage Act in 2002, English Heritage was charged, for the first time since its inception nearly twenty years earlier, with particular duties and responsibilities for the care and protection of submerged marine monuments, in, on, or under the seabed, within the English area of the U.K. Territorial Sea (to twelve nautical miles offshore), in order to preserve heritage values for the public good.

UNDERPINNING POLICY

English Heritage can and does take a proactive role in the management of sites, subject to limited powers, duties, and budgets, following as far as is possible the three elements of good sustainable management: policies, underpinning knowledge, and sound decisions on which to base action (English Heritage 2008a). There is also an explicit focus on heritage that is least understood, most threatened, most significant, and/or most valued by communities. In 2002 English Heritage published *Taking to the Water: An Initial Policy for the Management of Maritime Archaeology in England* (Roberts and Trow 2002), which set out how the organization intended to deliver its new responsibilities through a professional framework designed to encompass avocational involvement in the management of England's underwater cultural heritage. In particular, the policy refers to the desirability of a program of research designed to provide a more robust basis for the understanding and management of the maritime heritage and for studies designed to improve our understanding of marine site environments.

In 2005 the U.K. government announced its adoption of the Annex to the 2001 UNESCO Convention (UNESCO 2001), with its requirement to consider in situ preservation as the first option, as best practice for archaeology. In the wider context there are national marine policies and European instruments (English Heritage 2009) to which English Heritage aligns its work. It is more widely recognized that marine archaeological sites are a real component of the wider marine environment, which is not confined to what might be termed "natural," and it is entirely appropriate that such sites are managed within an overall approach to marine management policy (DEFRA 2009; Oxley 2004; Pater and Oxley 2014).

MANAGING CHANGE

To set out further an approach for the sustainable management of the historic environment, English Heritage developed the concept of *Conservation Principles: Policies and Guidance for the Sustainable Management of the Historic Environment* (English Heritage 2008a) to promote consistency across the organization's decision making. This has the ultimate objective of creating a management regime for all aspects of the historic environment that is clear and transparent in its purpose and sustainable in its application.

As such, "conservation" is taken to be the process of managing change in ways that will best sustain the values of the historic environment in its contexts, and which recognizes opportunities to reveal and reinforce those values. Therefore understanding change is crucial for establishing a baseline, tracking modification, and interpreting it with reference to an understanding of site formation.

DEVELOPMENT OF MANAGEMENT APPROACHES

Management approaches based on a high level of marine environmental knowledge are now preferred in many countries, and formal policy and proposal documents (often called "management" or "conservation" plans) based on comprehensive desk-based and field assessments are becoming common.

When English Heritage first assumed responsibility for marine resources in 2002, the subject of applied historic shipwreck resource management was still not well researched or published, and the available literature was often patchy, incomplete, or difficult to obtain (Oxley 2001a). It was also apparent that management strategies would almost inevitably fail if not taking full account of the actual factors governing causes of change to a site. Effective management should be responsive and adaptive (Oxley and Gregory 2002).

Management cannot be seen as being synonymous with preservation, and it cannot eliminate change completely but can only promote procedures that might reduce the detrimental effects resulting from recognized impacts. Deterioration cannot be completely avoided either, and therefore absolute preservation in situ is not achievable. All sites are dynamic, continuing to form in the sense that degradation processes keep on altering the material remains albeit at slow, often imperceptible rates.

The management of historic shipwreck resources is an ongoing, proactive necessity that should be backed up with quantified environmental information (i.e., data collected to a standard and using technique acceptable to the wider disciplines of marine science). The process should also be viewed within a wider spectrum of environmental awareness, incorporating concepts such as sustainable development and the precautionary principle.

In order to understand the management of historic shipwreck sites within their environmental context it is useful at this point to review the key factors driving resource management, such as:

- Good data is essential for good decision making.
- Identify users and stakeholders, and involve them.
- Understand the environment.
- Carry out comprehensive baseline surveys.
- Understand site formation and processes of change.
- Monitor periodically and effectively.
- Respond to change.
- Neutralize or diminish negative influences and build on positive ones.
- Increase appropriate involvement and promote nonintrusive access.

Table 10.1. Possible features of interest of the *La Surveillante* site together with the measurable attributes and the recommended methodology for monitoring them

Feature of Interest	Attribute	Assessment Methodology
Debris field	Exposure of artifacts	Visual, photo. video
Surrounding sediments	Stability of surface sediments	Sidescan/echo sounder (Quinn et al. 1998)
Inboard deposits	Tendency to promote deterioration of archaeological materials	Microbiological assay (Guthrie et al. 1996)
Accumulation/ erosion	Relative exposure to agents of degradation	Physical measurement
Guns and anchor	Coherence of concretion	Visual, photo, video
	Electro-chemical stability	Corrosion potential, pH
Copper sheathing	Coherence and stability	Visual, measurement
Anchor	Structural stability	Measurement
Hull structure	Percentage volume	Measurement

Note: After Oxley 2001b.

To achieve these aims, the concept of a management plan can be used as a mechanism for gathering, interpreting, and sharing data and turning it into information that is then used to provide robust and stable management advice to support justified and sustainable management decisions. These, in turn, contribute to maintaining and/or restoring conditions on the site conducive to the long-term aims of the plan, guided by the overriding aim of non–net loss of any part of the archaeological resource (table 10.1; Oxley 2001b).

Consequently in developing an effective program, and given the quantity of data and the number of potential sites of special interest, English Heritage's approach to the management of designated historic wrecks is informed by five principal factors:

- national and corporate policy;
- facilitating authorized public access and activities;
- strategic research and intervention;
- proactive interpretation/presentation; and
- ongoing dialogue with stakeholders (Dunkley and Oxley 2009).

ENGLISH HERITAGE'S STAGED APPROACH

English Heritage's publication *Conservation Principles* (English Heritage 2008a) provides a framework for decision making as it affects the historic environment, and the principles are translated into practice through the medium of projects. Its *Management of Research Projects in the Historic Environment* (MoRPHE) provides guidelines covering the management of research and development projects in the historic environment sector (English Heritage 2006). It is a model for archaeological projects undertaken or funded by English Heritage and has been influential in establishing benchmarks and standards for the archaeological profession as a whole (English Heritage 2006).

PRACTICAL CONSERVATION AND RISK-BASED MANAGEMENT

Gregory (2009) has suggested the fundamental steps to ensure the successful and responsible in situ management of underwater archaeological sites. These include extent to be preserved, the most significant threats to the site, the types of materials present and their state of preservation, the strategies to mitigate deterioration and stabilize the site from natural impacts, and subsequent monitoring and implementation of mitigation. Utilizing the content of the management planning concepts outlined earlier in this chapter, and addressing the factors driving resource management since 2002, English Heritage has developed an evidence- and ecosystem-based approach to frame the organization's role (Dunkley and Oxley 2009).

England's suite of "protected wreck sites," consisting of Late Middle Bronze Age cargoes through to early twentieth-century submarines, survive in a range of environments and to varying degrees. Quantification of a wreck's survival is a point-in-time measurement of the current state or condition of the wreck relative to some former state and reflects the cumulative effects of all the natural and human processes that have operated upon it.

It is recognized that natural processes, such as erosion, cannot always be prevented, but protected wreck sites that are subject to such forces will not be considered at risk if they are subject to a planned program of managed change, recording, and investigation.

In July 2008 English Heritage launched the first all-encompassing risk register of the country's heritage. This initiative, known as *Heritage at Risk*, assessed 30,687 listed buildings; 19,711 scheduled monuments; all 1,595 registered historic parks, gardens, and landscapes; all 43 registered battlefields; and all of England's protected wreck sites (Dunkley 2012).

The unpredictable nature of the historic environment makes the identification and management of risk characteristically difficult to anticipate, particularly as risks to marine archaeological sites have been identified as being derived from both environmental and human impacts. On this level it is also accepted that all wreck sites are at risk simply because of the nature of their environment. A methodology was therefore devised for the field assessment of risk to historic wreck sites to understand their current management patterns, their likely future trajectory, and how this can be influenced to ensure that their significance is maintained for both present and future generations (English Heritage 2008b; Dunkley 2012).

An English Heritage assessment indicated that the proportion of designated wrecks at high risk in 2008 was 24.4% (11 out of 45; Dunkley and Oxley 2009). By 2012 this had fallen to just 8.70% (4 out of 46) owing to strategic management intervention following the earlier assessment, such as site stabilization trials on the wreck of HMS *Colossus* undertaken between 2003 and 2005 (Camidge 2009).

All protected wreck sites are assessed using standardized terminology. Threats to sites are identified and a measure of risk is subjectively calculated. Then priorities are afforded to "high risk" sites and to "medium risk" sites that are in danger of becoming high risk. Where assessed, a protected wreck site will be considered to be at high risk if there is a significant likelihood of loss or further loss of historical, archaeological, or artistic significance from it, within the foreseeable future.

Significance, in this context, means *the sum of the cultural and natural heritage values of a place* (English Heritage 2008a). Assessment at medium risk indicates that there is a reasonable likelihood of loss of historical, archaeological, or artistic significance in the future if no change in the management regime takes place. "Low risk" indicates that the site is being managed in a way that is sympathetic to its historical, archaeological, or artistic significance (English Heritage 2008b).

Three broad factors have been considered when assessing the risk to the nation's protected wreck sites: the *current condition* of the wreck (whether in optimal condition, generally satisfactory, generally unsatisfactory, or having extensive problems); *vulnerability*, or an assessment of the natural and anthropogenic influences on the site; and *trajectory*, which is an assessment of the management regime and whether the monument condition is improving, remaining stable, or experiencing unmanaged or inappropriate decline.

Assessment Followed by Conservation Planning

To support understanding of the environment surrounding protected wreck sites, specific conservation management is informed in two principal ways. First, an assessment is performed for understanding of anthropogenic and environmental risks to a particular site. Second, the requirements for the conservation, maintenance, and enhancement of the values and features of a site are addressed (Oxley 2007). To address the former, an understanding of a site's environmental characteristics is required to inform intervention. Here a program of marine environmental assessment (MEA) is commissioned, examining chemical, physical, biological, and other parameters upon which informed decisions can be based (table 10.2; Camidge et al. 2006).

Table 10.2. Marine environmental assessment phases

Phase 1 Desk Based Assessment

Environmental
Identify all known sources of environmental data relating to the study area, including:
    Physical oceanographic status—waves, tides, water depth
    Sedimentological status—sediment transport, mobility
    Water quality status—chemistry, pollution
Assess the quality of data
Identify any areas that need further data collection
Archaeological
Establish the material type and known extent of archaeological site
Assess archaeological potential of site

Phase 2 Field Assessment

Collection of data relating to:
    Chemical—REDOX, salinity, PH, dissolved oxygen
    Physical—min/max depth, fetch, temperature, ground swell, tides, wave height, currents, sediment grain size, seabed strength, depth of sediment, bathymetry, sub-bottom profiling
    Biological—flora, fauna
Establish the effect of the above on the preservation of archaeological material
Identify material most at risk

Phase 3 Monitoring

Identify features of interest for monitoring
Identify attributes to monitor
Establish assessment methodology (stations, intervals) for each attribute
Monitor site for five-year period

MEA programs form one of the stages in a series of initiatives that will lead to the development of archaeological management plans for the sites that will inform English Heritage's future research, amenity, and education developments for the benefit of the wider community.

English Heritage continues to test or sponsor innovative methodologies for understanding how sites have developed and how they continue to change. These include advances in marine archaeological geophysics (Plets et al. 2009) and studies advancing our capabilities to manage metal-hulled ships and boats, such as using ultrasonic hull thickness measurement (Dunkley 2013).

CASE STUDIES

WARSHIP *HAZARDOUS*

Le Hazardeux was built in 1698 in France. In 1703 the ship was captured by the English and refitted as a fourth rate ship of the line with fifty-four guns (HWTMA 2006). In 1706 she was driven into shoal waters in Bracklesham Bay, West Sussex, in poor weather. There is evidence that limited salvage work was undertaken after wrecking, primarily aimed at recovering armaments. Due to the highly dynamic environment in which the site lies it is assumed that the wreck's upper structure would have broken up relatively quickly.

The wreck site had been under archaeological investigation by a local volunteer group, the *Hazardous* Project Team (Sub-Aqua Association 308), with the support of a range of archaeological advisors and organizations, for more than twenty-five years prior to the start of English Heritage's involvement in 2002 (Owen 1991). However, there had been only limited excavation on the site, undertaken in the late 1980s. Work since had been restricted to survey and surface recovery of artifacts that had been eroded from the sediment of what was clearly a dynamic site.

Active erosion of the site meant that archaeological survey had been essentially reactive as artifacts became dislodged and much of their contextual information was lost. It was clear that what was required was a comprehensive understanding of the site formation processes affecting the site in order to plan future work.

The first step was an archive project to safeguard the results of previous investigations. This would also provide the opportunity to assess how the site had been affected by the prevailing environmental conditions over the previous decades and to help managers gain an understanding of the processes causing the ongoing erosion. If necessary, the rescue excavation of exposed material could then be implemented.

The environmental assessment project addressed the need to quantify the extent and rates of erosion that are occurring on the site by looking at data on two principle scales: the wreck site (including data from archaeological, photographic, monitoring, distribution studies, and diver observation sources); and the coastal environment of the onshore, nearshore, and offshore zones (including data on sediment transport, coastal response, aerial photographs, beach monitoring, and charts; HWTMA 2006). The data were analyzed to identify particular areas of the site at risk from erosion in relation to areas with high archaeological potential. The result was an assessment of past and current environmental factors affecting the stability of the wreck site, the production of maps showing areas of most rapid degradation against those of highest archaeological potential, and the implications for the long-term future of the archaeological archive.

HMS COLOSSUS

HMS *Colossus* was a 74-gun warship built in 1787 and wrecked off Samson in the Isles of Scilly in 1798 after seeing action at Toulon, Groix, and Cape St. Vincent. In December of the latter year she was on her way home to England with wounded from the Battle of the Nile and a cargo including Sir William Hamilton's collection of Etruscan pottery. As the ship was sheltering from a gale in St. Mary's Roads, the anchor cable parted and she was driven aground. All members of the crew but one were taken off safely before she turned onto her beam ends and proceeded to break up (CISMAS 2005).

The site was modified by phases of intrusive activities including contemporary Royal Navy salvage, Admiralty contract recoveries, and unauthorized salvage, over many decades, before being designated under the Protection of Wrecks Act 1973. In 1975 Roland Morris worked on what was probably the bow section of the wreck, recovering a large number of pottery shards from Sir William Hamilton's collection (now in the British Museum) and other artifacts, including iron cannon.

In 2001 the current site was discovered some 350 meters (1,148 feet) to the east of Roland Morris's site. The rear half of the port side of the 74-gun ship of the line lies flat, preserved in the sand. The wreck includes the six aftermost gun ports on the upper gun deck, five of which still have 18-pound guns pointing through them, with their breech ends uppermost. The ship's structure appeared to be complete from the top of the gun ports on the quarter deck down to the turn of the bilge below the orlop deck.

The preservation of organic material appeared to be very good, including examples of decorative carving from the stern, although erosion due to recent lowering of sediment levels was a recognized threat. The reasons for this erosion were not known.

Following the assumption by English Heritage of management interests in protected wreck sites in 2002, a program of research has been developed and supported on the HMS *Colossus,* undertaken by Kevin Camidge and the Cornwall and Isles of Scilly Maritime Archaeology Society. Between 2003 and 2007 English Heritage sponsored two-year stabilization trials, including the assessment of burial parameters by data loggers, plus monitoring of sediment levels to establish prevailing sedimentation variation (Camidge 2009). Surveys of the debris fields around the main sites were carried out in 2004 and 2005 to investigate the wrecking process and locate additional material. Site stabilization of the vulnerable stern timbers, the installation of a diver trail including placement of an underwater information panel and waterproof booklets for licensed visiting divers, and a liaison program with dive charter boats were all undertaken in 2008. In 2010 testing of the mobility of artifacts and further site monitoring projects were carried out.

In 2012 the program included the targeted excavation and recording of newly exposed areas around a main gun deck port, examining the post-wrecking stratigraphy, monitoring mobile surface artifacts, and continuation of monitoring of sediment levels. The 2012 program also included investigation and appraisal of excavation methods and recording regimes, initiation of a long-term reburial trial using archaeological objects, as well as development of new opportunities for training and capacity building (Camidge 2012). Additional research focused on reburial and analysis of non-HMS *Colossus* wreck material and modern tokens, aiming to obtain complementary information about the degradation of different materials at the site's location (Middleton et al. 2012).

Royal Anne Galley

The *Royal Anne* was a fifth-rate oared frigate built at Woolwich (of the Preliminary Establishment of 1706–1718). The vessel was launched in 1709 with an armament of 40 guns and complement of 127 men. On November 10, 1721, while she was en route to Barbados, bad weather forced her to return to Falmouth, and she was wrecked on the Stag Rocks of Cornwall.

About two hundred crew and passengers were lost, including John, third Lord Belhaven, who was traveling to take up a new post as the governor of Barbados.

The wreck site was rediscovered in 1991 by local diver Robert Sherratt when a large sounding lead was found adjacent to two iron guns. Subsequently numerous objects were recovered from the seabed in the vicinity of the iron guns, including items of cutlery bearing the Belhaven crest, which led to the identification of the wreck. The wreck was designated in 1993 under the Protection of Wrecks Act 1973.

The *Royal Anne* lies close inshore, within an area surrounded by rocks that regularly experiences large Atlantic swells, even during periods of fine weather. A series of rock gullies on the seabed is filled with large rocks overlying coarse sand and small stones. Notably, the site has no known surviving organic material. The site consists solely of artifacts and some iron concretions, with no evidence of any ship's structure.

English Heritage commissioned the Historic Environment Service (Projects), Cornwall County Council, to carry out a staged MEA program. The Phase 1 desk-based assessment work included an archaeological and environmental assessment of the *Royal Anne* and also an investigation into the methods of data collection and a methodology to integrate all the disparate oceanographic data sets in order to provide high quality, auditable advice that is applicable not just to the management of the *Royal Anne* but to wreck sites in general. The Phase 1 assessment concluded with a strategy for a proposed Phase 2 field assessment to include obtaining data on waves, tides, water quality, sediment, and flora and fauna. The proposed field assessment also included airborne LIDAR bathymetry survey, artifact dispersal trials, monitoring corrosion of iron cannon, and assessing the biological degradation of wood (Camidge et al. 2006).

The Phase 2 field assessment was carried out during 2008 and 2009, and the following objectives were successfully accomplished: bathymetric survey, marine biological assessment, sampling for water quality, sediment analysis, installation of bricks and spheres for monitoring artifact dispersal, and setting up of objects to track wood degradation (Camidge et al. 2009).

The purpose of a Phase 3 monitoring stage was then to make an inspection of the site to recover the oak sample blocks for analysis and to locate the dispersal trials objects that had been placed on and below the seabed in April 2009 during the Phase 2 field assessment. In total, 21 of the original 40 objects were located and recorded: 8 spheres and 13 bricks. The spheres had been moved on the seabed by an average of 5.15 m (16.9 feet) and the bricks by an average of 4.89 m (16 feet). The distances moved by the spheres varied between 2.22 and 11.4 m (7.28–37.39 feet); the bricks moved between 0.80 and 9.79 m (2.62–32.11 feet). Although some of the objects may have been missed by the survey, it is more likely that many lay outside the 10 m (32.8 foot) radius searched. With a single exception, the objects were "sorted" by the environmental forces acting on the site—the spheres being moved west and the bricks to the east. This result was not anticipated. All the dispersal objects occupy a long thin corridor aligned northeast to southwest, and this is likely to be a good indicator of the direction along which the predominant seabed forces are acting. Analysis of the oak blocks exposed on the seabed shows they were subject to rapid attack by wood-boring organisms, indicating that survival of any timber from the wreck of the *Royal Anne Galley* is unlikely (Camidge et al. 2011).

AGGREGATES LEVY SUSTAINABILITY FUND (ALSF)

The Aggregates Levy Sustainability Fund (ALSF) was introduced in April 2002, initially as a two-year pilot scheme, to provide funds to tackle a wide range of problems in areas affected by aggregates extraction. English Heritage was a major distributor of the fund on behalf of the Department for Environment, Food and Rural Affairs, and collaborating entities were English Nature, the Countryside Agency (now Natural England), and the Centre for Environment, Fisheries and Aquaculture Science.

Described as a proactive, collaborative research program, it is regarded as a model of innovative heritage management involving public and private partnership to support strategic management of, and guidance upon, resources of benefit to all sectors (Flatman and Doeser 2010). The core objective of the English Heritage ALSF program was to reduce the impact on the historic environment of aggregate extraction, both terrestrial and marine.

The marine component of the ALSF in particular has been recognized by the heritage community, industry, and government as being one of the most successful components of the broader ALSF program. The ALSF has led to a significant improvement of relationships among all stakeholders and has had a considerable additional public relations benefit in promoting understanding of the marine historic environment to the general public.

ASLF included improving the development process through strategies such as mapping the distribution of unknown/unmapped heritage resources (particularly in the marine zone), the development of management strategies for such heritage (e.g., exclusion zones), and the provision of industry guidance and standards. All these activities assist the aggregates and other industries in identifying, planning for, and mitigating risk (including unexpected cost and delays) in the medium and long term.

Marine archaeological site formation understanding underpinned the development of the components of the marine ALSF program involving interdisciplinary approaches to research involving all stakeholders and both the natural and cultural heritage, as exemplified by the following English Heritage-supported projects.

Navigational Hazards

Developed by Bournemouth University using historical and environmental evidence of marine navigational hazards, the Navigational Hazards project aimed to characterize areas where a high potential for ship losses coincided with a high potential for archaeological preservation (Merritt et al. 2007).

Archives of historic sources, such as nautical charts and pilotage documents, produced from the medieval period to the present day, were assessed in order to identify historically significant hazardous sea areas, which were then presented spatially. A further approach was to categorize seabed sediment types by their preservation qualities.

The results of the project highlighted the scope for further refining the assessment of archaeological potential through the integration of further environmental and archaeological datasets and the analysis of relationships between them. This project introduced the possibility of mapping historical data of maritime activity together with marine environmental factors, thus giving heritage managers the opportunity to bring aspects of site formation and preservation into decision making.

Refining Areas of Maritime Archaeological Potential for Shipwrecks (AMAP1)

Building on the results of the Navigational Hazards research, completed in 2007, which used GIS to identify areas where a high risk to navigation coincided with a high potential for preservation, this project aimed to construct an interpretive GIS layer to provide the foundations for developing planning tools for assessing the potential existence of unrecorded shipwreck sites. A methodology for characterizing likely areas, Areas of Maritime Archaeological Potential for Shipwrecks (AMAP), was developed using statistical and spatial analysis of wreck data to define the relationships between known wrecks and the archaeological or environmental parameters affecting their preservation, in order to assess the potential for archaeological remains of shipwrecks to exist and survive within seabed sediments.

The project sought to compare trends in shipwreck data with marine environmental parameters, types and frequency of hydrographic surveys, and the nature and scale of coastal marine activity, such as ports, harbors, and anchorages. The identification of relationships between these datasets should improve the interpretation of wreck scatters and encourage a more comprehensive approach to predicting archaeological potential for unrecorded shipwrecks.

The project's GIS output provided a basis for developing a national dataset for Areas of Maritime Archaeological Potential (AMAPs), which could be used alongside other marine datasets for informing the management of coastal and offshore development. The benefits will be seen through a more accurate interpretation of the potential impact of marine development initiatives on the historic environment, leading to better mitigation planning.

The project ran as a pilot focusing on the development of a methodology using the Eastern English Channel as a study area. This was based on available digital data, with a long-term aim of developing a national GIS dataset. The results of the project highlight the need to develop and improve key environmental datasets to provide the basis to assist assessment of the potential for unrecorded shipwrecks and to improve heritage management in marine spatial planning. As well as further enhancing tools to aid decision making for heritage managers, the concepts developed in this project were also used to inform marine environmental managers and planners.

Characterizing the Potential for Wrecks (AMAP2)

Carried out between 2009 and 2011, this collaboration between SeaZone and the University of Southampton produced a characterization mapping developed through the integration of the methodology applied during AMAP1 with the modeling of marine environmental data, to produce a considered assessment of environmental character on a national scale (Merritt 2011; Carrizales 2010).

The aim was to improve management of the marine historic environment by increasing the understanding of relationships between historic wrecks and their environment; by developing a refinement of the baseline data for marine spatial planning; and by the development of a characterization of environmental variables affecting the shipwreck survival.

An analysis of the distributions of wrecks of shared characteristics in English waters was constructed that integrated physical properties of wrecks and their environment. The products of this research not only improved the understanding of the relationships between those two concepts for heritage managers but also produced additional insight regarding distribution of shipwreck sites, such as the age bias of wrecks and the relationships between physical characteristics and environmental parameters. The project demonstrated that the spatial tools developed revealed untapped value in the shipwreck databases that are available, including the records of the United Kingdom Hydrographic Office, showing the correlations made from modeling on a local scale with patterns in the distributions of wrecks of shared characteristics on a national scale. AMAP2 helped identify new areas for research and requirements for better data accessibility, highlighting the scope for using the results to improve heritage management decision making through an improved understanding of the potential impacts of marine environmental variables to specific groups of wrecks.

Wrecks on the Seabed

The Wrecks on the Seabed project consisted of two rounds running from 2002 to 2006. The project tested ways of assessing and evaluating wreck sites to assist with understanding the effects of marine aggregate dredging on shipwrecks (Wessex Archaeology 2007).

In all Wessex Archaeology investigated twenty wrecks using a variety of methods of hydrographic survey, remote sensing, and diving survey. The overall aim of the project was to provide industry, regulators, and contractors with guidance on the archaeological assessment, evaluation, and recording of wreck sites. Such a framework is important when considering the time and cost of marine investigations. The framework also promotes effective communication between industry, regulators, and contractors by defining comprehensiveness and detail for differing levels of investigations, suggesting specifications for surveys at each level.

Round 1 of the project started in July 2002 and addressed three levels of investigation, using both geophysical and diver-based techniques: field assessment, nonintrusive evaluation, and rapid in situ recording. Methodologies were developed on a sample of known (but generally unidentified) wreck sites off the coasts of Hampshire and Sussex, U.K. The wrecks included both metal and wooden-hulled vessels and aircraft. Investigations included side-scan sonar and magnetometer surveys of seventeen sites. In the second year detailed magnetometer, sub-bottom profiler, and multibeam echosounder surveys of seven sites took place. Diving investigations included assessment of nine sites, using surface-supplied divers equipped with video, digital still cameras, and underwater tracking. In Year 2 four out of seven wreck sites were dived on. In situ recording took place on three sites.

Round 2 of Wrecks on the Seabed commenced in 2005 and consisted of a geophysical section and a diving and remotely operated vehicle (ROV) section. During Year 1 of Round 2, aspects of geophysical surveys on sites over 30 m (98 feet) deep, area survey methods, and the geophysical identification of ephemeral sites were examined. Also during Round 2, Year 1 the diving and ROV section of the project dealt with the infrastructure of diving projects as well as the application of ROV survey methods on shallow wreck sites.

These deep-water geophysical surveys and the ROV work conducted on shallow sites served as the basis for the deep-water ROV wreck surveys conducted in Round 2, Year 1. The deep-water ROV surveys developed out of feedback received from the aggregate industry during Round 1 of the project, in which the question of the applicability of the tested methods to sites in up to 60 m (197 feet) of water was raised due to the possibility of the aggregate industry expanding its activities into deeper water in the future.

To assess whether the ROV survey methodologies developed during Round 2, Year 1 of the project could be applied to a deep-water environment, three unknown wreck sites in water depths between 50 and 60 m (164–197 feet) were surveyed with multibeam echosounder, side-scan sonar, and magnetometer in Round 2, Year 1 as part of the geophysical section of the project. The geophysical data acquired were used as the basis for the ROV survey, and all three sites were subject to an ROV survey during Round 2, Year 2 aimed at achieving level 2 or 3 site recordings.

Designed to test and develop ways of assessing, evaluating, and recording shipwreck sites, Wrecks on the Seabed provided an important analysis of the techniques available to heritage managers. Assessing the advantages and limitations of a range of recording technologies and methodologies as applied to a suite of wrecks lying in different marine environments provided a comprehensive tool for identifying appropriate and cost-effective methods for further investigation of such sites for many purposes, such as research, education, or amenity access.

WRECKS ECOLOGY

The ALSF Round 2 *Wrecks on the Seabed* study (Wessex Archaeology 2007) highlighted that there would be merit in developing a clearer understanding of the relationships between marine archaeological sites and their associated benthic ecology.

The objectives of the project were to assess the potential of archaeological data collected from a number of wreck sites off the East Sussex coast to provide useful ecological and biological information, and to gauge the value to archaeologists, ecologists, and seabed developers of integrating archaeological and ecological surveys of wreck sites in future.

The project proposed a cost-effective but ecologically sound methodology for recording the fauna and flora of wrecks during archaeological site survey, based on diver observations and/or still images and video footage. An increased understanding of the environmental interactions of wreck sites and the (potentially cumulative) impacts on wreck sites from aggregate extraction was developed. The potential for cost savings to the aggregates industry were also assessed based on the utility and potential of conducting both ecological and archaeological wreck site surveys in tandem (Wessex Archaeology 2008).

From an archaeological perspective, the project suggested that such data are useful to both archaeology and ecology, opening new opportunities with respect to better understanding site formation processes and the implications this has for managing wreck sites. It also builds important interdisciplinary links between archaeologists and ecologists, pointing the way to closer interactions in future. At a general level, this project sought to promote an awareness of the wider, in this case ecological, importance of the marine historic environment. All of these aims are central to the role of marine heritage managers in raising the awareness of a wide range of sea users to the potential to be gained by taking into account fully the environment of wreck sites. In addition, informed by wreck site formation theory and research, the project identified the potential of benthic studies and the suitable methodologies that heritage managers could both use and promote.

A FRAMEWORK FOR FUTURE RESEARCH AND MANAGEMENT ACTION

A National Heritage Protection Plan has been developed by English Heritage to determine priorities based on research (i.e., Ransley et al. 2013) and understanding (i.e., site formation theory and practice), with the goal of setting up processes for heritage protection and then implementing them.

The plan is a coherent national framework to bring together work by English Heritage and other partners within the sector, to protect the historic environment and to realign and apply the full range of our expertise and resources toward protection activities carried out either directly by English Heritage or by supporting others. The overall goal of the plan is to provide a framework for action for the entire sector, not just English Heritage (English Heritage 2012a).

The plan looks at the heritage itself (the assets) and the potential threats to heritage (issues). It is necessary to understand what resources exist, what threats are affecting them, and how to respond to those threats. Site formation research is fundamental to achieving that understanding and it will remain a vital component to many elements of the plan.

Conclusions

Since 2002 English Heritage has developed an evidence-based and ecosystem-based approach to frame the organization's role in the care and management of England's most important historic shipwreck sites designated under the Protection of Wrecks Act 1973. English Heritage's Conservation Principles provide the framework for making transparent, consistent, well-informed, and objective conservation decisions (English Heritage 2008a), while the innovative methodology for the Risk Management of Protected Wreck Sites assists with strategic prioritization. Site-specific Conservation Statements and Management Plans articulate a shared vision of how the values and features of particular sites can be conserved, maintained, and enhanced through local and regional stakeholder involvement. Any projects developed internally or funded by the organization are managed along the widely accepted guidelines of MoRPHE (English Heritage 2006).

All of these initiatives and the intervening research and mitigation projects that have been taken forward by English Heritage on wreck sites located in England's Territorial Seas have benefited from existing and developing wreck site formation understanding. In the short history of its involvement in historic shipwreck management, the organization has advanced both practice and research through systematic assessments and actions.

References Cited

Camidge, Kevin
2009   HMS *Colossus*: An Experimental Site Stabilization. *Conservation and Management of Archaeological Sites* 11(2):161–188.
2012   *HMS Colossus: Monitoring and Investigation 2012*. Report for English Heritage.

Camidge, Kevin, Charles Johns, and Phil Rees
2006   *Royal Anne Galley, Lizard Point, Cornwall: Marine Environmental Assessment Phase 1, Desk-Based Assessment*. Report for English Heritage. Historic Environment Projects, Cornwall County Council, Truro.

Camidge, Kevin, Charles Johns, Matt Canti, Miles Hoskin, and Ian Panter
2009   *Royal Anne Galley Marine Environmental Assessment: Phase 2, Field Assessment Report*. Report for English Heritage. Historic Environment Projects, Cornwall County Council, Truro. Electronic document, http://www.cornwall.gov.uk/idoc.ashx?docid=c59b2bef-7eec-461e-8a23-ced7c5383490&version=-1, accessed February 17, 2014.

Camidge, K., C. Johns, and I. Panter
2011   *Royal Anne Galley Marine Environmental Assessment, the Lizard, Cornwall: Phase 3, Monitoring: Initial Inspection and Recovery*. Report for English Heritage. Historic Environment Projects, Cornwall County Council, Truro. Electronic document, http://www.cornwall.gov.uk/idoc.ashx?docid=16e40adf-bed5-46be-9007-a800ced675d6&version=-1, accessed February 17, 2014.

Carrizales, Adam
2010   *Development and Refinement of Regional Sediment Mobility Models: Implications for Coastal Evolution, Preservation of Archaeological Potential, and Commercial Development*. Report for SeaZone Solutions Ltd., English Heritage funded project AMAP2. University of Southampton, Southampton. Electronic document, http://archaeologydataservice.ac.uk/archives/view/amap2_eh_2011/index.cfm, accessed May 24, 2013.

CISMAS
2005   *The Search for Colossus: A Story of Wreck and Discovery*. Cornwall and Isles of Scilly Maritime Archaeology Society, Penzance, Cornwall. Electronic document, http://www.cismas.org.uk/publication-dfs.php

DEFRA
2009   *Our Seas—a Shared Resource: High Level Marine Objectives*. Department for Environment, Food and Rural Affairs, London. Electronic document, http://archive.defra.gov.uk/environment/marine/documents/ourseas-2009update.pdf, accessed May 30, 2013.

Dunkley, Mark
2012   Civilising the Rude Sea: Assessing and Managing Risk to England's Protected Historic Wreck Sites. In *IKUWA 3, Beyond Boundaries: Proceedings of the 3rd International Congress on Underwater Archaeology 9th to 12th July 2008, London*, edited by Jon Henderson, pp. 105–111. Romisch-Germanische Kommission des Deutschen Archaologischen Instituts and Nautical Archaeology Society, Bonn, Germany.

2013   Petrolheads: Managing England's Early Submarines. In *Proceedings of the Advisory Council on Underwater Archaeology Conference, Leicester*, edited by Colin Breen and Wes Forsythe, pp. 179–184. Advisory Council on Underwater Archaeology.

Dunkley, Mark, and Ian Oxley
2009   The Management of Protected Historic Warship Wrecks in England's Waters.

In *Shared Heritage: Joint Responsibilities in the Management of British Warship Wrecks Overseas*, edited by Steven Gallagher, pp. 69–86. University of Wolverhampton and English Heritage, Wolverhampton. Electronic document, http://www.english-heritage.org.uk/publications/management-of-british-warship-wrecks-overseas, accessed January 17, 2013.

English Heritage

2006   *Management of Research Projects in the Historic Environment: The MoRPHE Project Managers' Guide.* English Heritage, Swindon. Electronic document, www.english-heritage.org.uk/publications/morphe-project-managers-guide/, accessed May 28, 2013.

2007   *Stirling Castle: Conservation and Management Plan.* Electronic document, http://www.english-heritage.org.uk/content/imported-docs/p-t/mgmtplan-stirlingcastlevfinal.pdf, accessed February 12, 2014.

2008a   *Conservation Principles: Policies and Guidance for the Sustainable Management of the Historic Environment.* Electronic document, http://www.english-heritage.org.uk/publications/conservation-principles-sustainable-management-historic-environment, accessed January 17, 2013.

2008b   *Protected Wreck Sites at Risk: A Management Handbook.* Electronic document, http://www.english-heritage.org.uk/publications/protected-wreck-sites-at-risk-handbook/, accessed January 17, 2013.

2009   *The European Landscape Convention: The English Heritage Action Plan for Implementation.* English Heritage, London.

2010   *Protected Wreck Sites: Moving Towards a New Way of Managing England's Historic Environment.* Electronic document, http://www.english-heritage.org.uk/publications/protected-wreck-sites/, accessed February 28, 2013.

2012a   *The National Heritage Protection Plan.* Version: 3rd December 2012. Electronic document, http://www.english-heritage.org.uk/publications/nhpp-plan-framework/nhpp-plan-framework.pdf, accessed May 28, 2013.

2012b   *Designation Selection Guide: Ships and Boats, Prehistory to Present.* Electronic document, www.english-heritage.org.uk/publications/dsg-ships-boats/, accessed May 28, 2013.

Flatman, Joe, and James Doeser

2010   *International Marine Aggregates Management Strategic Review: Short Report.* University College London, London.

Gregory, David

2009   In Situ Preservation of Marine Archaeological Sites: Out of Sight but Not Out of Mind. In *In Situ Conservation of Cultural Heritage: Public, Professionals and Preservation*, edited by Vicki Richards and Jennifer McKinnon, pp. 1–16. Flinders University Program in Maritime Archaeology, Past Foundation, Columbus, Ohio.

Guthrie, Jodi N., Linda L. Blackall, David J. W. Moriarty, and Peter D. Nichols

1996   Decomposers of Shipwreck HMS *Pandora*. *Microbiology Australia* 17:1–17.

HWTMA

2006   *Quantifying the Hazardous Threat: An Assessment of Site Monitoring Data and Environmental Data Sets. Project Report for English Heritage.* Hampshire and Wight Trust for Maritime Archaeology (HWTMA), Southampton. Electronic docu-

ment, http://archaeologydataservice.ac.uk/archives/view/hazardous_eh_2005/
index.cfm imaged 28 05 13.

Merritt, Olivia
2011   *AMAP2—Characterising the Potential of Wrecks.* SeaZone Solutions, Bent-
        ley. Electronic document, http://archaeologydataservice.ac.uk/archives/view/
        amap2_eh_2011/, accessed May 24, 2013.

Merritt, Olivia, David Parham, and Douglas M. McElvogue
2007   *Enhancing Our Understanding of the Marine Historic Environment: Navigation-
        al Hazards Project Final Report for English Heritage.* Bournemouth University,
        Bournemouth.

Middleton, Angela, Karla Graham, and Sarah Paynter
2012   Additional Reburial Objects. In *HMS* Colossus: *Monitoring and Investigation
        2012*, edited by Kevin Camidge, pp. 89–94. Report for English Heritage.

Owen, Norman
1991   *Hazardous* 1990–91 Interim Report. *International Journal for Nautical Archaeol-
        ogy* 20:4.

Oxley, Ian
1992   The Investigation of the Factors Which Affect the Preservation of Underwater
        Archaeological Sites. In *Underwater Archaeology Proceedings from the Society for
        Historical Archaeology Conference, Kingston, Jamaica*, edited by Donald H. Keith
        and Toni L. Carrell, pp. 105–110. Society for Historical Archaeology, Tucson.
1998   The In Situ Preservation of Underwater Sites. In *Preserving Archaeological Re-
        mains in Situ. Proceedings of the Conference of 01–03/04/96 at the Museum of Lon-
        don*, edited by Mike Corfield, Peter Hinton, Taryn Nixon, and Mark Pollard, pp.
        159–173. Museum of London Archaeology Service and University of Bradford,
        Department of Archaeological Sciences, London.
2001a   Towards the Integrated Management of Scotland's Cultural Heritage: Examin-
        ing Historic Shipwrecks as Marine Environmental Resources. *World Archaeology*
        32(3):413–426.
2001b   Towards a Sustainable Management Scheme for the *La Surveillante* Wreck Site.
        In *Integrated Marine Investigations on the Historic Shipwreck* La Surveillante: *A
        French Frigate lost in Bantry Bay, Ireland, January 1797*, edited by Colin Breen, pp.
        103–117. Centre for Maritime Archaeology Monograph Series no. 1. University of
        Ulster, Coleraine.
2004   Advances in Research into the in Situ Management of Historic Shipwreck Sites.
        In *Preserving Archaeological Remains in Situ? Proceedings of the 2nd Conference,
        September 11–14, 2001*, edited by Taryn Nixon, pp. 72–78. Museum of London
        Archaeology Service, London.
2007   Making the Submerged Historic Environment Accessible—Beyond the National
        Heritage Act (2002). In *Managing the Marine Cultural Heritage: Defining, Ac-
        cessing and Managing the Resource*, edited by Julie Satchell and Paola Palma, pp.
        87–95. CBA Research Report 153. Council for British Archaeology, York.

Oxley, Ian, and David Gregory
2002   Site Management. In *International Handbook of Underwater Archaeology*, edited

by Carol V. Ruppe and Jane F. Barstad, pp. 715–725. Plenum Series in Underwater Archaeology, Kluwer Academic–Plenum Publishers, New York.

Pater, Chris, and Ian Oxley
2014   Developing Marine Historic Environment Management Policy: The English Heritage Experience. *Marine Policy*. Special Issue 45: 342–348. Electronic document, http://www.sciencedirect.com/science/article/pii/S0308597 × 13002078, accessed February 12, 2014.

Plets, Ruth M. K., Justin K. Dix, Jon R. Adams, Jonathan M. Bull, Timothy J. Henstock, Martin Gutowski, and Angus I. Best
2009   The Use of a High-Resolution 3D Chirp Sub-Bottom Profiler for the Reconstruction of the Shallow Water Archaeological Site of the *Grace Dieu* (1439), River Hamble, UK. *Journal of Archaeological Science* 36:408–18.

Quinn, Rory, Jonathan R. Adams, Justin K. Dix, and Jonathan M. Bull
1998   The *Invincible* (1758) Site: An Integrated Geophysical Assessment. *International Journal of Nautical Archaeology* 27(2):126–138.

Ransley, Jesse, Fraser Sturt, Justin Dix, Jon Adams, and Lucy Blue
2013   *People and the Sea: A Maritime Archaeological Research Agenda for England*. CBA Research Report 171. Council for British Archaeology, York.

Roberts, Paul, and Steve Trow
2002   *Taking to the Water: English Heritage's Initial Policy for the Management of Maritime Archaeology in England*. English Heritage, London. Electronic document, http://www.english-heritage.org.uk/publications/taking-to-the-water, accessed January 17, 2013.

UNESCO
2001   *Convention on the Protection of the Underwater Cultural Heritage*. UNESCO, Paris.

Wessex Archaeology
2007   *Wrecks on the Seabed R2: Assessment, Evaluation and Recording*. Report for English Heritage. Wessex Archaeology, Salisbury. Electronic document, http://archaeologydataservice.ac.uk/archives/view/wrecks_eh_2006, accessed May 24, 2013 (further information from http://www.wessexarch.co.uk/projects/marine/alsf/wrecks_seabed/index.html).
2008   *Wrecks Ecology 2007–08 Final Report*. Report for English Heritage. Wessex Archaeology, Salisbury. Electronic document, http://www.wessexarch.co.uk/system/files/57456_Wrecks%20Ecology_web.pdf, accessed February 12, 2014.

11

Acoustic Positioning and Site Formation on Deep-Water World War II Shipwrecks in the Gulf of Mexico

DANIEL J. WARREN

Technology continues to open once inaccessible areas of the Earth's oceans and seas to exploration. Inevitably, these explorations reveal shipwrecks that have remained undisturbed since slipping beneath the waves years, decades, or centuries before. Often found far from shore and at water depths well beyond the limits of conventional scientific diving—defined here as 60 to 70 meters (197 to 230 feet) below sea level—these deep-water shipwrecks are challenging to document and assess. A key challenge for archaeologists investigating these sites is constructing accurate site maps. Archaeologists more often than not get only a single opportunity to visit a deep-water shipwreck, so accurate mapping is essential for understanding site distribution, assessing site formation, and providing data usable in future research. Water depths, time and cost limitations, site size, and seafloor terrain at these sites negate using traditional archaeological mapping strategies; instead archaeologists utilize acoustic positioning technology to document these deep-water sites to accuracy standards on par with that of investigations in shallow water or terrestrial sites. This chapter briefly discusses two types of acoustic positioning systems, ultra-short baseline (USBL) and long baseline (LBL), and examines the importance and use of acoustically positioned data in the determination of site distributions and formation on the 2003 *U-166* Project and 2004 Deep Gulf Shipwrecks of World War II Project, commonly known as the DeepWrecks Project.

Acoustic Positioning

Acoustic positioning is a proven, reliable technology that has been utilized internationally for years in the offshore exploration industry. The use of this technology for deep-water archaeology has been equally successful. Archaeologists use variations of both USBL and LBL systems for deep-water archaeological investigations.

Ultra-Short Baseline

USBL is used extensively by the offshore energy exploration industry. USBL systems determine position by measuring a beacon's range and direction relative to the surface vessel transceiver's known location and orientation. A typical USBL system consists of a transducer for sending and receiving acoustic signals, Differential Global Positioning System (DGPS), and a transceiver beacon for a subsurface vehicle, such as a remotely operated vehicle (ROV). The transducer contains three or more transceivers set in different planes at known, fixed distances from each other. The transceivers are in relatively close proximity to one another and therefore establish an "ultra short baseline" (C & C 2005).

To determine the position of the subsurface beacon on an ROV, the USBL transceiver transmits signals from the research ship on the surface to the transponder beacon on the ROV and receives signals back from the beacon. The beacon's range is determined by calculating the time between the signal being sent and the reply received. The beacon's bearing is determined by calculating the "time-phase" difference between signals on pairs of transceivers within the main transducer. The absolute position of the beacon is then calculated using the DGPS (C & C 2005).

Long Baseline

The long baseline system (LBL), also known as range-range acoustic measurement, uses an array of seafloor beacons, called compatts (Computing and telemetry transponder), to triangulate the position of a transponder beacon on an ROV within the array (fig. 11.1). The LBL system works by acoustically measuring distances from the compatts placed on the seafloor. The typical LBL setup consists of four or more compatts (five are preferable for redundancy), a transceiver integrated with a DGPS on the surface vessel, and a transponder on the ROV. The LBL system can be used without a DGPS system, but the positions of material will only be relative to positions within the array. Utilizing the DGPS systems provides an absolute

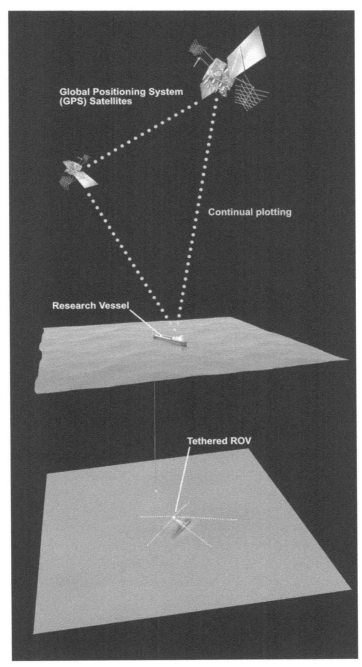

Figure 11.1. Depiction of a long baseline (LBL) positioning system array set up over a shipwreck site (courtesy of Andy Hall).

or real-world coordinate for seafloor objects, making the site map much easier to integrate into today's Geographic Information Systems (GIS; C&C 2005).

Initially the compatts are set in an array around the site, with each compatt's location surveyed in from the surface vessel so that its position is known. Once the array is set up and calibrated, the transceiver on the surface sends out a signal to the compatts, which send a signal back to the surface transceiver. The positioning software on the surface vessel calculates the two-way travel in order to triangulate the positions of the compatts and send this information to the beacon on the ROV. The ROV beacon then transmits a signal to the surface vessel, which allows the positioning software to calculate the ROV's absolute position using the DGPS data. This allows the real-world position of the ROV to be continuously plotted (C&C 2005).

LBL and USBL System Comparison

Each positioning system has its own specific advantages and disadvantages. LBL systems are more accurate than USBL systems. The accuracy of an LBL system is independent of water depth. Depending on the frequency of the system and the array size, positioning accuracies within 10 centimeters (3.9 inches) or less are achievable. The multiple transponders required for the LBL array provide redundancy for quality control of the positioning data and allow for accurate positioning over large areas. An additional advantage of the LBL array is that the compatt stands can be left in place, creating permanent datum points for future research at the site. The main disadvantage of the LBL system is in its need for multiple seafloor transponders and specially trained personnel to calibrate and monitor the array. The deployment, recovery, and calibration of the compatts are time-consuming tasks. Calibration of an LBL can take 18 to 24 hours to do correctly. Additionally, calibration of the system must be done each time the array is placed on a new site. Because of the extensive setup times required for LBL systems, they are typically used for mapping single shipwreck sites in high detail when there are not significant project time constraints (IMCA 2009; Vickery 1998).

USBL systems, although not as accurate as LBL systems, do provide very accurate positioning data. Typical accuracies of these systems range from 0.2% to 0.5% of water depth. Unlike LBL systems, USBL systems are ship based and do not use seafloor transponders, and once calibrated they do not have to be recalibrated between sites. This eliminates deployment, recovery, and calibration downtimes when documenting multiple sites or on time-limited projects. Additionally, the systems are relatively easy to use and require only a single shipboard transceiver that can be either permanently or temporarily mounted to the vessel's hull. The primary disadvantage of USBL systems is that their accuracy is dependent on other shipboard sensors, such as motion sensors, and system accuracy is influenced by water depth. Additionally, USBL systems are more susceptible to interference from outside noise sources than are LBL systems. For deep-water archaeological investigations USBL are typically used on projects examining multiple shipwreck sites or on projects where investigation times do not allow for the deployment of LBL systems. The appropriate system to employ on a project is determined by matching project parameters and objectives with the most suitable system (IMCA 2009; Vickery 1998).

Static Accuracy Testing

Once a USBL or LBL system has been calibrated, a static accuracy test is usually carried out to check calibration accuracies at each investigation site. Static accuracy tests involved the collection of multiple positions on a single-location fixed or relatively fixed point. The average and maximum standard deviations are then calculated for the recorded positions. From this data the relative accuracy of the system at a given site can be determined. For example, on the DeepWrecks Project, a static accuracy test of the USBL system was undertaken at the *U-166* and *Robert E. Lee* sites in 1,457 m (4,779 feet) of water. The ROV hovered stationary at one location while multiple positions were recorded. During the test, 64 USBL positions were recorded. The maximum deviation from the mean position was 2.48 m (8.13 feet). The accuracy for the USBL system was calculated to be 0.17% of the water depth (Church et al. 2007).

CASE STUDIES

The importance and necessity of acoustic positioning in the documentation of deep-water shipwreck sites in the Gulf of Mexico was demonstrated in 2003 during investigations of the German U-boat *U-166* and in 2004 on the DeepWrecks Project. Site maps constructed from the acoustic data allowed archaeologists to detail the artifact distributions at the site. This gave them a better understanding of the initial wrecking process and subsequent formation processes at the site. Archaeologists have subsequently used the site distribution data to determine the wrecking events of several vessels from the aforementioned studies (see Church, this volume).

Long Baseline Mapping at *U-166*

In 2001 the German submarine *U-166* was discovered during an oil and gas pipeline geophysical survey in the Gulf of Mexico. The initial ground truthing investigation in 2001 used an ROV without USBL or LBL positioning. That investigation only succeeding in collecting tantalizing video confirming the wreck's identity and raising many more questions about the site; it did not allow an accurate site map to be produced for the site, which covers over 8,100 square meters (26,575 square feet).

In October 2003 an investigation of *U-166* site was undertaken with a grant provided by the National Oceanic and Atmospheric Administration's Office of Ocean Exploration and Research. The project's objectives were to map the entire site in detail in order to determine its extent, how the wreck debris was distributed, and the wrecking events that formed the site. During the initial planning phase for the project, it was determined that a long baseline positioning system would be the best means of mapping the overall site. Using geophysical data including multibeam and side-scan sonar data, a rough estimate of site size was made. This estimate allowed the project team to determine the number of compatts and size of the array to cover the site as well as the approximate number of survey lines the ROV would have to navigate to survey the site completely (Warren et al. 2004).

The five-day investigation of the *U-166* in 2003 began with the deployment and calibration of five medium frequency compatts in an array with a diameter of 700 m (2,296 feet) around the site (fig. 11.2). Once the array was established, absolute positioning accuracy was between 15 and 30 cm (5.9 and 11.8 inches; Warren et al. 2004). In order to map individual wreck components and accurately correlate them with artifact photos, a vertically mounted digital still camera was used as the navigation centerpoint. Each position taken with the LBL system referenced this point. During the survey any wreck component or artifact was assigned a number and photographed, and then a navigation fix was recorded with the object centered in the camera's viewfinder. This allowed easy correlation of artifact descriptions, photographs, and positioning data. During the week-long project the ROV completed 63 north-south-oriented lines over the site at 4.5 m (14.8 foot) line spacing and documented 307 individual items or groups of artifacts (fig. 11.3).

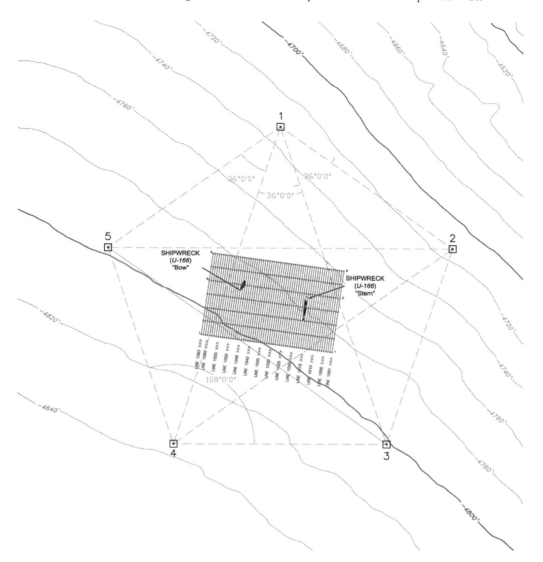

Figure 11.2. The orientation of the long baseline compatt array placed on the seafloor around the *U-166* site during the 2003 archaeological investigation.

During the post-survey analysis the position of each artifact was plotted on a digital map of the site. This map showed that the site consisted of two separate sections of hull remains and a large debris scatter covering an area of roughly 270 × 300 m (886 × 984 feet). It also showed that the distribution of materials around the site was so large that the mapping project could

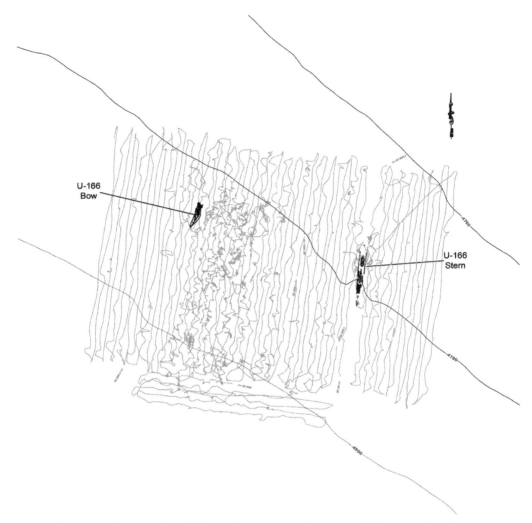

Figure 11.3. The map of the ROV trackline survey grid over the *U-166* site produced from positions collected with the long baseline positioning system during the 2003 archaeological investigation.

not have been done within the allotted timeframe using other deepwater survey techniques, such as mosaicking with an ROV.

The site map (fig. 11.4) indicated only a light scatter of materials in the eastern half of the site near the stern hull section, with the denser distribution in the western portion of the site associated with the bow remains. In general the main artifact scatter extends from the southern limits of the site to the north, increasing to its maximum density in the immediate vicinity

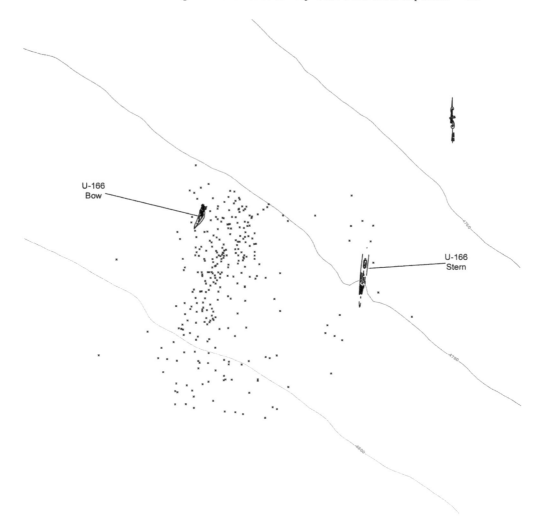

Figure 11.4. The site map of the *U-166* shipwreck showing artifact distribution base on acoustic positions recorded during the 2003 archaeological investigation.

of the disarticulated bow section. North and west of the bow, the seafloor is relatively devoid of artifact material other than a few outlying pieces of wreckage (Warren et al. 2004). Since the depth of the site, along with federal mitigations from oil and gas development, have protected it from anthropogenic impacts and influence by natural forces such as currents and siltation, the wreck scatter is believed to accurately represent how the remains were originally distributed when the vessel was lost in July 1942.

Using the artifact distribution map, archaeologists were able to reconstruct the wrecking events that formed the *U-166* shipwreck site. Based on the 2003 survey, it is apparent that during one of the depth charge attacks the navy patrol craft *PC-566* scored a direct hit that breached the hull just aft of the forward torpedo loading hatch, flooding *U-166* (as discussed in detail in Church, this volume). As the U-boat flooded, the loss of buoyancy led to an irreversible plummet to the seafloor. As *U-166* sank below its crush depth, it likely began to break up but did not implode, otherwise the debris would have been scattered over a much broader area. *U-166* neared the seafloor to the south of the current site location. Based on the seafloor distribution it is hypothesized that a second internal explosion tore the bow completely away from the stern section approximately 275 to 300 m (902 to 984 feet) above the seafloor. The stern, now absent its forward section, continued to the north, impacting the seafloor and settling on a near even keel. The bow planed forward and down by the prow, trailing debris. The prow eventually impacted the seafloor, but the forward momentum rotated the bow roughly 180 degrees, as the slight hook in the debris scatter shows, before settling to the seafloor.

Using USBL Mapping to Determine Site Distribution

In 2004, with interest in the Gulf of Mexico's World War II shipwrecks spurred by the *U-166* discovery, the Minerals Management Service funded the work commonly called the DeepWrecks Project, properly *Archaeological and Biological Analysis of World War II in the Gulf of Mexico: Artificial Reef Effect in Deepwater* (Church et al. 2007). This project investigated the sites of six World War II era shipwrecks in the Gulf, ranging in depth from 87 to 1,964 m (285 to 6,444 feet). The objectives of the DeepWrecks Project were to look at the archaeology and biology of each site, assess site preservation, and look at the function of these wrecks as artificial reefs (Church et al. 2007). Seven wrecks were slated for investigation, but adverse weather prevented researchers from visiting one site.

Investigating the sites provided a challenge for researchers. Never had so many deep shipwrecks in the Gulf of Mexico been examined at one time. The project called for seven sites, all beyond divable depths, to be documented within a single fourteen-day field season. As with the *U-166* project, the wreck depths made the use of traditional mapping techniques unrealistic, so acoustic positioning would have to be used. However, the number of sites and the two-week field window also made the use of an

LBL system impractical. To achieve the project's goals within the allocated time frame, researchers utilized an ultra-short baseline system.

As with *U-166*, the ROV was acoustically tracked as it surveyed a pre-established grid over each of the sites. The survey grids at each site were developed from data obtained from geophysical surveys or previous archaeological investigations. The size and layouts of the grids varied based on the existing information of the sites.

Over a two-week period in July and August 2004, six vessels were meticulously investigated and mapped using USBL positioning: *Virginia*, at 87 m (285 feet) below sea level; *Halo*, 143.3 m (470 feet); *Gulfpenn*, 555 m (1,820 feet); *Alcoa Puritan*, 1,964 m (6,444 feet); *Robert E. Lee*, 1,481 m (4,859 feet); and *U-166*, 1,457 m (4,780 feet). At each site the positioning accuracy of the USBL was calculated using a static accuracy test. These tests showed the USBL accuracies ranged from 0.17% to 1.24% of water depth at the six sites investigated (Church et al. 2007). The lowest two accuracies occurred at *Virginia* (1.24%) and *Halo* (0.80%), the two shallowest sites on the project. These low accuracies were likely the result of marine growth found on the USBL sensor head and subsequently removed (Church et al. 2007).

At all the wreck sites except *Virginia*, extensive debris zones were found. Detailed maps of each of the debris zones were created from the USBL positioning data. Analysis of these maps revealed three distinct distribution patterns. These patterns, designated A, B, and C, later formed the basis for a deepwater site formation predictive model and a more recent site analysis equation for deepwater shipwrecks (see Church, this volume).

All the shipwreck sites examined in the study had debris scatters representative of one of these patterns or a combination of patterns. Distribution Pattern A, observed on the *Robert E. Lee* and *Halo* sites, is identified by debris extending out from around the central hull remains (fig. 11.5). The wreck debris is distributed over the site unevenly with denser concentrations near the hull structure and lighter scatters on the site's periphery. This type of distribution is attributed to a ship sinking nearly vertically to the seafloor and the impact dispersing materials around the impact area (Church et al. 2007).

Distribution Pattern B, observed on the *Gulfpenn* site, is similar to a site distribution mechanism observed in shallow water (fig. 11.6). This pattern consists of a trail of wreckage leading to a site with denser concentrations near the core wreckage. On deepwater sites this pattern is attributed to materials continuing to move horizontally through the water column before

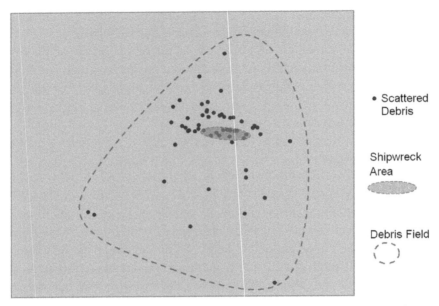

Figure 11.5. A scatter plot based on the 2004 DeepWrecks Project acoustic positioning data illustrating distribution pattern A at the *Robert E. Lee* wreck site.

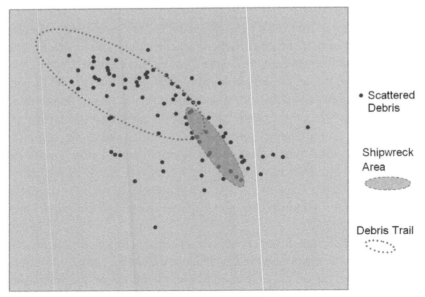

Figure 11.6. A scatter plot based on the 2004 DeepWrecks Project acoustic positioning data illustrating distribution pattern B at the *Gulfpenn* wreck site.

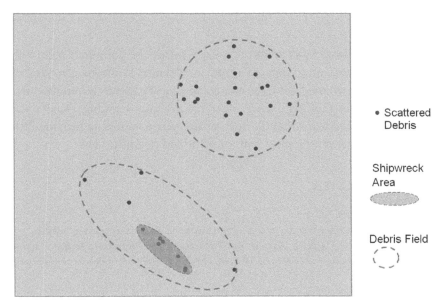

Figure 11.7. A scatter plot based on the 2004 DeepWrecks Project acoustic positioning data illustrating distribution pattern C at the *Alcoa Puritan* wreck site.

reaching the seafloor. In this type of pattern, the field density is directly proportionate to the amount of material dislodged from the vessel as it sank (Church et al. 2007).

Distribution Pattern C was noted at the wreck of the *Alcoa Puritan*. It is characterized by separate debris scatters (fig. 11.7). One or more scatters are located away from the core wreckage, while the main scatter is directly related to the main wreckage. In between the scatters, the seafloor is relatively void of wreck-related artifacts. This type of distribution occurs when materials are dislodged from a vessel on the surface, such as by an explosion, then the ship drifts or moves a substantial distance away from this point without additional loss of ship components, before finally sinking (Church et al. 2007).

Conclusion

The understanding of the site distribution patterns and site formation processes at the *U-166* and DeepWrecks Project shipwreck sites is based on interpretations of the detailed site maps created from the investigation data collected using an acoustically positioned ROV. Without the use of acoustic positioning systems on the ROV, the highly detailed mapping of these sites would not have been achieved because the sites extend over such large areas.

Analysis of deep-water archaeological sites must be done with accurately positioned investigation data. Without the detailed locations provided by acoustically positioned data, the associations and patterns inherently necessary for understanding a deep-water site are unobservable. Deep-water shipwreck explorations that do not use acoustic positioning provide little more than pretty site pictures with only limited scientific value.

References Cited

C & C Technologies, Inc.
2005   Company Files Written by C & C Scientists and Technicians (Unpublished).
Church, Robert R., Daniel J. Warren, Roy Cullimore, Lori Johnston, Morgan Kilgour, James Moore, Nicole Morris, William Patterson, William Schroeder, and Thomas Shirley
2007   *Archaeological and Biological Analysis of World War II Shipwrecks in the Gulf of Mexico: Artificial Reef Effect in Deepwater.* OCS Study MMS 2007-015. U.S. Department of the Interior, Minerals Management Service, New Orleans, Louisiana.
International Marine Contractors Association (IMCA).
2009   Deep Water Acoustic Positioning. Electronic document, www.imca-int.com, accessed September 30, 2014.
Vickery, Keith
1998   Acoustic Positioning Systems: A Practical Overview of Current Systems. Paper presented to the Marine Technology Dynamic Positioning Conference, Houston, Texas.
Warren, Daniel J., Robert R. Church, Roy Cullimore, and Lori Johnston.
2004   *ROV Investigations of the DKM U-166 Shipwreck Site to Document the Archaeological and Biological Aspects of the Wreck Site: Final Performance Report.* U.S. Department of Commerce, National Oceanic and Atmospheric Administration, Office of Ocean Exploration, Silver Springs, Maryland.

12

The *U-166* and *Robert E. Lee* Battlefield

The Equation of Site Distribution

ROBERT A. CHURCH

The Equation of Site Distribution was initially applied to the World War II casualty *Gulfoil* wreck site to understand the findings better at that deepwater site as part of the *Lophelia II* reefs, rigs, and wrecks study (Brooks et al. 2012). The equation provides a method to understand deep-water wrecking events better by examining the mathematical distribution of wreck material, particularly from steel-hull vessels that sank relatively quickly. Deep water is defined here as beyond scientific diving limits or greater than 60 meters (197 feet) below sea level (BSL), and the wrecks discussed in this section are between 1,480 and 1,490 m (4,856 and 4,888 feet) BSL. This methodology was applied to the battlefield site of the passenger freighter *Robert E. Lee* and the German submarine *U-166* not only to find additional remains that were key to understanding the battle but to help retrace each step of the battle itself (Church 2014).

Typically when a vessel sinks, it leaves a trail of debris as it plummets to the seafloor. This is a violent event with air rapidly escaping the internal compartments and water rushing in to fill the void. Some internal compartments simply implode under the pressure. Once a steel-hull vessel leaves the surface, it gains speed, quickly reaching a velocity of approximately 10 to 14 m per second (19 to 27.5 knots; Best et al. 2000; Garzke et al. 2000). The upper structures of most vessels are not designed to endure the forces of drag it is subjected to as it falls through the water column. As a result portions of the vessel break away, leaving a trail of debris as the vessel descends. A vessel typically impacts the seafloor forcefully, displacing massive amounts of sediment and producing a substantial impact crater. The hull frequently buckles and decks collapse from the impact, thereby forcing water back out of the interior spaces, further damaging the hull.

After such a destructive arrival on the seafloor, shipwrecks in deep water often sit nearly undisturbed for decades or centuries except for the slow biochemical deterioration of the site. The vessel slowly being consumed by microbes allows researchers a seemingly timeless glimpse of the wrecking event and site formation processes. Remarkably, the debris scatters of such wreck sites are typically distributed with mathematical consistency. The distribution of the debris at deep-water wreck sites can typically be measured as a function of water depth and vessel size, regardless of whether the wreck is the famed *Titanic*, one of numerous World War II casualties, or one of any number of other steel-hull vessels that have foundered in deep water. The Equation of Site Distribution, however, can help researchers understand more than just the distribution of the debris at the immediate wreck site. The bigger picture of the wrecking event also can be recognized using basic equations to examine the actions leading to a wrecking event, such as the torpedo and depth charges that led to the demise of the *Robert E. Lee* and *U-166*.

Robert E. Lee, U-166, and the Development of the Debris Distribution Model

On July 30, 1942, the passenger freighter *Robert E. Lee* was steaming across the Gulf of Mexico with U.S. naval escort *PC-566* running half a mile ahead. They were cruising at 16 knots on a heading of 282 degrees when a torpedo from *U-166* struck the starboard side of the freighter near the stern at 1637 hours (4:37 p.m.). *Robert E. Lee* went under in approximate three minutes, while the patrol craft maneuvered to search for the U-boat. *PC-566*'s lookouts spotted a periscope "2,000 yards" (1,829 m) to the south moving at 4 knots. They rushed to that location and dropped a spread of depth charges at 1645 hours as the U-boat attempted to dive and evade the patrol craft. By this time *Robert E. Lee* had already sunk. Within a few minutes of the first depth charge attack, *PC-566* regained sonar contact on the U-boat and made a second depth charge attack (USS *PC-566* 1942; Henderson 1942). Although it was not known at the time, this second spread of depth charges finished off the U-boat and sent it to the bottom. Going down in nearly 1,500 m (4,921 feet) of water, the freighter and the U-boat lay undisturbed within 1.5 kilometers (0.93 miles) of each other for the next 59 years.

In 2001 C & C Technologies, Inc. conducted a deep-water pipeline survey for BP Exploration and Production Inc. and Shell International using C & C's *C-Surveyor I* autonomous underwater vehicle (AUV). *C-Surveyor*

I's primary geophysical payload consisted of a Simrad EM2000, a 200 kHz swath bathymetry system, dual frequency EdgeTech side-scan sonar systems (120 kHz and 410 kHz), and an EdgeTech Chirp sub-bottom profiler providing acoustic imagery of the surface and subsurface of the seafloor. As a result C & C's marine archaeologists identified a sonar target in the area, which they thought might be *U-166*. On May 31 a research team from C & C, the Minerals Management Service (MMS), BP, and Shell conducted an investigation using a remotely operated vehicle (ROV). The investigation confirmed the identity and location of *U-166* and its last victim, the *Robert E. Lee* (Church et al. 2002). Over the next ten years C & C conducted several additional geophysical surveys over the wrecks while testing upgrades to their AUV sonars and other sensors. C & C archaeologists also led six visual site investigations using ROVs during various projects sponsored by the MMS (now the Bureau of Ocean Energy Management, BOEM), NOAA Office of Ocean Exploration and Research, and the National Oceanographic Partnership Program (NOPP).

Between 2004 and 2007 the *U-166* and *Robert E. Lee* wreck sites were investigated as part of the *Archaeological and Biological Analysis of World War II Shipwrecks in the Gulf of Mexico*, OCS Study MMS 2007-015 (Church et al. 2007). As a result of this project, a debris distribution model was developed based on the data from the *U-166* and *Robert E. Lee* wreck sites and four other deep-water World War II wreck sites. The distribution formula was conceived as a preliminary first step in developing a predictive model for shipwreck site distribution in deep-water. As such, it was based on a small sample of deep-water shipwrecks, but other sites have been added as data became available. The distribution model provides a method to estimate the potential distance debris will spread out as a steel-hull vessel sinks, taking into account the water depth. The model is intended to estimate a distance slightly farther than the actual spread of debris to provide an adequate search radius or an avoidance zone at a wreck site. The formula for that distribution is 20% of water depth plus the length of the hull and is listed below (Church et al. 2009).

$$0.20w + vl > \text{site boundary}$$
$$\text{Where: } w = \text{water depth}$$
$$vl = \text{vessel length}$$

The *Robert E. Lee*, with hull length of 114.3 m (375 feet) sits in water depth of 1,490 m (4,888 feet) BSL. The estimated debris distribution at the *Robert E. Lee* site based on the model is 412 m (1,352 feet), where the actual measured value is 320 m (1,050 feet) extending from the center of the hull. Based on the model the estimated debris distribution at the *U-166* site, with hull length of 76.8 m (252 feet), is 328 m (1,076 feet), where the actual measured value is 280 m (919 feet) at a water depth of 1,256 m (4,121 feet) BSL. *U-166* sits in water 1,457 m (4,780 feet) BSL, but the sinking depth is adjusted in the model because the U-boat was submerged at the time it began to break apart. Although it is not known from the historical record at what depth the U-boat's hull began to break apart, the crush depth of the Type IX-C U-boat is 200 m (656 feet) BSL. A depth of 1,256 m (4,121 feet) BSL represents the remaining water depth beneath the vessel at the time the *U-166*'s hull would have been subject to catastrophic failure.

The Equation of Site Distribution

The *Robert E. Lee* and *U-166* sites represent one of the few known deep-water battlefields in the Gulf of Mexico where both combatants are represented. The distribution of seafloor debris, however, was not enough to retrace exactly how the battle unfolded on the surface, even with historical accounts of the battle available. The orientation of the freighter and U-boat on the seafloor along with their associated debris fields did not provide sufficient information to determine the actual location of the initial attack, which was necessary to determine the starting point in the sequence of events. Therefore this deep-water battlefield was an ideal site to apply the Equation of Site Distribution methodology.

The estimated location of the torpedo attack can be determined by calculating the distance the *Robert E. Lee* could have traveled before sinking after the torpedo stuck the hull. The first step in this calculation was determining the freighter's rate of deceleration. This was calculated using the formula:

$$a = (Vf—Vi)/t$$
Where: a = acceleration in meters/second (m/s)
Vf = Final Velocity in m/s
Vi = Initial Velocity in m/s
t = time in seconds

Using a final velocity of 0 m/s, an initial velocity of 8.2311 m/s (16 knots), and an approximate time of 180 seconds (3 minutes), the *Robert E. Lee*'s deceleration (negative acceleration) after the torpedo impact would have been −0.04573 m/s. With a calculated deceleration rate, the distance the *Robert E. Lee* traveled before sinking was determined using the formula:

$$d = (Vf+Vi)t + (1/2)at^2$$

Where: d = distance in meters (m)

Vf = Final Velocity in m/s

Vi = Initial Velocity in m/s

t = time in seconds

a = deceleration rate in m/s

Using the calculated deceleration (−0.04573 m/s) to solve the equation shows that the *Robert E. Lee* would have covered a distance of approximately 741 m (2,431 feet) in the 3 minutes following the torpedo impact, decelerating from a velocity of 16 knots to near zero before sinking.

The *Robert E. Lee*'s engines however, apparently did not immediately stop when the torpedo hit. The freighter's engine order telegraph was found during the 2001 ROV investigation and showed that the engines were in the "Stop" position. It is not known how long it took the engine room to execute the stop engine command but only that they did. It must have happened quickly, as 382 of the 407 passengers and crew were able to abandon this ship before it sank. If the freighter continued under power for an additional 30 seconds before the engines were stopped, the vessel would have traveled 267 m (876 feet) under power and then 617 m (2,024 feet) during the remaining two and half minutes of deceleration for a total of 864 m (2,835 feet) before sinking. That is, however, speculation, and all that can be said for certain is that the freighter likely traveled more than 741 m (2,431 feet) after the attack and that a good approximation may be 864 m (2,835 feet). Nevertheless, this provides a direction and approximate distance to search for evidence of the torpedo attack.

The artifact scatter at the *Robert E. Lee* site is not characterized by a typical shipwreck debris trail, but rather a debris fan, making it difficult to estimate where the freighter left the surface. The percussion waves from the depth charges exploding as the freighter was sinking may account for the atypical debris pattern. No debris trail is present from the freighter's stern or bow. *Robert E. Lee* is lying on the seafloor on an eastward heading. The debris field spreads out the farthest toward the south-southwest, with one isolated artifact to the southeast. A location near the farthest edge of the debris field was selected as a starting point for the following calculations. Working backward from that point, two arcs are plotted 741 and 864 m

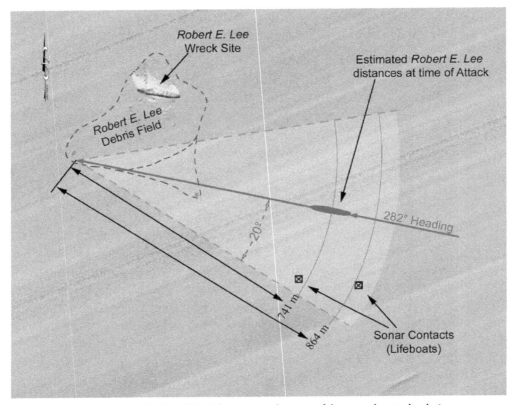

Figure 12.1. Estimate of *Robert E. Lee*'s location at the time of the torpedo attack relative to the wreck position and location of two of the freighter's lifeboats. Background image from the 120 kHz sonar mosaic collected in 2001 with the *C-Surveyor I* AUV (data courtesy of C & C Technologies, Inc., BP Exploration, and Shell International).

(2,431 and 2,835 feet) away from the wreckage on a reverse course to the freighter's heading of 282 degrees at the time of the attack. Vessels do not always move in a straight line after being attacked. Therefore a cone-shaped search area was set up to allow for possible deviation in heading after the attack. This provides a rough estimate for the *Robert E. Lee*'s potential position when the torpedo hit. Comparing this estimated location to the 2001 sonar data reveals that two sonar contacts are noted near that approximate area (fig. 12.1).

These two sonar contacts are located 663 m and 783 m (2,175 and 2,569 feet) respectively from the center of the shipwreck and 717 and 874 m (2,352 and 2,867 feet) respectively from the south-southwest edge of the debris field. The sonar contacts are 314 and 192 m (1,030 and 630 feet) to the south of the projected path of the *Robert E. Lee.* This places these sonar contacts within the southern portion of the search cone. Both sonar contacts were investigated with an ROV in 2003 and were identified as lifeboats from the sunken freighter (Warren et al. 2004). At the time they were thought to be isolated items that had drifted away from the wreckage before sinking. Their presence in light of the projected calculations indicates their location is a promising estimate for the area of the torpedo attack. If this is the correct location, however, a larger debris field would be expected. The 2001 survey was conducted with a 120-kHz side-scan sonar. It is possible that only the larger contacts such as the lifeboats were detected and that a more extensive debris field could be present in this area but went undetected during the 2001 geophysical survey.

In 2009 C & C conducted an AUV survey of the *Robert E. Lee* and *U-166* sites with a more advanced 230 kHz dynamically focused side-scan sonar with sub-meter resolution at full 225 m (738 feet) range. Although the data were originally collected for system testing and calibration purposes, when evaluated by archaeologists the sonar data provided significantly enhanced imagery over the estimated attack location. In addition to the two lifeboats, the 2009 data revealed an extensive scatter of debris around that location (fig. 12.2), providing strong evidence indicating that this was the position of the *Robert E. Lee* at the time the torpedo hit the freighter. In September 2013 C & C conducted an additional AUV geophysical, 3-D laser, and photography survey of the debris field, further strengthening these findings. The estimated position for the *Robert E. Lee* at the time of the torpedo attack can be adjusted, then, to correlate to the location of this debris field.

With the potential attack location established, the remainder of the battle can be plotted chronologically. From its location half a mile ahead of the *Robert E. Lee*, *PC-566* rushed toward the U-boat, which was spotted by its periscope 1,829 m (6,000 feet) from the patrol craft's location. Based on this information, it is estimated that the U-boat was approximately 1,000 m (3,280 feet) aft and to starboard of *Robert E. Lee*, which would place the *U-166* to the east-northeast of the freighter's position at the time the torpedo hit. *PC-566* reached that location within minutes and dropped the first spread of depth charges as the U-boat attempted to dive. Fifteen minutes later *PC-566* had regained sonar contact on the U-boat, reportedly near the area of the first depth charge attack, and dropped a second spread of depth charges that finished off the U-boat, sending it to the seafloor, as previously described (fig. 12.3) (USS *PC-566* 1942; Henderson 1942). *PC-566* reported that the U-boat was moving toward the sinking *Robert E. Lee*

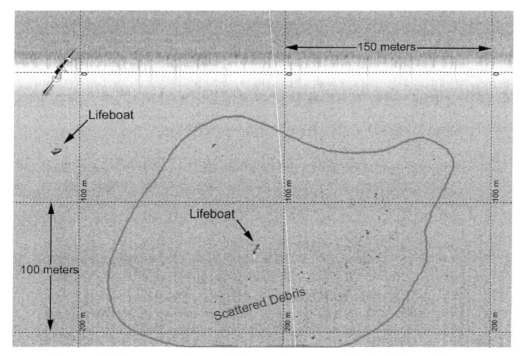

Figure 12.2. Side-scan sonar data, 230 kHz, revealing a scattered debris field near the lifeboats' position (data courtesy of C & C Technologies, Inc.).

to the south or southeast when they first spotted the periscope. The main hull of *U-166* currently sits on the seafloor on an 8 degrees north heading with a debris trail leading away from its stern. The U-boat likely changed course after the first depth charge attack, attempting to head away from the action, but did not get far before *PC-566*'s second attack. The range from the *U-166* wreck site to the estimated position of *PC-566* at the time they reported spotting the periscope is the same distance the patrol craft reported, "2,000 yards." It is possible that the first depth charge attack fatally crippled the U-boat, and the following sonar contact they established was on the hull of a sinking vessel. If the *U-166* was still under power at that time, the second depth charge attack certainly finished it off.

CONCLUSIONS

In the case of the *Robert E. Lee* and *U-166*, the Equation of Site Distribution methodology proved invaluable in understanding the battle and events of the sinking of both vessels. The ability to predict site distributions with

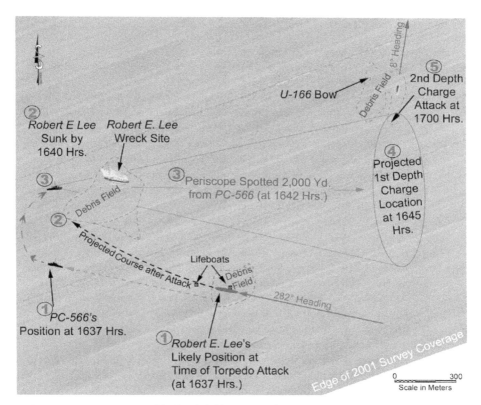

Figure 12.3. Progression of the battlefield scenario showing each vessel's location through the battle sequence. (1) *Robert E. Lee* and *PC-566*'s estimated location at the time of the torpedo attack at 1637 hours; (2) *Robert E. Lee* went under at 1640 hours; (3) *PC-566* spotted a periscope at 1642 hours; (4) *PC-566*'s first depth charge attack on *U-166* at 1645 hours; (5) *PC-566*'s second depth charge attach on *U-166* at 1700 hours.

higher precision, however, should also aid investigations of other shipwreck sites where vessels were lost through catastrophic sinking events related not only to warfare but also to collision, explosions, or other types of marine accidents. Using the same methodology, researchers could work forward to locate a sunken vessel if a location is known for the event that led to the vessel's demise, or if only the wreck location is known, they could work backward to locate the additional elements of the site. In either case, finding all the major components of a site and being able to retrace the sequence of events leading to the initial site formation are key in telling the complete story of each wrecking incident.

References Cited

Best, Angus I., William Powrie, Toby Hayward, and Max Barton
2000   Geotechnical Investigation of the *Titanic* Wreck Site. *Marine Georesources* and *Geotechnology* 18(4):315–331.

Brooks, James M., Charles Fisher, Erik Cordes, Lliana Baums, Bernie Bernard, Robert Church, Peter Etnoyer, Chris German, Elizabeth Goehring, Ian McDonald, Harry Roberts, Timothy M. Shank, Daniel Warren, Susan Welsh, and Gary Wolff
2012   *Deepwater Program. Exploration and Research of Northern Gulf of Mexico Deepwater Natural and Artificial Hard Bottom Habitats with Emphasis on Coral Communities: Reefs, Rigs and Wrecks—"Lophelia II."* Interim Report. OCS Study MMS 2012-106. U.S. Department of the Interior, Minerals Management Service, Gulf of Mexico OCS Region, New Orleans.

Church, Robert A., Daniel J. Warren, Andy W. Hill, and Johnathan S. Smith
2002   The Discovery of *U-166*: Rewriting History with New Technology. *Proceedings of the 2002 Offshore Technology Conference*. Houston, Texas.

Church, Robert, Daniel J. Warren, Roy Cullimore, Lori Johnston, Morgan Kilgour, James Moore, Nicole Morris, William Patterson, William Schroeder, and Tom Shirley
2007   *Archaeological and Biological Analysis of World War II Shipwrecks in the Gulf of Mexico: Artificial Reef Effect in Deepwater*. OCS Study MMS 2007-015. U.S. Department of the Interior, Minerals Management Service, New Orleans.

Church, Robert A., Daniel J. Warren, and Jack B. Irion
2009   Analysis of Deepwater Shipwrecks in the Gulf of Mexico: Artificial Reef Effect of Six World War II Shipwrecks. *Oceanography* 22(2):50–63.

Church, Robert A.
2014   Deep-Water Shipwreck Initial Site Formation: The Equation of Site Distribution. *Journal of Maritime Archaeology* 9(1):27–40

Garzke, William H., Robert O. Dulin, David K. Brown, and Kevin Prince
2000   Marine Forensics for Naval Architects and Marine Engineers. *Naval Engineers Journal* 112:249–264.

Henderson, E. D.
1942   *Summary of Statements by Survivors of the SS* Robert E. Lee, *U.S. Cargo-Passenger Vessel*. August 13. Navy department, Office of the Chief of Naval Operations.

USS *PC-566*
1942   Logs of the USS *PC-566*, Attached to the Gulf Sea Frontier, 7th Naval District, July 30, 1942. National Archives and Records Administration, Washington, D.C.

Warren, Daniel, Robert Church, Roy Cullimore, and Lori Johnston
2004   *ROV Investigations of the DKM U-166 Shipwreck Site to Document the Archaeological and Biological Aspects of the Wreck Site: Final Performance Report*. U.S. Department of Commerce, National Oceanic and Atmospheric Administration, Office of Ocean Exploration, Silver Spring, Maryland.

13

Conclusion

MATTHEW E. KEITH

THE ROLE OF SITE FORMATION IN SHIPWRECK ARCHAEOLOGY

As discussed throughout this volume, site formation processes are knowable, and following lines of inquiry that lead to understanding these processes can provide a greater understanding of submerged shipwreck sites. As the research in this volume demonstrates, site formation studies can provide important clues about the provenience of an entire site (chapters 2, 3, 4, 8, 10) or specific artifacts (chapters 5, 6). Site formation studies can provide valuable information about the site conditions for conservators (chapters 5, 6) and are an important component of applied archaeology as well. An expanded understanding of the marine environment is critically important in guiding the search for shipwreck sites (chapters 2, 3, 10) and ultimately can provide knowledge useful to heritage managers in better managing the resources under their care (chapters 7, 8, 10, 12).

THE IMPORTANCE OF CONTEXT

One of the guiding principles of archaeology is context, which is documented by mapping site distribution and provenience to develop a comprehensive understanding of the site matrix. There is no reason this should not be as pertinent for sites in the marine environment as it is for the terrestrial environment. By understanding the mechanisms and processes at a given site, we can make it possible to interpret that shipwreck site better. The provenience and distribution of artifacts and site components provide important information regarding a wrecking event (chapters 11, 12) and the events leading up to the wreck (chapters 9, 12). To this end, we have given examples (chapters 5, 6) of how site formation is used to understand context better within a site and to inform the interpretation of the site matrix.

To date, excellent work has been conducted in which site formation is a major component of research, including but not limited to work performed by the U.S. National Park Service on the *Hunley* (Murphy 1998), *Housatonic* (Conlin 2005), and *Arizona* sites (Lenihan 1990) and work performed on the Red Bay wrecks by Parks Canada (Bernier 2007).

Despite these examples, such detailed studies have largely been underutilized in shipwreck archaeology. One major reason for this is cost, another is the availability of personnel with the specific expertise needed to perform such detailed studies, and yet another is a lack of emphasis on the importance of site formation within the field of nautical archaeology as a whole. This volume helps address the lack of emphasis, and there are also solutions for the others.

MULTIDISCIPLINARY APPROACH

It has been noted elsewhere (Murphy 1998; Conlin and Russell 2009) that partnering with other fields to perform multidisciplinary (or interdisciplinary) studies can not only defray costs for expensive research but also reach funding sources that may not typically fund archaeological projects while advancing mutually beneficial research. Examples include sediment analysis performed on the *Mary Rose* (Murphy 1998:387); the *Lophelia* studies performed under contract to the U.S. Bureau of Ocean Energy Management (Church et al. 2007; Brooks et al. 2012); as well as work on submerged landscapes discussed within this volume (Ford et al., chapter 2). Conlin and Russell (2009) make a distinction between multidisciplinary and interdisciplinary studies, arguing that while a multidisciplinary approach brings together scientists from multiple fields, they typically produce independent reports specific to their field of study that are provided to the archaeologist to synthesize (or are discussed separately from the archaeology altogether). In the case of interdisciplinary studies, the research team members collaborate to address the research design and to consider new questions as the project progresses. A true interdisciplinary approach ensures collaboration at all stages, from development of research design through analysis of the results, and can provide a broader and more pertinent assessment of an archaeological site.

TOWARD THE FUTURE

Terrestrial archaeologists have learned to specialize in order to conduct the level of research they need but also to ensure their marketability in a competitive field. Marine archaeology students can take advantage of programs in their institutions to develop specializations in the physical sciences that will allow them to grow the field and enhance their erudition. Even a little exposure can help develop the knowledge of other fields necessary to develop research designs, collaborate with those in other fields, oversee projects, and review results.

It is hoped that future scholarship will continue to expand site formation studies and integrate them into maritime archaeology. Development of a comprehensive theory of site formation (as advocated by Gibbins 1990; Stewart 1999; O'Shea 2002; Martin 2011) is an important start. However, the obvious limitations of such work must also be acknowledged. This volume focuses on a number of specific aspects of site formation as detailed by archaeologists and scientists who specialize in those areas. To date, though, studies that do include site formation have typically focused on one or two aspects and have not addressed the full breadth of variables influencing site formation processes. It is acknowledged that a unifying theory that advocates an all-encompassing approach to site formation is unlikely to be applied except perhaps on high profile and well-funded long-term projects. More practically, lead researchers need to identify those areas that will provide the most value to the understanding of their site, based on its unique environment and wreck variables, in order to maximize the information garnered from their research.

Despite an increased focus on site formation studies in recent years, and outstanding contributions by a few scholars, our understanding of how these processes relate to archaeology is still in its infancy. Potential areas of future research are numerous and include burial and preservation processes of wooden wrecks in shallow and moderate water depths; preferential establishment of sessile communities on archaeological features; impact of archaeological sites on dominant current and/or wave regimes; corrosion rates and the long-term stability of metal-hulled wrecks; and improved understanding of human impacts to wreck sites. It should also be noted that as deep-water archaeological finds increase and technology allows us to work in ever increasing water depths, the limitations of our knowledge of the deep-water environment and how it impacts shipwreck sites become more evident. Expanding our understanding of the biologic, chemical, oceanographic, and geologic processes that impact shipwrecks in deep-water environments is one area of inquiry that is rapidly expanding.

Conclusion

The goal of this volume is to introduce the primary variables that influence shipwreck sites while providing examples of research specific to each area of inquiry. Although the organization of the topics covered in this volume is not unique (see Muckelroy 1978; Stewart 1999), often such research is published in disparate volumes and journals specific to the specialized field of study of each set of researchers. Bringing these concepts together in one volume makes the breadth and range of topics more accessible.

It is expected that the rise of heritage management, coupled with the use of in situ preservation as a viable management tool, will continue to facilitate an increased emphasis on site formation studies within the field of maritime archaeology. Those conducting purely academic research can also continue to integrate and expand upon site formation studies. Further developing and refining methodology to understand site level processes will aid archaeologists in interpreting the site's context in order to develop more accurate cultural inferences about the ship and its crew. Site formation studies can even help to advance large-scale regional analysis (as advocated by Murphy 1997:388) that can provide understanding beyond just a single site. The continual expansion and development of site formation studies throughout the field of maritime archaeology, coupled with an increased emphasis on site formation within educational institutions and a focus on interdisciplinary studies, can aid in expanding our understanding of submerged shipwreck sites in order to improve our understanding of the past and to protect these nonrenewable resources.

References Cited

Bernier, Marc-André
2007   Site Formation Process and Break-Up of the 24M Vessel. In *The Underwater Archaeology of Red Bay: Basque Shipbuilding and Whaling in the 16th Century*, vol. 4, edited by Robert Grenier, Marc-André Bernier, and Willis Stevens, pp. 215–290. Parks Canada, Ottawa.
Brooks, James M., Charles Fisher, Erik Cordes, Lliana Baums, Bernie Bernard, Robert Church, Peter Etnoyer, Chris German, Elizabeth Goehring, Ian McDonald, Harry Roberts, Timothy M. Shank, Daniel Warren, Susan Welsh, and Gary Wolff
2012   *Deepwater Program.: Exploration and Research of Northern Gulf of Mexico Deepwater Natural and Artificial Hard Bottom Habitats with Emphasis on Coral Communities: Reefs, Rigs and Wrecks—"Lophelia II."* Interim Report. OCS Study MMS 2012-106. U.S. Department of the Interior, Minerals Management Service, Gulf of Mexico OCS Region, New Orleans.

Church, Robert, Daniel J. Warren, Roy Cullimore, Lori Johnston, Morgan Kilgour, James
    Moore, Nicole Morris, William Patterson, William Schroeder, and Tom Shirley
2007   *Archaeological and Biological Analysis of World War II Shipwrecks in the Gulf of
    Mexico: Artificial Reef Effect in Deepwater.* OCS Study MMS 2007-015. U.S. De-
    partment of the Interior, Minerals Management Service, New Orleans.
Conlin, David L. (editor)
2005   *USS* Housatonic: *Site Assessment.* National Park Service, Submerged Resources
    Center, Naval Historical Center, and South Carolina Institute of Archaeology and
    Anthropology.
Conlin, David L., and Matthew A. Russell
2009   Site Formation Processes Once-Removed: Pushing the Boundaries of Interdis-
    ciplinary Maritime Archaeology. In *ACUA Underwater Archaeology Proceedings
    2009, Toronto, Canada,* edited by Erika Laanela and Jonathan Moore, pp. 83–90.
    Advisory Council on Underwater Archaeology.
Gibbins, David
1990   Analytical Approaches in Maritime Archaeology: A Mediterranean Perspective.
    Antiquity 64:376–89.
Lenihan, Daniel J. (editor)
1990   *Submerged Cultural Resources Study: USS* Arizona *Memorial and Pearl Harbor
    National Historic Landmark.* Southwest Cultural Resources Center Professional
    Papers no. 23. Santa Fe.
Martin, Colin
2011   Wreck-Site Formation Processes. In *Oxford Handbook of Maritime Archaeology,*
    edited by Alexis Catsambis, Ben Ford, and Donny Hamilton, pp. 47–67. Oxford
    University Press, New York.
Muckelroy, Keith
1978   *Maritime Archaeology.* Cambridge University Press, Cambridge.
Murphy, Larry E.
1997   Site Formation Processes. In *Encyclopedia of Underwater and Maritime Archaeol-
    ogy,* edited by James P. Delgado, pp. 386–388. Yale University Press, New Haven.
Murphy, Larry E. (editor)
1998   *H. L. Hunley Site Assessment.* National Park Service, Submerged Resources Cen-
    ter, Naval Historical Center, and South Carolina Institute of Archaeology and
    Anthropology.
O'Shea, John M.
2002   The Archaeology of Scattered Wreck-Sites: Formation Processes and Shallow
    Water Archaeology in Western Lake Huron. *International Journal of Nautical Ar-
    chaeology* 31:211–227.
Stewart, David
1999   Formation Processes Affecting Submerged Archaeological Sites: An Overview.
    Geoarchaeology: An International Journal 14(6):565–587.

Contributors

Michael L. Brennan received his Ph.D. in oceanography at the University of Rhode Island's Graduate School of Oceanography in 2012. His dissertation research focused on quantifying the impacts of trawling on shipwrecks. He is currently director of marine archaeology and maritime history and project manager for Ocean Exploration Trust and the Nautilus Exploration Program. He has a B.A. from Bowdoin College in archaeology and geology and an M.A. from URI in history. His archaeological fieldwork experience consists of more than ten years of excavations at Maya sites in Belize as well as projects in Italy and Greece.

Robert A. Church is senior marine archaeologist for C & C Technologies, Inc. in Lafayette, Louisiana. He received his M.A. in maritime history and nautical archaeology from East Carolina University in 2001. His work has included many aspects of historical underwater archaeology on sites ranging in date from the seventeenth to the twentieth centuries. His primary research has focused on deep-water archaeology and has included numerous investigations at depths of 100 meters to more than 3,000 meters.

Justin Dix is senior lecturer in marine geophysics and geoarchaeology at the National Oceanography Centre Southampton. He is interested in the development and integration of geophysical (particularly acoustic), geological, archaeological, and hydrodynamic approaches for the solution of a suite of scientific problems.

Brad Duncan is state maritime archaeologist responsible for the Maritime Heritage Program at New South Wales Heritage Branch, Parramatta, Australia. He specializes in maritime cultural landscapes, historic maritime infrastructure studies, and fishing and defence landscapes. His current research projects include regional interpretation of the maritime cultural landscapes of coastal and inland waterways, the archaeology of shipbreaking and adaptive reuse of hulks, deep-water wrecks, WWII sites in the Solomon Islands, and remote sensing of convict sites on Norfolk Island. He is coauthoring a book with Martin Gibbs on community responses to shipwrecks.

Amanda M. Evans is senior marine archaeologist for Tesla Offshore, where she specializes in interpreting remote sensing data for submerged archaeological resources and directing offshore archaeological investigations. She has conducted federally funded research on historic shipwrecks in the Gulf of Mexico, site formation processes, and submerged prehistoric archaeological landscapes.

Katherine Farnsworth is associate professor of geoscience at Indiana University of Pennsylvania. She received her Ph.D. from the College of William and Mary School of Marine Science with a focus on marine geology. Her research specialization is the interaction between terrestrial and aquatic systems, often focusing on the flux and fate of sediments in coastal oceans. She is a coauthor of *River Discharge to the Coastal Ocean: A Global Synthesis*, as well as of numerous research articles.

Antony Firth is director of Fjordr Limited, a consultancy based in the United Kingdom that carries out research and provides advice relating to the marine and historic environment for a range of public authorities and private developers. He first became involved in archaeology as a volunteer diver investigating submerged prehistoric landscapes and a sixteenth-century shipwreck. His doctoral research examined the management of archaeology underwater in the United Kingdom and across a range of European countries, encompassing law, policy, and practice. Subsequently he became heavily involved in the emergence of development-led marine archaeology, working on a wide range of projects in the ports, marine aggregates, and marine renewable energy sectors.

Ben Ford is associate professor specializing in maritime and historical archaeology at Indiana University of Pennsylvania, where he is faculty in the Masters of Applied Archaeology program. His Ph.D. from Texas A&M University was preceded by several years of cultural resource management experience and degrees from the College of William and Mary and the

University of Cincinnati. He has edited the *Oxford Handbook of Maritime Archaeology* and *The Archaeology of Maritime Landscapes* and is the editor of the Society for Historical Archaeology Technical Briefs Series. His current research focuses on a Revolutionary War–era town in Pennsylvania and the maritime cultural landscape of Lake Ontario.

Martin Gibbs is professor of Australian archaeology at the University of New England, Australia. He specializes in the archaeology of maritime industries, cultural aspects of shipwreck site formation, shipwreck survivors, and the processes of maritime colonization. His current research projects include the archaeology of the sixteenth-century Spanish explorations of the Solomon Islands and the maritime cultural landscapes of Sydney Harbour. He is coauthoring a book with Brad Duncan on community responses to shipwrecks.

David Gregory trained as an analytical chemist prior to obtaining degrees in archaeology (B.Sc. Hons, University of Leicester, 1991; M. Phil., Andrews University, 1992; Ph.D., University of Leicester, 1996), with a special focus on the application of natural sciences to archaeological and conservation science focusing on the deterioration and conservation of waterlogged archaeological wood and iron. He has worked on numerous maritime archaeological projects as a diver, in both archaeological and conservation capacities. He is currently a research professor at the museum's conservation department, where he is investigating the deterioration of waterlogged archaeological wood, assessment of its state of preservation, and methods of in situ preservation of archaeological materials in underwater environments. He is author and coauthor of more than eighty scientific articles and book chapters on this research.

M. Scott Harris is associate professor of geology and environmental geosciences at the College of Charleston. He received his Ph.D. from the University of Delaware Department of Geology, M.S. in environmental sciences from the University of Virginia, and B.S. in geology from the College of William and Mary. His research focuses on paleolandscapes and evolution of coastal regions with an emphasis on the coastal plain and continental shelf of the southeastern United States. Recent geoarchaeological studies include geology of the *H. L. Hunley*, the search for Barney's War of 1812 Flotilla in Maryland, sedimentology of the Topper Paleoamerican site, and coastal studies in Greece.

Matthew E. Keith is vice president and geoscience manager for Tesla Offshore, LLC. He received a master's degree from Florida State University. He specializes in interpreting remote sensing data for submerged archaeological resources and site characterization and has conducted research into the site formation processes that impact both historic shipwrecks and submerged prehistoric archaeological landscapes in the Gulf of Mexico.

Ian D. MacLeod is executive director of the Western Australian Museums in Fremantle and has been solving deterioration problems with shipwreck artifacts since 1978, when he joined the museum's Department of Materials Conservation. He has studied shipwrecks in Canada, Scotland, Finland, the United States, and the Federated States of Micronesia. He is a chartered chemist and a fellow of the Royal Society of Chemistry, International Institute for Conservation of Artistic and Historic Works, Royal Australian Chemical Institute, Australian Academy of Technological Sciences and Engineering, and Society of Antiquaries of Scotland. He is an advisor on the conservation of the Confederate submarine *H. L. Hunley* and on the USS *Monitor* projects.

Ian Oxley began his career in 1980 for the Mary Rose Trust as an archaeological diver, progressing to archaeological scientist. He then joined the U.K. government's Archaeological Diving Unit based at the University of St. Andrews, ending as deputy director. During these periods of employment he embarked on an archaeological sciences degree at the (now) University of East London and an M.Sc. by research at the University of St. Andrews. After moving to Historic Scotland's Inspectorate of Ancient Monuments, he joined English Heritage in 2002 to set up and manage the Maritime Archaeology Team. He is currently the historic environment intelligence analyst marine for Historic England providing leadership in forecasting long-range issues, assessing threats and impacts to the marine historic environment, and delivering workable and cost-effective responses.

Ruth Plets is lecturer in the School of Environmental Sciences at Ulster University. Her research interests include the use of geophysical techniques for underwater archaeology. Such investigations focus on shipwreck and submerged landscape imaging, characterization, and visualization.

Rory Quinn is reader at the School of Environmental Sciences, Ulster University. His research interests are in marine geoarchaeology, specifically shipwreck site formation processes and submerged archaeological landscapes.

Robin Saunders received his Ph.D. from the University of Southampton in 2005. He is a chartered building engineer and a member of the British Hydrological Society. With his background in civil engineering (B.Eng. Hons., University of Southampton, 2000), his doctoral thesis combined his understanding of hydraulic flow with his keen interest in maritime archaeology to investigate seabed scour around submerged three-dimensional objects.

Carrie Sowden is archaeological director of the Great Lakes Historical Society in Toledo, Ohio. Her master's degree is from the Nautical Archaeology Program in the Anthropology Department at Texas A&M University. She has worked on archaeological projects across the world and now focuses primarily on Great Lakes archaeology in the late nineteenth and early twentieth century. She is the assistant editor of *Inland Seas*, a quarterly journal highlighting Great Lakes history.

Daniel J. Warren is senior marine archaeologist at C & C Technologies, Inc. He received his M.A. from East Carolina University's Program in Maritime History and Nautical Archaeology in 1998. His research focuses on the location, documentation, and analysis of deep-water shipwrecks. He is currently serving as co–principal investigator for the archaeological analysis component of the Bureau of Ocean Energy Management's project Comparative Analysis of an Oil Spill on the Biota Inhabiting Several Gulf of Mexico Shipwrecks.

Kieran Westley is research associate at the Centre for Maritime Archaeology, Ulster University. His current research focuses on the reconstruction of submerged prehistoric landscapes using geophysical, geotechnical, and archaeological methods. He also has wider interests in the use of marine geophysics for mapping shipwrecks and the impact of coastal erosion on archaeological sites.

Index